The Art of Augustus John

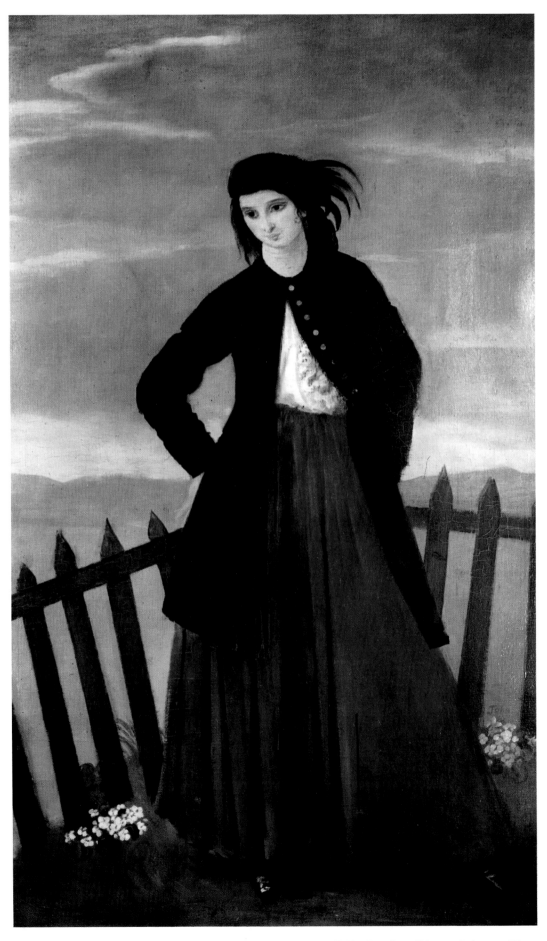

DORELIA STANDING BEFORE A FENCE, *c.* 1903–4 (Miss Jemima Pitman) (*see p. 45*)

THE ART OF

❧ AUGUSTUS JOHN ☙

Augustus Edwin John

Malcolm Easton

&

Michael Holroyd

David R. Godine

PUBLISHER

BOSTON

First published in America 1975 by
David R. Godine
306 Dartmouth Street, Boston
Massachusetts 02116

Text and Selection of Works by Augustus John
Copyright © Michael Holroyd and Malcolm Fyfe Easton 1974

ISBN: 0–87923–113–0

LCC No: 74–84335

Printed in Great Britain by
Westerham Press Limited, Westerham, Kent

Contents

❧ List of Plates ❧

vii

List of Figures in the Text

Acknowledgements

We are indebted above all to the artist's family, particularly to Admiral of the Fleet Sir Caspar John and Mr Romilly John. We have also received invaluable assistance from Mme Poppet Pol, Mrs Vivien White, Mr Edwin John, and the late David John.

While respecting the wishes of others to remain anonymous, we thank the following owners for permission to reproduce their property: Sir Robert Adeane; Mr Richard Burrows; Mr Cass Canfield; Mrs Thelma Cazalet-Keir; Mr Richard Driver; Miss Amaryllis Fleming; Mr Brinsley Ford; Mr and Mrs John Gardner; Mr Peter Harris; Mrs R. M. Hughes; Lady Kleinwort; Gwen Lady Melchett; Miss Jemima Pitman; Mr Peter A. Salm; Mr and Mrs Benjamin Sonnenberg; Mr Anthony Speelman; Mr and Mrs Stephen Tumin; Mrs Julian Vinogradoff; Sir Charles Wheeler. We gratefully acknowledge leave to reproduce works by Augustus John in the National Portrait Gallery; the Tate Gallery; the Imperial War Museum; the National Gallery of Ireland; the National Museum of Wales; the National Gallery of Victoria, Melbourne; the Art Gallery of Ontario; the Beaverbrook Art Gallery, New Brunswick; Boston Public Library (Department of Prints); the Detroit Institute of Arts; the Fitzwilliam Museum, Cambridge; University College, London; the City Art Gallery, Manchester; the Walker Art Gallery, Liverpool. Messrs Thomas Agnew and Sons and P. and D. Colnaghi very kindly supplied us with photographs of prints in their possession.

We have been fortunate in the help given us at various stages and in various ways by Miss Dobi Adeane, Miss Miriam J. Benkovitz, Mr Rollo Charles, Mr Joseph Darracott, Mr Arthur Driver, Dr M. Roy Fisher, Mr Geoffrey Green, Mr Clifford Hall, Mr Max Harari, Mrs Sarah Jacobs, Mr John Lumley and Mr Godfrey Pilkington; and privileged to consult the archive of Augustus John photographs in the National Museum of Wales, the Witt Library at the Courtauld Institute, and the collection of exhibition-catalogues belonging to the Library of the Victoria and Albert Museum.

For newly-commissioned photographs we have been largely dependent upon the skill of Miss Eileen Tweedy.

The Art of Augustus John

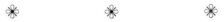

1

OVER-EXPOSURE OF the creator is peculiarly unfortunate in the visual arts, where one expects to have eyes only for the thing created. And it was Augustus John's whim to transform himself into the kind of 'picturesque man' against whom Nietzsche has issued a special warning. He hit the headlines with unwearying zest and lived long enough to make his final truculent bow on television. What did he care for the critics and their accumulating stocks of gelignite? In the end, and long before he died in 1961, aged eighty-three, his great reputation had been blown sky-high.

The fragments of that reputation, however, as at last they drift down to earth again, seem to the authors of the present essay to form a new, exciting pattern. Like the man himself,[1] the artist demands reappraisal. When a figure of importance in the history of our time is currently underrated both by the State's appointed guardians of culture and by Royal Academicians at Burlington House, something must be wrong somewhere. Without attempting a 'rescue operation' (John's own contemptuous phrase in rejecting an offer of the kind from Wyndham Lewis), we think the plain facts, many of them freed from distortion or presented for the first time, may provide a refreshingly different image of the painter.

❋   ❋   ❋

Augustus Edwin John was born in Tenby, Pembrokeshire, on 4th January 1878, the younger son and third child of a family of four. His mother (formerly Augusta Smith, whose roots were in Brighton) died at a very early age. It had been from her, however, not from his father, a Welsh solicitor, that he and his sister Gwen, the elder by two years, inherited their insatiable desire to draw. At the time of Augustus' birth in a seaside boarding-house, Haverfordwest (inland) was still the family home. The motherless children were not moved to Tenby till 1884, and the two budding artists among them endured rather than enjoyed its self-conscious gentility.

A short spell in Clifton, Bristol – not at the College – excepted, Augustus received his education in Tenby; for a few months, in his seventeenth year, at the Tenby School of Art, though he afterwards appears to deny it.[2] Was it here under the general supervision of the Principal, Edward J. Head,[3] or at an earlier stage that a Miss O'Sullivan taught him the smudge-and-stipple way of going about things known as 'stumping'?[4]

The Slade School of Fine Art soon put a stop to this, and for the tightly-rolled paper 'pencil' dipped in pulverized chalk substituted a brittle stick of charcoal much less easy to handle. His son's decision to

[1] Michael Holroyd's *Augustus John*, the official biography, will be referred to here, from now on, as 'M.H.'.

[2] '. . . though I attended no official Art School': Augustus John, 'A Note on Drawing' in Lillian Browse's *Augustus John Drawings* (1941), p. 9.

[3] A painter of landscape and still-life, Head came to Tenby from Scarborough. He exhibited sporadically at the R.A. between 1893 and 1921.

[4] Lillian Browse, *op. cit., loc. cit.*

renounce an Army career in favour of art may seem to have been accepted by Edwin William John with surprising equanimity. In fact, no heavy sacrifice threatened him. It is often forgotten that Augustus was master of a tiny but vital income of £40 a year, perhaps £400 in present-day terms. With this and the remission of fees earned by scholarships and a prize or two thrown in, he could keep his head above water. He arrived in London in October 1894.

The legendary Slade acclamation, 'There was a man sent from God, whose name was John', does not date back to those earliest days in Gower Street. Evidence exists to show that John began as a quiet, painstaking and anything but cocky pupil. The bevy of talented girls was daunting enough. The men students dazzled less; but he stood in some awe of Tonks, the Principal's second-in-command.[5] It has been the fashion to decry as affected John's highly personal approach to drawing, as if one so well endowed by nature needed – *ad captandum* – to elaborate a 'style'. On the contrary, the fastidiousness was all objective. The simpler the statement, too, the better pleased the artist. Characteristically, his initial rendering of the Discobolus in the Antique Room at the Slade sported no flourishes of any kind. Its economy almost shocked – before it delighted – the prowling Assistant Principal. What leaped to the eye was a gift for the form-revealing contour which the Slade, following Ingres, regarded itself as pledged to inculcate. Had Tonks been French, instead of merely francophile, he would have fallen on John's neck. Here was the student he had been waiting for.

The advantages for John himself in having Tonks as mentor rouse some doubts. Bedevilled always by a central core of indecision, he was particularly grateful to be led just at this moment. London confused as well as charmed him. Art was still unknown country. Tonks drove his students hard; but John welcomed a discipline he could not have supplied had he been left to his own devices. The industry was there, its direction lacking. But at this distance in time, the drawbacks of becoming Tonks' star pupil are even clearer than the undeniable advantage or two. Because Tonks himself so outshone Steer[6] as a teacher, what he taught – drawing – acquired an isolated significance, instead of linking up with Steer's sleepy commentary on colour. Tonks' own works in oils or pastel tend to be hesitant and insipid. John could have learned little from them; and as he could learn nothing from Steer either, he seemed doomed to remain (the term was Tonks') a 'methodical' draughtsman and no more.

Then, in the summer of 1897, a serious accident befell him. Bathing off Giltar Point along the coast from Tenby, he struck his head on a submerged rock. The wound, which had to be extensively stitched, was regarded by the doctor who undertook the task as the 'worst of its kind he has had to deal with'.[7] A lengthy convalescence – rather than the blow itself – seems to have unleashed new forces in John. He returned late to the Slade for the 1897–8 session, a changed man. Not only had his appearance altered (he gave up shaving and ceased to clean his shoes): in character, even, this was a *blagueur* and rebel. Strange to relate, the grisly experience he had just been through left him anxious to risk his neck again at every opportunity. In the Life Class, too, scene of only cautious master-strokes up till then, he began to achieve an excellence that positively alarmed: 'methodical' still, but with a streak of madness in the method now.

A sheet of studies drawn about 1897 (Pl. 25) gives us a glimpse of the new virtuosity. It is a Slade exercise and rightly belongs within those grey walls. Here, exalted to an independent art-form, is a rendering of the human body by a 'succession of rhythmical lines following the surface and explaining

---

[5] Henry Tonks (1862–1937) had been invited by the Principal, Frederick Brown (1851–1941), to join the staff in 1893: this was a daring move, since Tonks' experience had been wholly medical.

[6] Philip Wilson Steer (1860–1942), at the height of his powers in the late Eighties and early Nineties, had been appointed by Brown in 1892. With Tonks, he remained at the Slade till 1930.

[7] The victim, in a letter to Ursula Tyrwhitt. M.H., p. 51.

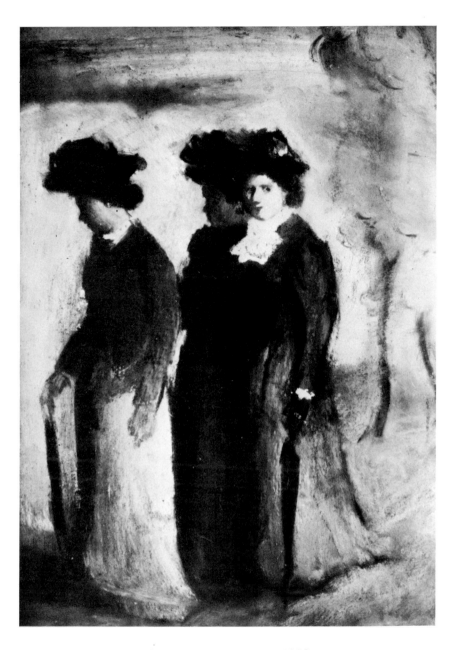

i   The Promenade, *c.* 1900

its structure'[8] which perfectly fulfils Tonks' *religio medici*. No one could have competed with John in such a task – or produced anything at once so brilliant and so hideous.

Fortunately, sitters other than professional models, and from a world outside the suffocating Life Room, soon presented themselves. One of the bonuses of John's convalescent inactivity was that the boredom and loneliness of it seem to have put to flight all his former shyness. Gwen had arrived at the Slade in 1895. The once daunting band of girl-students led by the sisters Waugh (Edna and Rosa) and by Louise Salaman could not be expected to withstand the entreaties of an always handsome and now bolder Augustus; and their portraits must be numbered among his most sympathetic early works.

[8] Lillian Browse, *op. cit.*, p. 10.

With Gwen, on one occasion, posed a couple of the Slade's particular beauties, Ursula Tyrwhitt and Ida Nettleship (Pl. 26). Both, at different times, might be called objects of his 'unhesitating devotion'[9]: an Augustan phrase not to be confused with any irrevocable plighting of one's troth. The drawing is in pencil. Whatever the superior richness of charcoal, its breadth and warmth, pencil was to be John's most characteristic medium. For some reason, this is held against him, as was a predilection for the small sable against Stanley Spencer. Both tools, it has been supposed, ration the full vigour of genius. One cannot actually observe that they do. In fact, the drawing just mentioned has none of the suavity, offensive to the same critics, of the long procession of silvery Dorelias which was to follow later. Nor do the lines in this group-portrait obediently hug the surface and report on structure. They are as higgledy-piggledy as Sickert's, in adapting themselves to a new topic. No swooning arabesques here, but a multitude of short, coarse jabs with the pencil, blunt for preference, oblique and cross-hatched without reference to the underlying form.

A number of other drawings traceable to the late 1890s survive to show the artist's independence of what, through his own influence, was coming to be known as the 'Slade manner'.[10] Sometimes they are hardly recognizable as John's. He was searching for the ideal medium. In several fancy pieces, particularly rustic idylls (of which the Tate has an example), he tried his hand at pastel. It may be that voluntary departure from easy elegance had to do with first experiments in etching, where it is not in the needle's power to sustain a single, expressive line for very long.

Sir William Rothenstein no doubt saw the thing in correct perspective when he wrote, years later, that while John's 'drawings and pastels got better and better', about this time, 'his painting was still uncertain; he found it difficult to control his palette, but now and again he gave promise of astonishing genius'.[11] Where painting was concerned, John had, in one sense, no master; in another, too many masters. An uncertain colourist himself, Tonks was a strong advocate of what could be picked up through constant visits to the National Gallery and other public collections. John returned from these visits bewildered, his head swimming with Rubens, Rembrandt and Watteau. To pass out of the Slade with the highest honours, he had to score one resounding triumph in oils. It is not astonishing that, having concentrated all his remarkable powers on winning the Summer Composition prize of 1898, he easily succeeded; nor that the result proved very much a pastiche of the masters dearest to him.

But we are not for that reason obliged to dismiss his 'Moses and the Brazen Serpent' (Pl. 28) as a feeble echo. In the circumstances, it may be reckoned a wonder of wonders: that is, given John's age (under twenty-one) and the poverty of Slade painting-instruction in the hands of Steer and W. W. Russell.[12] At a recent exhibition in the Royal Academy Diploma Galleries,[13] 'Moses and the Brazen Serpent' could be seen hanging next to Gwen John's 1900 self-portrait, now owned by the Tate Gallery. This juxtaposition prompted some mock-sympathy for Augustus on the part of the cataloguer: one cannot think why. Of course, we all enjoy Gwen's painting of herself in cameo and tartan-striped blouse. But it is a small picture (less than eighteen inches high) and, of its very nature, intimate and inward-looking. Her brother's 'Moses' was planned – quite properly – as a public demonstration of his powers and occupies a canvas five feet by seven. To 'do Poussin over again', to out-Rembrandt Rembrandt, was Augustus' prime business here. Naturally, he failed in that endeavour, but he gave

[9] The words are inscribed on a drawing in the British Museum, given by the artist to a 'Miss Emily'.

[10] Several early self-portraits and at least three Slade-period drawings of Gwen (one in the Archive of the National Museum of Wales, the others belonging, respectively, to Mr Michael Salaman and Mr John Lumley, are well known to us) display the harsher approach.

[11] Sir William Rothenstein, *Men and Memories* (1931–2), Vol. I, p. 340.

[12] Later, Sir Walter Russell (1867–1949), Assistant Professor at the Slade from 1895 till 1927.

[13] *The Slade, 1871–1971: a Centenary Exhibition*, 20th November–12th December 1971.

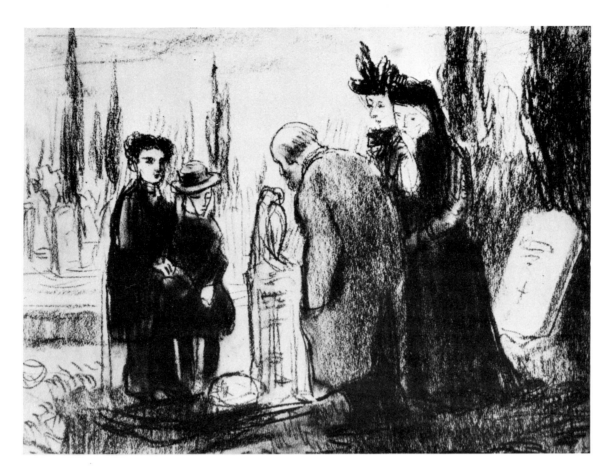

ii   Churchyard Scene, *c.* 1901

his large-scale decorative ambitions a notable first airing and attained a fine, blond harmony and a subtle texture of paint throughout. The more often this derided work leaves cold storage the better, in fact. One has only to look at the next prize-winning composition, the much vaunted 'Hamlet' by young William Orpen,[14] to perceive the difference between precocious mimicry and a student's genuine determination to learn from the best models.

Oddly enough, the surfeit of explanatory gesture which somewhat tries one's patience in 'Moses and the Brazen Serpent' points also (if we are right) to an admirable, and in 1898 quite extraordinary, appreciation of El Greco. Paris was then the capital of the art world; yet Arsène Alexandre tells us that there were probably not more than ten men in that city during the last decade of the century who knew or cared about the Toledan master.[15] John visited Spain for the first time in the spring of 1922, and his enthusiasm never waned. It was all very well for him to poke fun at 'two gigantic old gentlemen [presumably, the 'St Andrew with St Francis' in the Prado], lightly clad in paper dressing-gowns' tripping 'buoyantly in a landscape of cork and bottle-green, under the illumination of a gibbous moon

[14] To give it its full title: 'The Play Scene from Hamlet'. It is even larger than John's entry, and now hangs in Houghton Hall, Norfolk. Sir William Orpen (1878–1931) was a student at the Slade from 1897–9.
[15] The El Greco craze really began in 1902, with an exhibition of his work at the Prado, Madrid. A. F. Calvert and G. C. Huntley's monograph appeared in Calvert's *Spanish Series* in 1907, Barrès' in 1912 and David Katz's *War Greco astigmatisch?* in 1914. A plethora of works on the subject followed after the First World War and has continued ever since.

which shines balefully between the incandescent shuttle-cocks of a sky in uproar'.[16] Frivolous himself, when under the Greco influence, John indulged eccentricities which, being at second hand, are a good deal less easy to pardon. He could have been more sparing with the imitative upcast glances, the spavined knees, the flourish of excessively tapered fingers and the very limited repertory of contra-puntal poses borrowed from El Greco's Roman portfolio. But to be sparing was not John's way.

He left the Slade in the summer of his 'Moses and the Brazen Serpent' triumph, and there followed an interlude of feckless industry, during which his chosen companions were most often Orpen – 'Orpsie-boy', self-styled, a stage Irishman almost, but having a hard enough head for business – and Ambrose McEvoy;[17] with the indefatigable Will Rothenstein always helpfully at hand. In Will's wake came his brother Albert, and Charles Conder, of whom Will painted what is arguably the finest of all portraits of the 1890s.[18] John's departure from the silhouette, typified by this canvas, of attenuated silk hat and hour-glass, ankle-length overcoat finished off by a pair of sparkling pumps, cuts him adrift at once from the Beardsley world of 'Lady Gold's Escort'. In the heyday of the Decadence, John was never of it. Whistler, its father-figure, whom he met through Gwen, made little impression upon him. When the opportunity came to join the circle of flatterers round Wilde, an evening or two was as much as he could take. Though addicted to café life, especially to that of the Café Royal, John had constant need to fill his lungs with copious draughts of fresh air.

In this respect, Rothenstein's shadowy glimpse of him, in the summer of 1899, posed with Alice Rothenstein for the picture called 'The Doll's House', is highly uncharacteristic: he couldn't, one feels, have remained at the foot of that cramped staircase in the stifling little hall a moment longer, even with Alice's agreeable good looks to console him.[19] He swam prodigiously, during this stay near the Channel coast, and the drawing he did was all out of doors.

Nevertheless, John would have to continue a prisoner of cities for a while yet. It is the artist's – and particularly the young artist's – fate that he must live where he can sell his work. John had had his first one-man show at the Carfax Gallery in the spring of 1899. Backed by D. S. MacColl,[20] whose goodwill expressed in *The Saturday Review* was very well worth having, he sold enough to think himself successfully launched. In the same year, at its summer and winter exhibitions, the New English Art Club accepted a total of four drawings. Though rather less hostile to the Royal Academy as the years passed (and this was the Club's thirteenth), it offered wall-space to almost every anti-Establishmen-tarian from Stanhope Forbes[21] to Sickert (even welcoming Beardsley in his brief hour of health and strength). Promising Slade students had an entrée to the N.E.A.C. through its Secretary, none other than their Principal, and through two other members of the Gower Street staff, Steer and Tonks. No 'faithful dog', as he expressed it, in affairs of the heart, John had a strong professional sense of loyalty, and he remained a regular exhibitor with the Club for the best years of his working life. But showing

[16] Augustus John, *Finishing Touches*, edited and introduced by Daniel George (1964), p. 134. These notes, entitled 'The Prado Revisited', were composed as late as 1954. The 'St Andrew and St Francis' remained unknown until 1937 and did not enter the Prado until 1942. In spite of the irreverent manner in which El Greco is here discussed by John, the spell was never quite dissolved.

[17] Ambrose McEvoy (1878–1927) entered the Slade in 1893: he became a fashionable portrait-painter. His wife, Mary Spencer Edwards, was also a member of the Johns' circle, and Augustus did some notable early drawings of her.

[18] Albert Rutherston (1881–1953) changed his name from Rothenstein during the First World War. He arrived at the Slade in 1898 and won the Summer Composition prize himself in 1901. Charles Conder (1868–1909) had no Slade con-nexions. Rothenstein's portrait of him, of 1892, is in the Toledo, U.S.A., Museum of Art.

[19] In the Tate. A scene from Ibsen's play is intended, John playing Krogstad, Alice Rothenstein Mrs Linde.

[20] Dugald Sutherland MacColl (1859–1948), champion and biographer of Steer, and later Keeper of the Tate Gallery and the Wallace Collection.

[21] Stanhope A. Forbes (1857–1947), chiefly associated with the Newlyn School and paintings of Cornish seafaring life. For a fresh examination of the N.E.A.C., its later connection with the Slade, and a complete list of John's contributions to its exhibitions, see M.H., pp. 109–113 and Appendix.

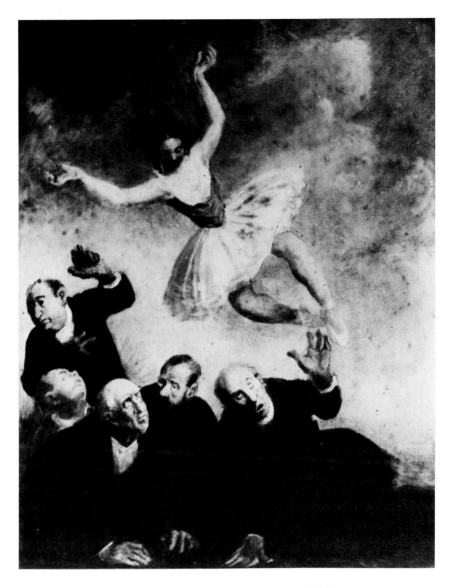

iii   Désespérance d'Amour, *c.* 1902

and selling an occasional drawing, or even a sheaf of drawings, wasn't sufficient to keep him.

Still less the two of them: for on 12th January 1901, with McEvoy, Evans and Gwen as witnesses, he married Ida Nettleship.[22] His indigence had hitherto required no apologies, but under the Nettleships' disapproving eye it began to embarrass him. Thus, when MacColl was asked to suggest someone for the post of instructor at an art school affiliated to Liverpool's University College, John, after some natural hesitation, allowed his name to go forward.[23] He was offered the job and accepted it, arriving in Liverpool with Ida very early in 1901. Artistically, the importance of this migration cannot be

---

[22] This relationship began at the Slade. Ida Nettleship was the daughter of Jack Nettleship, an animal painter in the tradition of J. M. Swan and Briton Rivière, but less successful. Her mother kept the pot boiling by designing and making dresses, in particular for leading personalities in the theatre.

[23] He was never, as has often been stated, Head of a University Department of Fine Art, nor occupant of a Chair. (Liverpool achieved full university status only in the summer of 1903, a year after the Johns' departure.)

overestimated. Among its results was the pile of copperplates which established him at once as a master of the etching medium. Something much less predictable, however, was to be born out of Merseyside pea-soupers and the drab grove of Academe on Brownlow Hill: something gay and grand. Here began in earnest the Romany cult. The persistence of this theme through the years is as remarkable as the suddenness of its coming to life. All at once, we may say, the song in John's heart expanded from a mere nationalistic *Mae Hen Wlad Fy Nhadau* to a Schubertian *Das Wandern*, the young artist accepting as the Land of his Fathers any wild shore or stretch of desolate heath patronized by the Gypsy-kind.

Fallen now into disrepute as the province of photographic hacks, etching has more than once served the noblest cause. Rembrandt's free play of invention on the copper held up to ridicule the elaborately systematized plates issued by the royal (and Papal) presses of his day. In the late eighteenth and early nineteenth centuries Goya and Blake, each in his different manner, used the technique with subtle polemical effect. Later in the nineteenth century, and in the hands of men like J-F. Millet, Charles Meryon and Rodolphe Bresdin, it became one of the most telling instruments in the attack on materialism. In England, John's ageing contemporary Whistler waged with it his personal war against British bad taste, rejecting for a fastidious delicacy of touch the crude approach that marked his own philistine beginnings as a naval cartographer in the United States. Added to which, the introduction of photomechanical processes during the 1880s had more to do with the revival of etching as a studio activity than has been generally supposed, just as the discovery of the zincograph gave new prestige to non-commercial wood-engraving.

Such historical considerations are not irrelevant, for if John took to etching like a duck to water, it was at least in part because he adored Rembrandt, Goya and Millet, could be as spookily Romantic as Meryon and as sentimentally Realistic as Bresdin. And no one of his generation was able to ignore the exquisite series of plates etched by Whistler in London and Venice, together with portraits and figure-studies less open to criticism than the Master's later oils.[24] Etching, too, as has just been said, had become the traditional vehicle of the rebel; and the bearded, be-ringed, moleskin-suited John who arrived in Liverpool for the spring session of 1901 was certainly that. Nor must one forget either the part played by Benjamin Evans,[25] his fellow-student and crony at the Slade, in first acquainting him with the mysteries of the acid-bath, or – a determining factor, perhaps – the existence in the Brownlow Hill art school of the essential but least easily acquired item of printmakers' equipment, an etching-press.

Evans received his reward in the form of a portrait, thought to be John's opus no. 1 in this field (Pl. 27). It survives in two impressions, a rare, light print and a second, from the rather heavily-inked later state. But competing with this for first place are the three square inches of copper bearing a Rembrandtesque self-portrait and signed and dated on the plate 'John 1901'.[26] Indeed, this introductory period is Rembrandt, Rembrandt all the way, Liverpool's seedy supernumeraries – 'The Mulatto', 'The Old Haberdasher', 'Old Arthy' – standing in for Amsterdam's and culminating in an 'Old Man in a Fur Cloak' straight out of the Jodenbreestraat. That the plates are tiny and the persons figuring on them captured sight-size reinforces the Rembrandt comparison: not much to John's

---

[24] Less open to John's criticism, that is. Whistler's tentativeness on canvas during his old age led John to an apt, if cruel, comparison with Balzac's Frenhofer, a fictitious painter who lingers so long over his work that nothing intelligible ultimately emerges from it. Ironically, the problem of not knowing where to stop would equally afflict John himself.

[25] Benjamin Evans was a boyhood friend of John's, having attended the same private school at Clifton. With McEvoy he made up a threesome on sketching expeditions.

[26] The proof we examined in the National Museum of Wales was marked 'John's first etching'.

advantage, for he has neither his hero's insatiable curiosity nor his patience. There is as little variation in technique as in subject-matter, and fine early states too often disappear under the burr ploughed up by reckless afterthoughts in drypoint.

Though such an example as the celebrated and slightly larger 'Tête farouche' (Pl. 29)[27] shares these weaknesses, too, it expresses a dash and abandon that are wholly John's, and further suggests the 'wild man of the woods' constantly in dispute with the salaried art-teacher. John Sampson[28] (Pl. 31),

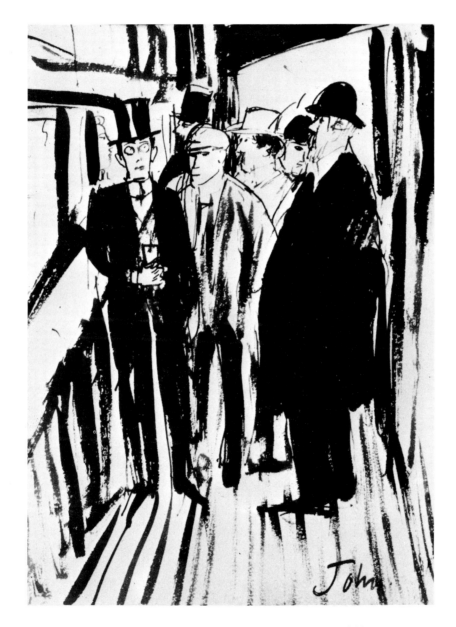

iv   Spectators in a Picture-Gallery (?), *c.* 1912

[27] No. 10 ii, in Campbell Dodgson's *A Catalogue of Etchings by Augustus John, 1901–1914* (1920). The later state, not shown here, is heavily slashed with drypoint.

[28] John Sampson (1862–1931). Appointed in 1892, he remained at the University College and the University for thirty-six years.

the Liverpool University College Librarian and national expert on Gypsy words and ways, became the artist's favourite companion. 'Under his tutelage and by personal contact with the Gypsies,' John wrote later, 'I soon picked up the English dialect of Romani.'[29] Sampson took John with him on expeditions to Romany camps at Aintree and on the Wirral; and a portrait of Walter Boswell, kinsman of Watts-Dunton's Rhoda, makes its appearance among the early etchings. The Liverpool episode is closely examined in Michael Holroyd's biography of John.[30] Here we need do no more than record the artist's inevitable wearying of the three days' teaching a week, as well as – Sampson, Mackay and Kuno Meyer excepted[31] – of the stuffy little College circle. Out of patience at times even with Sampson, a *Rai* who indulged some excusable delusions of grandeur, John and Ida discovered a more endearing kindred spirit in Mary Dowdall, daughter of Lord Borthwick and wife of an ambitious Liverpool lawyer whom we shall meet again in these pages.[32] Gypsies and aristocrats have a spacious way with them: picketed middle-class domesticity filled John with horror. In January 1902 Ida's first child, David, had been born. Though welcoming the event, the artist trembled for his freedom. When Ida left Liverpool for a short visit to her ailing father in the spring of that year, he wrote to Will Rothenstein: 'Decidedly it is inspiring to lie alone at times. I fear continued cosiness is risky . . .'[33]

With the aim, therefore, of escaping the deadly tentacles of this cosiness, the artist gathered up his family and left Liverpool for London in July 1902. The return without regular salary to Fitzroy Street and its happy-go-lucky economy increased, of course, his need to find solutions to the financial problem. In another form, teaching itself would have to be resumed. Ida was again pregnant. If the butcher and baker (devil take the landlady!) were ever to get paid, tiny images on copper would have to give way to more acceptably-sized equivalents on canvas. It had already become obvious that John, a natural catcher of likenesses, must expect to earn the best part of his living as a portrait-painter. Though he lacked the tricks of the trade, he was often enough, if glumly enough, going to pick up his palette for the same purpose as the years went by.

Consider his current diploma-pieces in the vein. There was the initial commissioned portrait of 1899, the anonymous 'Old Lady' (Pl. 1).[34] She lived in Eaton Square: scanty information, but still worth having. For it reminds us how, even at the earliest stage, the anti-social John managed to land feet first in the midst of the most enviable of all quarters of patronage in London, that which divides Sloane Street from Grosvenor Place. Belgravia was a world of high ceilings as well as great wealth, and most of these town-mansions (before so many of them were snapped up as embassies) had their twin establishments in the country, with walls similarly able to accommodate canvases of Sargent-style dimensions and splendour. The 'Old Lady', however, does not woo us like Sargent's sleek 'Mrs Asher Wertheimer'. She is all dignity and reserve. A single patch of scarlet, the cover of the book she holds, acts as foil to the sombre background and sitter's black silk gown. It is sad to read John's almost contemptuous dismissal of the picture in *Chiaroscuro*, revealing his utter incapacity to distinguish

---

[29] Augustus John, *Chiaroscuro, Fragments of Autobiography: First Series* (1952), p. 58.

[30] M.H., Ch. III, *passim*.

[31] A sensitive sketch (untraceable now) of Sampson is reproduced in *Chiaroscuro*, facing p. 58; John's portrait of J. M. Mackay, Rathbone Professor of Ancient History at Liverpool, is a particularly fine one; and that of Kuno Meyer the eminent Celtic scholar – Pl. 52 – is perhaps the most impressive example of the artist's work in the National Gallery of Ireland: see our footnote 49, p. 21.

[32] Harold Chaloner Dowdall, later County Court Judge and Lord Mayor of Liverpool, became a few years later the subject of the grand, formal portrait rejected by Liverpool and now in the National Gallery of Victoria, Melbourne (Pl. 49).

[33] M.H., p. 134.

[34] Thought by Mrs Arthur Clifton to represent John's landlady (!), the picture was rediscovered by the then Director of the Tate Gallery in 1941 and added to its collection. See also M.H., p. 85.

[35] *Chiaroscuro*, p. 147. This incapacity was the cause of great embarrassment to those who, like Mr Brinsley Ford, attempted from time to time to bring together an anthology of his best productions.

between good and bad in his own work.[35] Indeed, he was to sheer right away from this Pre-Raphaelite attention to detail – and too often, more regrettably, from the warm sympathy for his sitter which (in spite of his protests to the contrary) seems to light up the features, Rembrandtesque again in their golden hue, of the frail but still formidable dowager in her *petite coiffe*.

John's next portrait of consequence, 'Merikli' (Pl. 30), was hung at the N.E.A.C.'s 1902 winter exhibition. The anxieties inseparable from a commissioned work did not bother him here, for his model was Ida. Like several early portraits of favourite sitters, particularly of this one, the painting is carried out almost as a pastiche of a seventeenth-century master: is it Rembrandt, Velázquez or one of those Roman or Neapolitan artists hardly known to the British public until after the Second World War?[36] Whatever the answer, 'Merikli' was perfectly acceptable – indeed, reckoned fresh and exciting – in its own day. The dark, almost masculine beauty of the head, the exquisite painting of the left hand, naturally made a deep impression. And yet the picture is more curious than attractive. Those who turn to the account of John's married life will find themselves wondering what, consciously or un-consciously, the artist was saying here about the courageous but often uneasy partner of his moods and vagaries.[37] They will be puzzled that out of her plaited-straw basket, stock-in-trade of Zurbarán and Caravaggio as well as of the Gypsies, and loaded with finer blooms, Ida selects and proffers a simple daisy. If the gold band on her finger is what it appears to be, a wedding-ring, then why does she display it so proudly to the spectator *on the wrong hand*? At least it has been possible to settle the meaning of the word 'merikli' (Note to Pl. 30). Yet there was sufficient of John's aggressive character as a painter in this ambiguous and not altogether satisfactory mixture of old and new for the work to be acclaimed by the N.E.A.C. its Picture of the Year.

The honour done it may seem the more remarkable when we remember that 'Merikli''s companion-piece at the 1902 exhibition was the portrait of Signorina Estella Cerutti (Pl. 4). Very conveniently, we have been able to examine the two works side by side in the City Art Gallery, Manchester. They are utterly different in technique and spirit. At odds with the old-masterish pose and Stradivarius browns, Ida's features are laid in broadly and spontaneously and without the least regard for elegance. In the painting of the Signorina, on the other hand, all is subordinated to sinuous contour and an ultra-refined mapping of the shadows. The 'Merikli' might have been inspired by Hals, the 'Estella' by Ingres. Excellent proselytizers both: but for John to swing between antithetical poles in one and the same year suggests an artist in a quandary. He was still, in fact, in search of an idiom of his own. Other dilemmas, too, of the heart rather than the hand, are suggested here. Of the pair, it is the wife who lacks self-assurance. Estella, or 'Esther' (she lived, easily summoned, in the same house in Fitzroy Street), fixes Augustus with a glance, long and languorous, in which the certainty of pleasing is rendered more piquant by the ballooning curves of her ribbed muslin dress. Indeed, the whole creamy-gold silhouette, which takes in the sitter's clasped hands and trailing handkerchief, provides an irresistible effect of movement: so that, with the Signorina, we seem suddenly to glide forward – up to and just across the threshold of the twentieth century.

It was not, however, till the following year, 1903, that John met Dorothy McNeill, the 'Dorelia' whose discovery led to his first unequivocally personal work, from charming little studies like the early 'Ardor' (Pl. 5) to the magisterial set-piece called 'The Smiling Woman' (Pl. 9). This time, Ida's dilemma was to be resolved only by her death, which took place in Paris, in 1907.

[36] John certainly appears to have been drawn to the Caravaggisti, employing at the same time many contradictory features of Mannerism. We have come across only one painting of Ida, that belonging to Mr and Mrs John Gardner (Pl. 2), which, though still emerging from brown shadow, seems genuinely of John's own day.
[37] M.H., pp. 113–154.

[11]

❧ 2 ❧

A FTER HIS return from Liverpool to London and hoping to 'make pocket-money out of it at least', John decided to join forces with Orpen in founding an art school in Chelsea.[1] His own privacy was secured nearby at 4 Garden Studios, Manresa Road: an arrangement which, despite its convenience, left him characteristically ungrateful. He hated (he could also, he sometimes forgot, love) London. 'A studio,' he growled, '–what is it? . . . 'tis a box wherein miserable painters hide themselves and shut the door on nature . . . .'[2]

By the summer of 1903, when he wrote in these terms, an escape-route had been organized. Ida, with her boys David and Caspar (Robin would be born in the following year), settled into Elm House, Matching Green, Essex, where Augustus joined them from time to time. The small children in a hitherto unpublished sheet of pencil-studies (Pl. 33) may represent the David and Caspar of this era. If so, it provides a foreglimpse of the long series of sketches and more deliberate compositions in which John's sons – they reached, at one point, a total of seven – serve as models, either by themselves or in company with his womenfolk.

Just as there is a hunter's moon, so perhaps we can speak of a painter's moon, when daring, skill and opportunity are all in miraculous accord. For John, this splendid moment extended from Dorelia's first appearance in his life[3] to the outbreak of the 1914–18 war.

Beyond its almost exclusive concentration on his own children and womenfolk as models, the period is remarkable for its open-air settings, for it was now John's aim to live in high Gypsy fashion. In 1905 he took a positive step towards the realization of his desires by acquiring a picturesque, 'cottage'-style van from an old Slade-School crony, Michel Salaman.[4] Late that April, or early in May, it provided shelter and seclusion for the birth of Dorelia's child. But soon after the arrival of the baby, the seraphically beautiful Pyramus (Pl. 12), they were joined by Ida, with her own sons, and by John himself. The site was Dartmoor; and there survives one little sketch of the distant caravan, dark against a late-evening sky (Pl. 34), that is both romantic and eerily reminiscent of Conan Doyle's description of the place in his *Hound of the Baskervilles*, then not long published. In another, much larger canvas, the two mothers and their children pose together beside the dipped shafts of the *vardo*.[5] Most evocative of all, and now in a private collection, is a second oil sketch, showing the same group in

---

[1] Orpen played the leading rôle: John himself taught for one day a week only. The establishment, with Rothenstein's brother-in-law Knewstub as secretary, opened in the King's Road for the autumn session of 1903, and was called, not very daringly, 'The Chelsea Art School'.

[2] In a letter to Will Rothenstein. M.H., p. 180.

[3] She did not become a permanent member of his household till towards the end of 1904.

[4] Salaman died, in his nineties, in 1971. At the R.A., 1954 (No. 373), was a portrait of him in hunting pink entitled 'The M.F.H.', for he soon gave up art to return to the normal recreations of a country gentleman.

[5] Reproduced in John Rothenstein, *Augustus John* (1945, 2nd ed.), Pl. 6: now in Lord Cowdray's collection. *Vardo* (Romani) = van.

bright sunlight framed by the dark opening of a tent (Pl. 6). In the two latter pictures, the artist leans over the caravan's half-door, smoking his clay pipe, the perfect Romany Rye.[6]

All this, however, was in the nature of a vacation. A grudging traipse-back had to be made to sordid street and claustrophobic studio. But the school in Chelsea wearying him, and France calling with a new insistence, John decided he had had enough of London for the moment; thus, though the Elm House lease had not quite run out, he removed women and children and himself *en bloc* to Paris, where he rented a studio in the rue Dareau, Petit Montrouge, on the southern outskirts of Montparnasse.

France had called to John – with whose voice? A stronger French influence has been noticed in his work about this time by connoisseurs on the other side of the Channel as well as by our own.[7] John's numerous private utterances on the subject confirm the principal source of inspiration:[8] apart from what was freely available in reproduction, he seized every opportunity to familiarize himself with Puvis de Chavannes' large decorative paintings, all carried out during the 1880s and 1890s, in the Sorbonne, the Hôtel de Ville and the Panthéon. Never is the quiet lyricism of these canvases (for such they are: not frescoes) interrupted by any of the brash, fortissimo passages characteristic of John. On the other hand, both Puvis and his Welsh admirer subscribe to the same canon of Meaninglessness[9]: the picture is the thing, its message a secondary affair. And we can easily recognize a blood relationship between the gesturing dreamers of the Paris decorations and Ida and Dorelia, forever waving explanatory hands (explaining nothing) while the babies scream and the milk boils over. Even Campbell Dodgson's enthusiasm petered out at times in the somnolent presence of these *belles paresseuses* abstractedly gathering to themselves an enigmatic Caspar or a sulky Robin. It was under pressure from Dodgson, however, that John produced an avalanche of freshly-etched copperplates in 1906. Their purpose was twofold: to add to the *corpus* of prints Colvin[10] had begun to collect for the British Museum, and to fill the walls of an exhibition-room at the Chenil Gallery.[11] From the historian's viewpoint they are of little interest, though there creep in some further souvenirs of the Dartmoor visit. In portraiture, the crisp likeness of Wyndham Lewis,[12] of an earlier date (Pl. 32), as indeed that of Benjamin Evans, first portrait and plate of all, would never be improved upon. The dependence on Rembrandt, at the same time, noticeably slackens.

John did much more than slough off the seventeenth century by his thirtieth year. With a wild leap he landed in the present. The vogue for the Primitive certainly fascinated him. Looking through a cache of his ephemeral sketches recently, we were struck by the heavy incidence of Easter Island heads, doodled on scraps of paper, which must date from the early 1900s. The attempt to break away

[6] The caravan craze, as part of a widespread Gypsy cult, is discussed in Malcolm Easton, *Augustus John: Portraits of the Artist's Family, Catalogue of an Exhibition*, etc. (1970), 'Wheels within Wheels', pp. 43–59. One can add that by 1908, with the publication of Kenneth Graham's *The Wind in the Willows*, this craze penetrated the nursery.

[7] E.g., René Gimpel, in his notes on the Quinn sale of 1927 (*Journal d'un collectionneur*), speaks of 'trop de réminiscences françaises'.

[8] In letters to Alice Rothenstein and Alick Schepeler (see footnote 15, p. 15), only a year later, he could refer to Puvis as the 'finest modern' and speak of revisiting the Panthéon 'to encourage myself with a view of Puvis' decorations'. M.H., pp. 253 and 224.

[9] Though few of us like *every kind* of 'meaninglessness' in John's work *at all times*, it is of the essence of his art. Nor, as has often been suggested, can it be written off as an old-fashioned or reactionary trait. In fact, had John bothered to lay down the principles of his attitude in print, they would read today quite as impressively as Clive Bell's analysis of 'significant form'.

[10] Sir Sidney Colvin (1845–1927), then Keeper of the Department of Prints and Drawings at the British Museum.

[11] There were two exhibition-rooms at the Chenil Gallery, directed by Knewstub, who had purchased premises (with Orpen's help) next to the Chelsea Town Hall in the winter of 1905. One of these rooms housed a permanent collection of the McEvoy–Orpen group. John exhibited his etchings in the other, in May 1906. The show proved a great success.

[12] Percy Wyndham Lewis (1884–1957) was introduced to John in the summer of 1902. The rich comedy of their relationship was first dealt with in Michael Holroyd, 'Damning and Blasting', a radio talk, published in *The Listener*, 6th July 1972. See also, M.H., pp. 139–142. John's two fine etchings of Lewis belong to 1903.

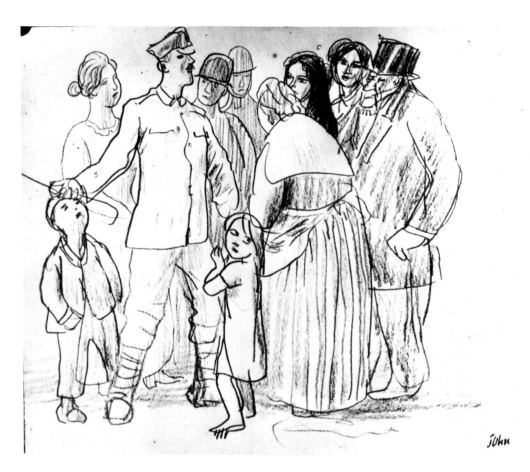

v   The Bragging Soldier, 1915

from what is now regarded as an excessive facility in rendering the superficial appearance of things, to stop being (as his contemporaries termed it) an 'ill-mannered camera', to change his whole approach, in fact, may be connected with the tragic death of Ida, following the birth of her fifth son Henry,[13] on 14th March 1907. While the artist appeared to armour-plate himself against grief or self-reproach, he had passed through an experience which left the world a different place. And to describe this different world artistically, some changes of procedure were called for.

By April, he was explaining to Rothenstein his need to abandon models, to paint phantasy-figures, Polynesian-eyed. These, he told Will, entered into a primeval vision which included mighty 'chanting in the flushing palm tree groves' and 'thumping of the great flat feet of ecstatic multitudes' aglow with sacred oil.[14] Quite logically, John's first French exemplar, Puvis de Chavannes, had been followed by Gauguin and then by Picasso – the painters of 'Te Reriora' and 'Les Demoiselles d'Avignon' having both expressed their debt to Puvis' 'Le Pauvre Pêcheur'. The year of Picasso's crucial 'Demoiselles', this same year of 1907, witnessed a meeting between the two men. 'I saw a young artist whose work is

[13] A fourth son, Edwin, had been born soon after the Johns' arrival in Paris, in November 1905. Henry, whose birth Ida survived by only five days, was brought up by the Nettleship family. He died in 1935, drowned off the Cornish coast.
[14] M.H., p. 258.

wonderful in Paris,' wrote John, on 5th August, to Henry Lamb;[15] and not long afterwards he was confirming this first impression (to which the 'Demoiselles' most forcefully contributed): 'Picasso is a wonder!'[16] The immediate results may be seen in a few large, lugubrious canvases so untypical of their begetter in most people's minds that they caused a good deal of astonishment at the Studio sales of 1962 and 1963.[17] In a 'Peasant Woman with Baby and Small Boy' (Pl. 42) John has banished the sinuous poses most tempting to him. The red-haired mother is dour, charmless and uncomfortably rectangular. The 'outcast' note has been sounded with as much emphasis as in the string of similar subjects already carried out by Picasso; and the maternal feet, flat enough certainly, thump one of those lonely beaches so often to be seen in the works of the young Spanish master. A 'French Fisher-Boy' (Pl. 7), of even greater dimensions, can be seen in Mr and Mrs Tumim's Collection. Will the critics ever warm to this aspect of John's talent? One may shrug it off as too derivative, yet there is an act of self-immolation here that demands our respect. Endlessly dissatisfied with his own pleasing gifts, he was to return again and again to the austerity and simplification practised by the early Picasso, most notably, though not particularly successfully, in the vast 'Mumpers' (Pl. 55), now in Detroit.

There were important events on other fronts in 1907. He met for the first time Dick Innes, a brother Celt whose personality soon exercised a powerful spell over him.[18] And he paid an initial visit to Ireland, to stay with Lady Gregory at Coole Park, so that studies could be made of a fellow-guest, W. B. Yeats. At least one fine etching resulted, and more than one oil portrait, with the inscrutable touch required by their hostess. The best – and the least fey – is undoubtedly that in the City Art Gallery, Manchester (Pl. 8). If the object of his going to Ireland had been, quite simply, to make some much-needed money, there were unexpected fringe-benefits. The beauty of the countryside, Yeats' fairy-lore, and Lady Gregory's researches into the language of the Irish tinkers (Shelta, strictly, but having close affinities with Romani), ended by captivating him. Ireland he would return to many times, its peasant-girls and fishermen taking on, though less perceptibly as the years went by, something of the character of Picasso's Blue and Rose Harlequinades. Even the Manchester Yeats is provided with one of those 'viridian vistas' which had been part of the vision communicated to Rothenstein.

No doubt, these stylistic flirtations helped to prepare the way for the full-length picture – unadorned simplicity, in terms of form – of the woman who had succeeded Ida as manager of his affairs and mother-general to all his children, the bright particular Dorelia of 'The Smiling Woman' (Pl. 9), painted in 1908 and probably the most familiar of all John's works. So familiar was this animated *genre*-portrait for at least twenty-five years after its first appearance at an 'Exhibition of Fair Women' at the New Gallery, in February–March 1909,[19] that those who directed public taste grew to resent its

[15] Henry Lamb (1883–1960) was for long the artist's favourite disciple, modelling himself on everything that was most flamboyantly Johnian. Being equally mercurial, and often a rival for the same women's favours, Lamb outlived his original warm welcome. His wife Euphemia shared with Alick Schepeler a first place among John's subjects for pencil-sketches outside the family circle itself.

[16] M.H., p. 273.

[17] At the first of these Christie sales, 184 items were put up for auction; at the second, 173. After this, we still counted exactly 100 paintings in a warehouse in Salisbury many of which were later acquired by the National Museum of Wales. Few, even among art-lovers, realize both the prolific and the self-critical character of the artist which led him thus to hoard and hide during his lifetime.

[18] James Dickson Innes (1887–1914) painted mainly landscapes, especially Welsh ones. Their character is harsh and subdued in colour; and though many are supposedly actual views, as of Mount Arenig (there is a typical example in the Hull University Art Collection), most are imaginary. He shared with Picasso a preference for the non-retinal image, which may account for the same envious admiration felt for him by John.

[19] Roger Fry initiated the chorus of praise in *The Burlington Magazine*, in 1909. In 1930, it could still be chosen as the colour frontispiece for Sir Joseph Duveen's *Thirty Years of British Art*.

ebullient vitality, its almost indecent powers of mesmerism. The picture was withdrawn to the vaults of the Tate Gallery where, a little anxious that the fire might have gone out of it and only the flourishes remain, we were privileged to have the vast canvas hauled out for our inspection. It is pleasant to record the delight aroused in us by what we saw. Many people share Wyndham Lewis' perfectly understandable prejudice against the Gypsy themes that engrossed John about this time: the sterner draughtsman found them altogether too stagy. And nothing could be more stagy than 'The Smiling Woman'. At the top of Lewis' proscribed list, therefore, she ought by sheer inches to overwhelm us with embarrassment. She doesn't. Neo-Gypsy or not, this is a complex human being, still mischievously fresh and alive after solemn burial by the highbrows. The plum-red – *prune sauvage* – of the dress and cerement-yellow of the spotted background curtain, which is its foil, have never before been rendered full justice in reproduction. The hands are exquisite; the mouth a triumphant vehicle for mirth, by no means owing all to Hals. We have here, from John, not a mother of two of his sons,[20] but an eternally enticing mistress. Dorelia had played him up a good deal before and after Ida's death, and now he makes good-humoured capital out of her infidelities:

> *Du kannst nicht treu sein,*
> *Nein, nein, das kannst du nicht!*

– to the rhythm, it could very well be, of a German band blaring away outside his most recent studio in Church Street (now Old Church Street), Chelsea.

Having an anchorage in London did not prevent him from indulging his wanderlust. In the summer of 1908 there had been trips to Rouen, Cherbourg and Dielette with Dorelia and the children.[21] By the spring of 1909 he was ready to take to the road again, having incarcerated himself in his studio long enough to paint the flamboyant portrait of William Nicholson (Pl. 48),[22] and he began by bringing up the caravan from its last resting-place (Dartmoor) to Wantage, and so by equine forced-marches to Effingham, where the horse collapsed between the traces. In April, a further van was acquired, along with a light cart and a relay of stouter-hearted animals under care of a groom. The family (nine strong, including Dorelia's sister Edie) were thus transported, a home-made tent supplementing their sleeping-quarters, from Effingham to Cambridge. Here the artist stopped off to paint the Principal of Newnham College, Miss Jane Harrison, who, like Mme Récamier, adopted a reclining pose. The cortège then made for Norwich, whence John himself left for the north, to produce, under some stress and strain, the gigantic picture of Chaloner ('Silky') Dowdall – attended by an even more commanding flunkey – as Lord Mayor of Liverpool. This (Pl. 49), together with his famous 'Mme Suggia' (Pl. 20), represents John's most serious effort to come to grips with *grand salon* portraiture. One regrets that the attempt, finely dignified yet witty, should not have met with Merseyside's approval, though no doubt it is well enough appreciated in its final home in Australia at the National Gallery of Victoria, Melbourne.

The caravan-jaunt, though nostalgically recorded in a number of amusing snapshots,[23] proved as dismal as the weather. The groom neglected his job. The horses (when they remained on their feet at all) made wretched progress. John returned to London quite disenchanted with this method of transport. But, immured once more in Church Street, he continued to gasp for air. To his aid hurried a

[20] Romilly was born in 1906.

[21] It should be noted that (to begin with!) Dorelia had an itch for the open road quite as imperious as Augustus'. See, in particular, M.H., pp. 272–3.

[22] One of the present collaborators must confess that he has never liked the Fitzwilliam's 'William Nicholson'. Nicholson (1872–1949) won deserved admiration as a designer and still-life painter, but his whimsical personality was not really strong enough to stand up to such *magnifico* treatment.

[23] The photographer was Charles Slade, whose brother Loben married Dorelia's sister Jessie.

new admirer, John Quinn,[24] conjuring up with the magic wand of wealth gayer modes of travel in climes sunnier than East Anglia. On his side, Quinn promised himself a great deal of fun. Alas, his humourlessness was monumental. These, however, were the early days of the partnership. 'He's a treasure,' Augustus informed Dorelia, in the late summer of 1909. 'He's offered me £250 a year for life and I can send him what I like.'[25]

Though no such contract was ever formally drawn up between them, Quinn made it possible for John to visit Italy in mid-January 1910 and remain abroad for nine months, the last six of them spent with Dorelia and a sampling of sons in Provence. Often he departed by himself for a few days' parleying and junketing with a chieftain of the Coppersmith Gypsies and members of the Demeter family: as a result of which he was able to furnish the *Journal of the Gypsy Lore Society* with an unusually detailed vocabulary, supported by transcriptions of songs and tales.[26] Earlier, renewing acquaintance with the Italian fifteenth-century masters at first hand, he had delighted in their 'primitivism', and fallen avidly upon works by Piero della Francesca, Ghirlandaio and Botticelli.[27] But he lacked patience for sightseeing and picture-galleries soon damped his spirits. On the train from France, furthermore, he had observed a tiny inland sea glittering invitingly in the sun. It was the Etang de Berre, between the hills of Estaque and the Mediterranean. When he began to tire of Italy, he remembered the sense of excitement with which this stretch of water had filled him.

In March, accordingly, having picked up Dorelia, Pyramus, Romilly, Edwin and a friend, Helen Maitland,[28] at Arles, he conducted them by the route he himself had taken earlier to the charming little town of Martigues, a fishing-port on this same Etang de Berre, where Dorelia (in a white cowboy hat or Leghorn straw) with or without the children would be 'snapped' on celluloid and panel while bathing in the mere or sunning herself on the steps of their house (retained for many years), the Villa Ste Anne.[29] 'What I have been doing here', John wrote to Quinn, after five months in Martigues, 'is rapid sketching in paint.'[30] In November 1910, fifty – no less – of these oil sketches, under the title of 'Provençal Studies', were exhibited, together with a splendid group of drawings, at the Chenil Gallery in London, whither the trek back had been made late in September.

It would be difficult, if not impossible, to account for each and every one of these fifty little paintings, some on canvas but the most characteristic on panel. Quinn's own enormous holding has been scattered to the four winds. Since Percy Moore Turner,[31] on this side of the Atlantic, had a great deal to do with their disposal, many found their way into British private and public collections. Others remained in America, or were carried across the border into Canada.[32]

The exact dating of John's work is rarely easy, and the painting of his family in an outdoor setting continued, of course, after 1910, from models who had altered little. Occasionally, the hard facts are provable, when a date follows the signature, or a fancy title, that of Mrs Wilkins' 'Notre Dame de Martigues', say, has survived. There are sketches near the Villa Ste Anne (Pl. 10). But it is often difficult to distinguish between Martigues and Normandy (Pl. 41), and to know in which pool or

[24] (1870–1924) lawyer and collector of books and works of art. See B. L. Reid, *The Man from New York: John Quinn and his Friends* (New York, Oxford University Press, 1968).

[25] M.H., p. 319.

[26] *Journal of the Gipsy Lore Society*, New Series, Vol. V, July 1910–April 1911, pp. 217–35.

[27] The clearest echo of his hours in the galleries must be the rhapsodic portraits of Pyramus, already referred to (Pl. 12), and Caspar in a beret (Pl. 50).

[28] Dorelia's close friend, that is, who had met the John family on Hampstead Heath. Helen Maitland married a man well known to Augustus, Boris Anrep, the Russian mosaicist; after the marriage broke up she lived with Roger Fry.

[29] There is a contemporary series of snapshots in the family album.

[30] Letter of 25th August 1910. M.H., p. 348.

[31] Proprietor of The Independent Gallery, in London.

[32] Entering, for example, the Vincent Massey collection.

mere the children paddle under the eye of the lady in the Leghorn hat. Some, however, fit effortlessly into the first Martigues epoch, evoked for us by Romilly John's book.[33] The most beautiful of these gay productions, and as spontaneous as any, we believe to be a picture in the possession of Mr Harris, a quick sketch of Dorelia and the children, known quite simply once as 'Provençal Study' (Pl. 11). Typically, it is on panel, either sized or (as Clifford Hall suggested) lightly glass-papered and oiled, of a type John carried with him in a slotted box on his travels. The artist drew on the wood in pencil, often taking up the pencil again later to define the form over a thin skin of pigment. The jewel-like effect of this little work, its primitiveness, the painterly relation of sitters to an outdoor background: here were elements unusual in a production of the English School before the end of the first decade of the twentieth century.

We can afford to be so specific about the *terminus ante quem*. It was in November 1910, and during the three months bringing us up to January 1911, that the full impact of modern movements in art across the Channel made itself felt in Britain. The importance of 'Manet and the Post-Impressionists', an exhibition organized by Fry,[34] is now very generally understood. Not merely the uninstructed public, but artists and art critics, too, reacted in the strongest way to what was set before them at the Grafton Galleries. Nothing has damaged John's reputation so much as his comment on this first introduction of works by Cézanne, Van Gogh, Gauguin and Picasso to Londoners. It was, he told Eric Gill, in words reported back to Will Rothenstein, a 'bloody show'.[35] A moment's thought, however, must correct the false impression that John disliked the artists we have just named (as well as others less crucial to the immediate effect of the exhibition). For these men he had already expressed a deep personal admiration.[36] What offended him was the hullabaloo. He had not seen the show when he expressed himself thus irascibly. Later, he went twice, declaring himself on the second occasion much impressed. The reason for his enthusiasm was that a fine new batch of Van Goghs had arrived during the interval. He found the Gauguin reinforcements a delight, too. As for Cézanne, 'he was a splendid fellow, one of the greatest'.[37]

These later tributes, unfortunately, are not as well known as the first explosion of ill-temper. One has been led to think of Roger Fry as the grand cosmopolitan and John as the Little Englander. Fry organized a splendid exhibition of all the French artists we now admire most, and John turned his back on it: thus, greatly to the English painter's discredit, the events of 1910–11 have been arbitrarily interpreted. The truth could not be more different. John had as intimate an understanding of the contemporary French situation as Fry and the Bells[38] in Bloomsbury. Pictures which astonished tyros like Gilman,[39] sitting at the feet of Sickert and Lucien Pissaro, just across the Tottenham Court Road, were more familiar to John than the creaking signboard of The Cooper's Arms. How nearly his exhibition at the Chenil Gallery approached the Fry show in its revolutionary character may be judged by reviews of the time, reviews whose significance we can only now begin to appreciate.

To the critics, Augustus Edwin John seemed more wilfully eccentric than the 'Frenchmen at the

---

[33] Romilly John, who is also a poet, excels, in the opening chapter of *The Seventh Child* (1932), in conveying the brilliant colours of Provence.

[34] Roger Eliot Fry (1866–1934). John admired his ideas, while deploring the woodenness of his art.

[35] Sir William Rothenstein, *Men and Memories*, Vol. II, p. 213.

[36] The only important French modern whom John then really disliked, Matisse, had not been included in Fry's first Grafton exhibition.

[37] Letter to Quinn, 11th January 1911. See M.H., p. 362.

[38] Arthur Clive Howard Bell (1881–1964) married, in 1907, Vanessa Stephen (1879–1961). The one, in his criticism, the other, in her pictures, paid witty and graceful tribute to the natural superiority of 'la belle peinture'.

[39] Harold Gilman (1876–1919), though the most promising of our younger artists, would have been introduced by his mentors to vintage Impressionism only.

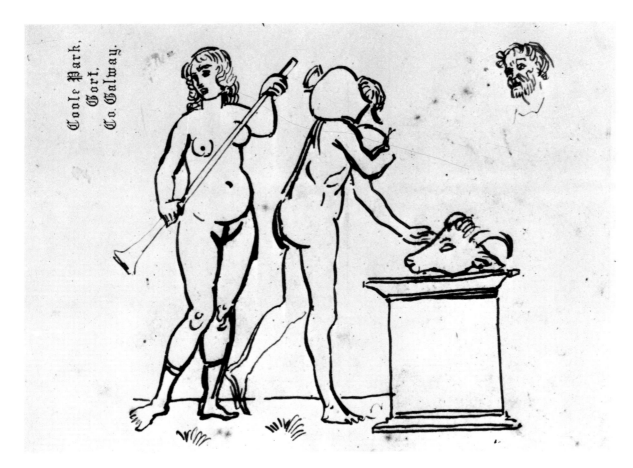

vi   A Classical Subject, ? 1915

Grafton'. In *The Times*, one read of the Chenil show: 'What does it all mean? Is there really a wide-spread demand for these queer, clever, forcible, but ugly and uncanny notes of form and dashes of colour? . . . for our part we see neither nature nor art in many of these strangely-formed heads, these long and too rapidly tapering necks, and these blobs of heavy paint that sometimes do duty for eyes.'[40] 'At his worst', another critic noted, 'he can outdo Gauguin . . . uncouth and grotesque . . . It is unfortunate that Mr John should go on filling public exhibitions with these inchoate studies, instead of manfully bracing to produce some complete piece of work.'[41]

Thus were the exquisite 'Provençal Studies' received in their own day: that is, with the same cater-waul of horror which greeted the exactly contemporary showing of 'Manet and the Post-Impressionists'.

In the following year, John risked another misconstruction of intent by off-handedly turning down Clive Bell's invitation to contribute to the second Post-Impressionist exhibition, which was to include, besides Matisse and others, living British painters. No particular clash of principle detached John from this enterprise: his own territory had easily absorbed the pre-Cubist Picasso; it could be

[40] *The Times*, 5th December 1910.
[41] *The Queen*, 10th December 1910.

[19]

stretched to admit Derain; he was even beginning to think better of Matisse.[42] Nothing, we may suppose, prevented his appearing in public alongside Epstein, Kramer, Gilman, Gore and Nevinson,[43] all artists he had more than once recommended to Quinn in private. Unlike these artists, however, he himself neither needed nor wanted any additional publicity. The Chenil, Knewstub still erratically presiding, was always at his service. If laziness had also something to do with his rejection of Bell's overtures, loyalty played its part, too. Entering Fry's camp would have amounted to a break with the N.E.A.C., to which John felt strong obligations, and would have been regarded by Will Rothenstein, Fry's rival and his own faithful, if sometimes embarrassing, impresario, as a savage act of betrayal. One ought to add that the painter was never really at home with art politics or gatherings dedicated to some particular aesthetic purpose. Though his name was on the books of the Camden Town Group, formed in the early summer of 1911, he contributed to the Group's first exhibition only.[44] He is known to have dropped in occasionally at 19 Fitzroy Street; but there was hardly room on such restricted premises for both himself and Sickert, whose taste for plain, even debilitated, women would have embarrassed John, in hot pursuit of a beauty required to be robust.[45] Then there were the long and frequent absences in France and, as he got fonder of Innes, in North Wales. Finally, in the summer of 1911, Lady Wimborne daringly leased Alderney Manor,[46] near Parkstone, Dorset, to the John family; and who could better assess its isolation than Henry Lamb, whose admiration extended to the lady of the house. 'She [Dorelia],' he wrote to Lytton Strachey, 'lives in an amazing place – a vast secluded park of prairies, pine-woods, birch woods, dells and moors with a house, cottages and a circular walled-garden.'[47] John, therefore, from then on, redoubled his elusiveness.

It has been necessary to relate in some detail the reasons, possible and probable, for the artist's keeping clear of the Second Post-Impressionist Exhibition. We hope we have made our points: that John was neither insular nor reactionary. If he has been damned as both, we can trace this to the well-known inferiority complex (supported by 'European-minded' historians) which insists that England's only course has been to imitate, always insensitively and very late in the day, the chain of events on the Continent.

In fact, among the most interesting features of John's work during the years 1912–14 is its 'primitive' lode, to which we have referred already. This primitivism is neither native-heath nor European, but universal. Dick Innes, therefore, a born 'naïf' (the rarest thing in the world), made a perfect companion for him. The Carmarthen painter was fighting a hopeless battle against tuberculosis, yet stimulated by its bacilli (as had been Beardsley earlier) into never-ending activity. He introduced John to some of the loneliest painting-grounds then known, in the neighbourhood of Lake Bala and Mount Arenig. Superficially, Innes' small panels and canvases have a good deal in common with John's: the work is flat, harsh, not often spectacularly brilliant (in bright colour, his possessive

[42] By 1928, Matisse had become for John the 'best, the most sensitive, of French painters': article in *Vogue*, written in that year.

[43] Sir Jacob Epstein (1880–1959) had just become a British citizen and was currently engaged on his sculpture for the Wilde Memorial; Jacob Kramer (1892–1962), a mere boy at the time, was exhibiting extraordinary promise, never quite fulfilled: Spencer Gore (1878–1914), understandably, impressed everyone in every camp; C. R. W. Nevinson (1889–1946) transferred, about this time, from the Slade to Julian's.

[44] The works were Welsh landscapes, 'Lynn Cynlog' and 'Nant-ddu', and gratefully listed Nos. 1 and 2 in the catalogue. John never attended a formal meeting of the Group: see Malcolm Easton, *Art in Britain, 1890–1940* (1967), for an examination of the Minutes.

[45] It is significant that in the most intimate study of Sickert to appear recently (Marjorie Lilly, *Sickert: The Painter and his Circle*, (1971)) John's name occurs but once, in a single clause of a single sentence: and in Dr Wendy Baron's scholarly monograph, the obvious conclusion receives further confirmation.

[46] The house has since been demolished.

[47] Letter of 24th July 1911. M.H., p. 385.

friend John Fothergill thought him 'supreme among English landscape painters');[48] but there is no evidence that John cribbed from Innes. His own 'Provençal Studies', which preceded any close acquaintance with the other's manner of painting, were already flat, harsh and brilliant. On the other hand, Innes' integrity thrilled him into fresh ambitions, especially in the province of landscape. But whereas Innes improvised before the *motif* more often than directly rendering it, and painted many a scene of Brontë-like gloom, John rarely exonerated himself from the debt to nature; and nature, for him, almost always smiled. A splendid example is the Tate's 'Llyn Treweryn' (Pl. 13), a small area of water in North Merioneth – not to be confused with the Dorset 'Blue Pool' (Pls. 16, 53, 54) – to which Innes had guided him.

Though John occasionally turned out a commissioned portrait, he had not yet become identified with professional face-painting. Those fortunate enough to have been entertained in Liverpool University's staff dining-room in recent times will have been impressed by the John likenesses of distinguished members of the old Dining Club which now hang there. In 1911, another was added to the series, that of Dr Kuno Meyer (Pl. 52)[49]: but one has to journey to Dublin for a glimpse of it – a journey well-rewarded, since it is a fresh, bold, honest work, without doubt the most successful of the Club commissions. Between that time and 1914, he was still making do with family and friends as models. Grand as its high heathlands are, the country around Alderney Manor never appealed to John as pure landscape: the garden of this odd, castellated bungalow, however, provided many a background for sketches, Martigues-style, of Dorelia and the children. The gem is perhaps the Tate's 'Washing Day', but for those who feel they are getting to know this too well we recommend a study of Lady Kleinwort's enchanting 'Romilly, Robin and Edwin' (Pl. 14). The latter work's gentle primitivism, though, hardly prepares us for the stark – and even more appealing – naïveté of the 'Edwin and Romilly' (Pl. 51), formerly with the Piccadilly Gallery.

Passing reference has already been made to something of a very different order, that strange amalgam of Gauguin and Gower Street, Parkstone and Picasso, Gypsies and Johns, entitled 'The Mumpers' (Pl. 55).[50] Vagrants of all kinds were encouraged to make themselves free of the Alderney grounds. Many sat for John (Pl. 15 shows Mr Harris' glorious portrait of one of the younger generation). Others were generally 'observed' and, the mood overtaking him, John wove them into more schematic compositions. But why the huge scale of the Detroit picture? Fry it was who kept active in John's mind the idea that he had a special gift for vast decoration.[51] Since Fry had given close study to the history of British art, he can hardly have been unaware that any mural project in this country is a very risky enterprise. We take it, however, that the suggestion had been made with the best of intentions. Fry must have received a shock when, in 1912, 'The Mumpers' at the Chenil came in for a worse drubbing than the simultaneous second exhibition of Post-Impressionists at the Grafton.

We have not, in this present section, returned as yet to the drawings. Since John has been apologized for as the draughtsman who also painted, we have wished to redress the balance: and, to us, his painting is so often more exciting than his drawing. Granted, the lapses from grace hit us harder in the oil medium; yet his insistence that colour-context and milieu are as important as the figure itself and his contribution to the lightening of the British palette place him for a moment – for a brief moment – well ahead both of Sickert and Gore. Certainly (in the period up to 1912 which we are now discussing)

---

[48] John Fothergill (intro.), *James Dickson Innes*, Ariel Books on the Arts (1956), p. 12.

[49] Kuno Meyer (1858–1919) was the leading authority of his day on Celtic language and literature.

[50] Mumper means beggar. It appears to be a term of scorn directed by Gypsies themselves against the humbler tribes in their community.

[51] As early as 1909, Fry had urged that 'Mr John should have a great wall in some public building and a great theme to illustrate': *The Burlington Magazine*, Vol. XV, No. 73, April 1909, p. 17.

John had advanced a great deal further from traditional anecdotal art than any other British painter.

By preferring his paintings to his drawings, we do not mean we subscribe to the notion, much canvassed in the art schools of today, that John 'couldn't draw'. It must be obvious to the intelligent person that there are a hundred good ways of drawing and that John's is one of them. After his early essays in chalk (black or red: sometimes both together), one can say that the lead-pencil – Sir Caspar John recalls how, as boys, he and his brothers were sent out to purchase mottled-green 'Venus' replacements by the bundle – was the artist's favourite as well as most characteristic instrument. It is especially true of this, his finest period, when Dorelia, Alick Schepeler and Euphemia Lamb[52] constituted his chief sitters among the grown-ups, with his sons brought up as supernumeraries. In fact, drawings of Dorelia outnumber all the rest by hundreds (lost or undeclared sketches of the artist's most beautiful model must bring the total up to the thousand-mark). We reproduce here a sample only of the most exquisite (Pls. 43, 44, 45), one taken from the Tate, one from Mrs Thelma Cazalet-Keir's collection, and the third from the Fitzwilliam Museum. However, the drawings of Euphemia Lamb can often be extremely disappointing. In the present circumstances, we thought it more instructive to reproduce instead two drawings of Alick Schepeler (Pls. 37, 40), in which the oblique shading has been compared with that of Leonardo's silverpoints.[53] Till advancing years brought on a 'flicker', by which contours are uncertainly multiplied, John's line was unusually strong and sustained. Accused of developing little, he made the disarming reply that he had sought to preserve something he valued above all else, the spirit of his youth.[54]

But if a top half-dozen had to be decided upon among the vast output of drawings surviving from between 1903 and 1914, they might very well turn out to be delicate chalk or pencil studies of the boys. We have had many of our pleasantest surprises in private houses, coming suddenly, in a passage-way or as we climbed a staircase, upon a 'David', an 'Edwin' or a 'Robin'. Less well-known than most is the 'Caspar' actually rejected by the artist, belonging to Mr Brinsley Ford (Pl. 46). And (to depart for a moment from crayon or pencil) the drawing of 'Pyramus Asleep' (Pl. 39) is a particularly refined example of John's penwork from the period under review.

The artist used, in the main, Whatman paper, Not or Hotpressed, made up into blocks from which the sheets could be extracted. But there are plenty of alternatives to Whatman's dimpled white surface: grey papers, blue-grey, pink, yellow-pink. Then one must not forget the drawings coloured with monochrome washes or a wider range of pigment. Among these, are the Ontario 'The Blue Scarf' and the Fitzwilliam's 'The Blue Shawl' (Pl. 45), where the scarf and shawl alone have been tinted.

So much for the drawings. We return to the artist's activities just prior to the First World War. In 1913, as so often before, he was in Paris. There, one April day, Epstein introduced him to Modigliani.[55] Had we not previously encountered John's passion for the primitive, it would seem unbelievable, bearing in mind the elegant, old-masterish quality of the drawings just discussed, that their author should have been so deeply affected by the two stone heads Modigliani showed him. 'For some days afterwards,' John recalled, 'I found myself under the hallucination of meeting people in the street

[52] Alick Schepeler has been barely mentioned. Her real name was Alexandra and, like Dorelia, she earned her living as a typist (on *The Illustrated London News*). Euphemia had been a Slade student before Henry Lamb married her. She appears in countless John studies, particularly in and around 1907. The Lambs were divorced towards the end of the 1920s, and Euphemia later became Mrs Grove.

[53] With the difference that Leonardo, unlike John, was left-handed.

[54] 'A Note on Drawing', in Browse, *op. cit.*, p. 10. 'Does it not seem,' wrote John, 'as if the secret of the artist lies in the prolongation of the age of adolescence with whatever increase of technical skill and sophistication the lessons of the years may bring?'

[55] Amedeo Modigliani (1884–1920), Italian sculptor and painter who settled in Paris in 1906.

who might have posed for them, and that without myself resorting to the Indian weed [Modigliani took hashish].'[56] Though Brancusi and African carvings (the other's principal models) left no mark on John's own style during the years following, there is a late echo of the enthusiasm engendered by this meeting, the still-life with flowers, featuring one of the sculptured heads draped in a widow's veil, entitled 'In Memoriam Amedeo Modigliani' (Pl. 64).

In 1914, John got so far as drilling with other Army volunteers in the forecourt of Burlington House. Entry into the Forces was denied him, however, through a knee-injury. At first, in any case, his mind dwelt little on the war. More real to him was the death of Innes.[57] No other man would ever mean so much to John; no fellow-painter so inspire him to grapple afresh with the problems of his art. From that moment, the wavelets of Treweryn lost their sparkle. The moon began to set in John's artistic heaven. The rest is a disappointing – and, year by year, a more disappointing – story.

[56] *Chiaroscuro*, p. 131.
[57] Innes died from tuberculosis on 22nd August 1914. He was twenty-seven.

❧ 3 ❧

THE DECLINE, to begin with, was scarcely perceptible. Spared the restrictions of military service, John could profit from what freedom of movement remained, and in the autumn of 1915 crossed to Ireland. Once again he had been commissioned by Lady Gregory to paint a portrait at Coole Park: this time, of George Bernard Shaw. The three studies that resulted, and we reproduce the best (Pl. 56), have an undeniable vigour – but they ring a knell. A boldly accelerated 'drawing with the brush' has succeeded the Ingres-like *facture* of the Cerutti portrait and the solidity of 'The Smiling Woman'. From now on, and in the same broad, bright, fatally breezy manner, John would become (except in rare instances) almost as banal a recorder of the wealthy and celebrated as Orpen himself. If a buccaneering touch was often added, this rarely upset his clients. We applaud him, of course, for refusing to compete with the more submissive portrait-painters of the day; but there is irony in the fact that, war having permitted a new freedom of manners, John became as petted for his crustiness as they for their flattery.

No sirens yet sang from Belgravia, however. Eaton Square withheld its custom. And for Sampson's pupil the gayest mansions were still green ones. From 1911 onwards, there had been a baffling 'Lyric Fantasy' (Pl. 16) on his hands, its background a horse-and-trap journey from Alderney Manor. 'Lyric Fantasy' was the first and last large-scale composition of John's that promised real success. The Pitmans,[1] after it came into their possession, tactfully turned aside all offers to 'finish' – and so, predictably, to ruin – the picture, which had been undertaken originally as a mural for the house of Sir Hugh Lane[2] at a time when several very large canvases or cartoons, 'Forza e Amore', 'The Mumpers' (already referred to) and 'The Flute of Pan', were in process of realization,[3] and when, even while grinding his teeth over 'Lyric Fantasy', John could propose a companion-piece of similar dimensions.[4]

This last proved a mirage. The 'Fantasy' itself was abandoned after Lane's death in the *Lusitania* disaster of 1915. For many years it glowed with the warmth of a fine tapestry out of the shadows of Mrs Pitman's drawing-room at Odstock. In 1972 it appeared in the Tate, to which she had bequeathed it. The picture stood up to public gaze with dignity, preserving as it does all that was best in John, in particular his beguiling elegance and the charm inseparable from any early work inspired by Ida, Dorelia and the two broods of children. Unlike most other trial flights on the same scale, 'Lyric Fantasy' is *conceived in colour*, and nowhere more expressively than in the passage dovetailing the

---

[1] The late Hugo Pitman and his wife Reine, friends and generous patrons of the artist.

[2] Sir Hugh Percy Lane (1875–1915), art patron and Director of the National Gallery of Ireland.

[3] 'Forza e Amore' appeared at the New English Art Club's winter exhibition in 1911; 'The Mumpers' exactly a year later. In November 1912 he was engaged on an 'immense drawing of the Caucasian Gypsies'. Again at the New English, in the winter of 1913, John showed a large cartoon, 'The Flute of Pan'.

[4] Letter of 24th June 1914: 'As for Lane, I have told him I will do him another design which will harmonize with the big one I am doing for him now.' See M.H., Vol. II, Ch. 1.

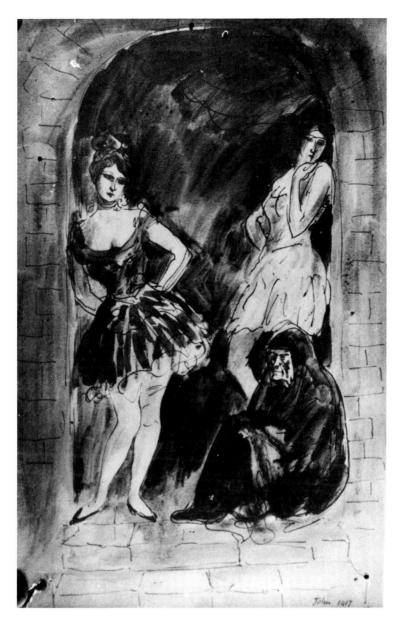

vii   Entrance to a Brothel, 1917

scarlet tunic of the young drummer to the blue-green water of the clay-workings.[5]

The most ambitious of all John's mural compositions, the 'Galway' triptych (Pl. 57), belongs to the same year as the Shaw portraits. Leaving Coole, the artist fell in with Francis Macnamara, hereditary squire of Ennistymon.[6] Together, they made the steamer-trip from Aran to Galway city, 'clustered above the water in a pattern of grey and white'. Before examining the vast canvases in the Tate's Acton warehouse, one should read the brief account in words John gives of the western capital. It well conveys how much the place and its fisherfolk meant to him artistically. An impression is produced, too, of plunging pavements as well as of plunging seas; of endless glasses of the 'hard stuff' in

[5] Mr Romilly John has thus identified the mysterious 'blue lake'.
[6] Francis Macnamara, born in 1885 or 1886, died in 1946.

Flaherty's bar on the New Dock.[7] John's long-suffering liver was obviously under duress again: the temptation would be to try it too hard.

Art, however, being seldom strictly autobiographical, 'Galway' now appears the soberest of paintings. Reading from left to right (the three sections, coupled up, would amount to more than forty feet of canvas, measured horizontally), we begin with an al fresco banquet to which, in a trial sketch, the title 'Bank Holiday' has been appended.[8] The central panel, the best known and the one reproduced here, shows a highly stylized group of shawled women with their children. In the right-hand, concluding section, a dozen men in billicocks and braces converse together. Even in its over-simplistic centre-piece, 'Galway' is a work of real bone and brawn; though whether John could have taken it much beyond its present semi-monochromatic, sketched-in state may be doubted. Closely connected with the Tate triptych is a similar subject owned by Gwen Lady Melchett (Pl. 17). This is lighter and gayer and constitutes perhaps the most successful of John's fragmentary recollections of his 1915 visit to Ireland. If the observed and invented elements do not always work in well together, it has to be remembered that an artist's opportunities were severely restricted in wartime Galway.[9]

Though his portraits of Lloyd George and Admiral Fisher[10] might have been regarded as contributions to the war effort, John dearly longed to reach France. He applied for a temporary commission as a war-artist early in 1916, but had to learn patience. A year and more passed before Lord Beaverbrook was able to get him gazetted Major with the Canadians. Writing from Corps Headquarters, near Arras, shortly afterwards, John saw his task as 'immense and magnificent'.[11] But when, in the spring of 1918, this brief episode ended, the results fell short, in quality, if not in quantity. He had painted a number of portraits of soldiers and had accumulated a long series of studies for a Canadian War Memorial picture on the scale of 'Galway' which was not, however, continued beyond the stages of charcoal cartoon and oil sketch.[12] Had he been able to adapt to this enormous frieze the fine, low-keyed palette which characterizes 'Fraternity' (Pl. 59), the result might have been a triumph.

The war itself did little, its aftermath more, to alter the tenor of John's life. In 1919, besides painting official portraits at the Peace Conference in Paris,[13] he visited Deauville, meeting there the duchesse de Guiche and the duchesse de Gramont: 'You see what elevated company I'm in,' he told Gwen.[14] But if two seem an overplus of duchesses, this was, after all, the age of artists like de László who kept company with half the Almanac de Gotha. And Deauville soon palled. John's daughter, Vivien,[15] accompanied him to many grand houses and confirms for us that his social digestion was a delicate one, boredom always breaking in. Contemplation of heavily mascaraed marchesas (Pl. 18), like consumption of the hard stuff (though more and more of that was required), only momentarily rescued the artist from his fits of black despair. He knew – if the general public did not – that his work was going downhill; that, through his continual burning of the candle at both ends he had already contracted what, abusing musicians' terminology, we might call *wrist-flutter*. Yet, still adding here and there to his

[7] *Chiaroscuro*, pp. 92–3. The account of Aran characteristically follows that of Galway, a reversal of the historical sequence.

[8] *Cf.* Anthony Bertram, *Augustus John* (1923), Pl. 31.

[9] Letter to Dorelia, autumn 1915, from Galway: 'Sketching in the harbour is strictly forbidden so that is another drawback and a big one'. M.H., Vol. II, Ch. 2.

[10] Painted in April 1915.

[11] Sir William Rothenstein, *Men and Memories*, Vol. II, p. 311.

[12] The cartoon has always been described as for a 'Canadian War Memorial', whereas the small canvas sketch, identical in composition (Pl. 60) and now owned by Beaverbrook Foundations, is called 'At Liévin Castle'.

[13] E.g., of Hughes, Massey, Borden, Cecil, Cunliffe, Summers, Goode. The work continued into 1920.

[14] M.H., Vol. II, Ch. 2.

[15] Born in 1915, Vivien is the younger of Dorelia's two daughters; her elder sister Poppet was born in 1912.

family, he needed more money. He needed it, in any case, to underwrite a lordly carelessness and generosity, to maintain studios and a home in England and a house abroad. His three trips to America in the 1920s were cynically undertaken to rake in the dollars; yet, when it came to the point, he would often desert his Wideners and Fullers and Mellons for the humbler pleasures of Harlem. At the beginning of the decade he let his name go forward for election to the Royal Academy.

As an Associate, therefore, he could be sure, in 1923, of getting his huge portrait of Madame Suggia (Pl. 20) into the Burlington House shop-window. The reputation which had sagged since 'The Smiling Woman' of 1908 suddenly revived. Here was a challenge to which John rose magnificently. The celebrated cellist is herself a witness to the time and care the artist lavished on this work.[16] She posed for two hours consecutively, some days both during the morning and afternoon, and work on the picture continued over a period of three years. A nearly square canvas has been selected to accommodate Suggia's expansive pose and the cascade of skirt flowing down into the lower right corner as she rides her way through an austerely splendid suite of Bach. It is to be supposed, however, judging by the number of alterations involved, that the artist was more often sweating with anxiety than revelling in the grand C Minor. The dress, occupying about a quarter of the picture-area, went through a gold, then a white, then a red (and final) stage. The arms were painted in and out half-a-dozen times. Physically and nervously extravagant as these shifts may seem, 'Mme Suggia' must be accounted the last late masterpiece of John's professional career.

Another portrait belonging to 1923 is that of Thomas Hardy (Pl. 66), now in the Fitzwilliam. Lightweight after the Suggia, it offers an agreeably crisp and clear impression of a man John genuinely admired. This is a convenient place in which to speak of the 'English Men of Letters' series in the artist's *oeuvre*. Since the pen is demonstrably mightier than the brush, there has always existed a love-hate relationship between practitioners of the two arts. But in *Chiaroscuro* and *Finishing Touches*, one must admit, literary reputations are disposed of with exceptional severity and we read with surprise the stinging comments on writers who were also John's close friends. Can it be that the author nursed some secret ambitions in the same field, making him doubly jealous? Certainly, a fine, Romantic correspondent earlier on (see the brilliant letters first published in *Men and Memories*), he continued to pursue the *mot juste* in his 'Fragments of Autobiography', over which much midnight oil was burned.[17] In his paintings, this carping spirit is absent or concealed, however. During the years from 1917, he did handsomely by Arthur Symons, Ronald Firbank and W. H. Davies (Pls. 58, 61, 63). The paintings of T. E. Lawrence are, not surprisingly, somewhat café-style: John portrays here the celebrity rather than the painstaking compiler of the *Seven Pillars of Wisdom*. We have preferred to reproduce one of the National Portrait Gallery's three drawings (Pl. 62).[18]

There is some kinship between these portraits of writers and the various studies of Lady Ottoline Morrell,[19] of which the most memorable, painted about 1919, appears here (Pl. 19). It will be mistaken years hence for a caricature of some haughty and horsy Edwardian aristocrat. In fact, like Goya's Maria Luisa of Parma, John's Ottoline is a straightforward presentation of a splendidly ugly woman broadminded enough to accept the visual truth about herself. Passions having died down, she remains a dear friend; and, again as Goya saw the consort of Charles IV, John sees Ottoline as a

[16] On 8th April 1923 *The Weekly Despatch* published the article: 'Sitting for Augustus John'. Guilhermina Suggia (1888–1950), born in Oporto, in 1914 settled in England. There are at least two charcoal sketches and an earlier and smaller oil painting of the sitter.

[17] See Mr Daniel George's witty and perceptive Introduction to *Finishing Touches*, particularly p. 11.

[18] John continued to portray Lawrence, though (as it seems to us) with diminishing excitement, after he became Aircraftsman Shaw.

[19] Kinship, because of Lady Ottoline's chosen role of literary (and artistic) muse.

person, not as the representative of a class. A strong wash-drawing of the same subject (Pl. 47) is included here as a foil to the over-familar work. 'Memorable' Plate 19 undoubtedly is, but histrionically rather than artistically. The drawing of a decade earlier explores profounder depths. From now on almost all John's portraits are high-voltage sketches, little felt and only worked up to the minimal degree of finish. A remarkable exception, however, is the subtle, feathery painting of Joseph Hone (Pl. 72), executed some years after less rewarding sessions with Hugh Walpole and Sean O'Casey.[20]

To 1925 is ascribed the first flower-painting. In the family it is understood that not so much desire as desperation drove John to this activity. When all else failed and the artist turned in disgust from the latest portrait which wouldn't come right, Dorelia, that great gardener, thrust one of her potted plants or a selection of cut flowers in front of him with instructions to get to work at once: so great a liability was the master of the house unemployed. In these circumstances, therapeutic rather than anything else, we should hardly expect fine works, yet we do find them. It was Manet, with his peonies, who infused life into flowers at the expense of botanical detail. John, with a touch far less sure, works on in this manner, himself often attracted to the peony, though other canvases feature magnolias, mimosa, gloxinia, cineraria, cyclamen, sweet williams, primulas and sunflowers. We shall restrict ourselves to the handsome 'Peonies in a Jug' (Pl. 21), which belongs to Mrs Thelma Cazalet-Keir, and an unusually ambitious 'Mixed Flowers' (Pl. 24) from a private collection in London.

If John admired Hardy, he does not seem to have felt any very great affection for the Wessex landscape, except as a summary backcloth for the 1911–14 open-air studies of his family. After an interlude of dazzling Llyn Treweryns and small panels inspired by (though not in any way imitations of) Innes' work, and the war over, he was able to concentrate on the arid countryside round his Villa Ste Anne, at Martigues; and when the Villa was sold in 1928, to visit gayer areas of France, with the wilds of Ireland thrown in for variety. He was soon back in Provence again, however, where from 1937 he rented the Mas de Galeron, St-Rémy-de-Provence. What has been said about the flower-paintings covers equally well the landscapes, at least those belonging to the later years. It was in 1928 that he painted 'The Little Railway, Martigues' (Pl. 69); and most of the St-Rémy views, like the example shown here (Pl. 75), were produced during the late Thirties. John seems to have been automatically roused to action by the sight of the olive-orchards nestling under the pink foothills of the Alpilles. This style of landscape looks like a diluted Matthew Smith,[21] the fine artist whom he loved and respected and of whom he painted a worthy old-man's portrait (Pl. 77).

In 1927 the John family moved from Alderney Manor to Fryern Court, and in the following year Augustus became a full member of the Royal Academy. He was now, however flamboyantly he tried to disguise it, a country gentleman and an honoured pillar of the Establishment. There can be no doubt, too, that poor health (in 1930 he was driven to take a 'cure') sapped, besides his talent as an artist, the old spirit of rumbustiousness which had enjoyed such a fling over the Leverhulme affair.[22] Of the meeting they had in 1931, when John was a mere fifty-three, Lady Mosely recalled: 'He seemed old, his hair was grey, his eyes bloodshot . . . He had aged very much in those years [from 1926–30]'.[23] A full-length portrait of Viscount D'Abernon (Pl. 67a) had been occupying John about

[20] The Walpole portrait is at King's School, Canterbury. Of the two portraits of O'Casey, one belongs to the writer's widow, the other to the Metropolitan Museum, New York. John contributed to the décor of O'Casey's *The Silver Tassie* in 1929.

[21] Sir Matthew Smith (1879–1959). The portrait was not painted till 1944.

[22] In 1920 John's portrait of Lord Leverhulme was returned to him with the head cut out of the canvas. John saw to it that such vandalism received world-wide publicity (*Chiaroscuro*, pp. 150–1).

[23] Letter to Michael Holroyd.

the same time. Shown at the Academy in 1931, and a sensation of the day, it looks more like an 'instant' Old Master now than a brave piece of satire, which last conception a photograph of D'Abernon (Pl. 67b) seems finally to dispose of.

No admirer of the best in John will wish to linger over the merely pretty models increasingly employed by him towards the end of the Twenties. There were exceptions, of course, as when in 1929 he painted the late Lady Adeane, formerly Miss Kit Dunn (Pl. 22), who perfectly expresses the irresistibly beautiful yet emancipated heroine of the contemporary light romance, from Arlen to Dornford Yates. We add, in a different category though probably belonging to about the same year, the Gerhardie-style 'Poppet' (Pl. 68). Two drawings of James Joyce (Pls. 70, 71), dated 1930, consort oddly with these adorable creatures.

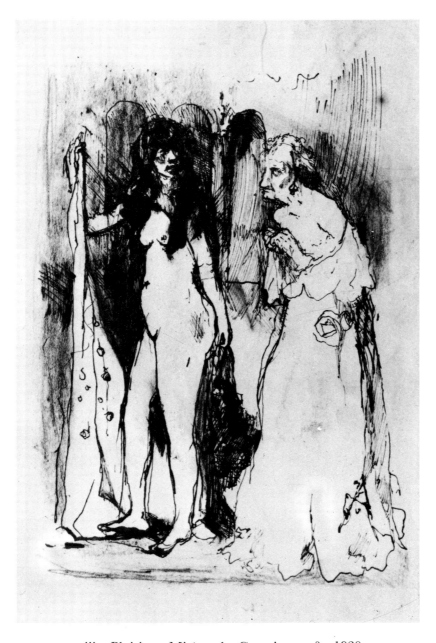

viii   Plaisirs et Misères des Courtisanes, ? *c.* 1920

[29]

One episode out of which John came with flying colours was a visit to Jamaica in 1937 (the unpleasant taste of *The Boy David* still in his mouth[24]). There is a humanity about this series of portraits unique in John's entire production. Staying just outside Kingston, he persuaded the hotel servants and any other native girls available to pose for him in portrait after portrait labelled 'Ivy', 'Daphne', 'Phyllis', 'Aminta', etc, sometimes singly (Pl. 23), sometimes paired (Pl. 74). But with these, the artist seems to have tapped his last fresh source of inspiration.

The outbreak of the Second World War (whose bombs were to interrupt John's portrait of the Queen) brought its familiar limitations of personal freedom, particularly aggravating to the artist. Too old to follow the troops to France, he marked time at Stulik's[25] or in the Fitzroy Tavern, often in the company of Dylan Thomas (Pl. 73). Interspersed with the drawings of pretty, too pretty, girls, an occasionally fine likeness of a worthier sitter emerged (Pls. 76, 78, 80). From looking old, John began to look battered. The nicotine that dyed his white beard and moustache here and there gave him a piebald appearance; his deafness grew worse; the whites of his eyes gleamed in a permanent myopic glare, as an astonishing profusion of self-portraits has recorded (*cf.* Pl. 79).

As far as his public image was concerned, however, he had no rival. After a widely-publicized resignation,[26] one hardly noticed his graceful reception back into the Royal Academy's ranks only two years later. For the man in the street John remained the bad bold Bohemian, attracting in this character an unsolicited affection. To the student, on the other hand, as the war receded and the art schools of the fifties were going through the teething stage of the next decade's revolution, the Slade draughtsman and the fashionable portrait-painter (as he appeared to be) equally became anathema. The 1954 exhibition at the Diploma Gallery of Burlington House, the first great comprehensive retrospective of the artist's work, all the more sharply divided John from the generation then growing up. But the reformed rebel of British art, with his Order of Merit (1942), was not and never had been a self-satisfied virtuoso content to repeat himself indefinitely.

No one understood this better than Sir Charles Wheeler,[27] whom John admitted to his confidence during the last years. Others were aware of the execution of a delicately-hatched drawing or two by the trembling hand and a number of paintings of the ageing Dorelia (Pl. 81); what the world did not know was that a projected triptych based on the legend of Les Saintes-Maries-de-la-Mer occupied all the artist's spare moments (Pl. 82). He had returned to his old dream of a vast canvas, this time to commemorate the landing in the Camargue of the two Marys, Mary of James and Mary Salome, with a servant, Sara. Sara, cared for by the Gypsies, became their patron saint – and so, one might say, John's. In 1960 Wheeler went down to see the triptych in progress. 'The sureness of hand and mind of the earlier day was waning,' he afterwards recalled of this visit to Fryern Court. More than ever, John was scraping-out and altering. Wheeler adds: 'Each time I saw it [the Saintes-Maries decoration], it became less and less resolved and was never finished.'[28]

By 9th March 1961, John felt that the task had defeated him: he wrote to tell the President that the Abbey Trust would have to relinquish the idea of a commission. The letter reveals the artist's bitter

[24] For this play of Barrie's, which turned out a fiasco, John had been engaged to design the scenery and costumes. Long before its brief run ended on 31st January 1937, he had given up the costumes and his principal scene had suffered catastrophic alterations. See Malcolm Easton, 'The Boy David', *Apollo*, Vol. LXXXII, No. 44, October 1965, pp. 318–325.

[25] The Tour Eiffel, or Eiffel Tower, Restaurant in Percy Street, owned by Rudolf Stulik.

[26] Ostensibly, John took this step when he heard of the Academy's rejection of Wyndham Lewis' portrait of T. S. Eliot in 1938. In fact, he looked on the event as a welcome opportunity to express his temporary displeasure with the then President, Sir William Llewellyn. Later, on actually seeing Lewis' picture, he confessed to a sympathy with the Academy! See Michael Holroyd, 'Damning and Blasting', in *The Listener*, 6th July 1972.

[27] Sculptor, born 1892, and President of the Royal Academy from 1956 to 1966.

[28] Sir Charles Wheeler, *High Relief* (1968), p. 116.

distress.[29] Indeed, Michael Ayrton remembers him in tears, declaring: 'My work's not good enough.'[30] Fortunately, the public's last view of him, in a 'Face to Face' programme of May 1960 on B.B.C. Television, was of a genius hoarfrosted and frail – but still defiant.

Augustus Edwin John died at his home in Fordingbridge, three months short of his eighty-fourth birthday, on 31st October 1961.

[29] And was followed by another, thanking Wheeler for a wire and a letter, and adding: 'They saved [my reason] and I am almost myself again': Wheeler, *op. cit.*, pp. 118–9.

[30] M.H., Vol. II, Ch. 5.

Notes on figures in text

i THE PROMENADE, *c.* 1900

Pastel: from a photograph (original untraced)

The John Estate

Sir William Rothenstein felt that John's early pastels were superior to his paintings, and spoke of the influence of Daumier: though where the Tate's 'Rustic Scene' is concerned, Millet might be nearer the mark. But it was Degas whose successful handling of this medium took away its stigma as the perquisite of maiden aunts. John himself recalled that the great majority of his own pastels were produced shortly after leaving the Slade; say, about 1898–1903.

ii CHURCHYARD SCENE, *c.* 1901

Black chalk on buff paper, $10\frac{1}{2} \times 14$ *(26·6 × 35·6), S*

Collection: Mrs Valentine Fleming
Miss Amaryllis Fleming

This is extremely difficult to date. If the costume is contemporary with the drawing itself, then it must be early; and John made the greatest number of drawings in black chalk about the turn of the century. On the other hand (and the style would seem to corroborate it), this might be a 'period' reminiscence. Any allusion to deep human feeling, especially grief, is rare in John's work: hence this drawing's particular interest. Mrs Valentine Fleming's title for it was 'A French Funeral'; but some memory going back to childhood days in Tenby could have been utilized.

iii   DESESPERANCE D'AMOUR, *c.* 1902

From a photograph by Mowl and Morrison, Liverpool
(original untraced)

Collection: Judge Dowdall
The John Estate

It was an article of faith with John that the bourgeoisie is racked by the passions it condemns. Throughout his work appear disapproving elders, male or female, holding up their hands in horror at the lovers who pass them on the primrose path. Here youth, for a change, expresses its contempt for age. In style and composition, as well as fancy, this lost picture resembles another, showing Orpen 'escaping from his relatives', recently with Mr Anthony d'Offay.

iv   SPECTATORS IN A PICTURE-GALLERY (?), *c.* 1912

Pen, brush and black ink: from a photograph (original untraced)

The John Estate

The interest here is the baffling strangeness of the style, more reminiscent of Edvard Munch (1863–1924) than of John who, nevertheless, appends an irreproachable signature.

v   THE BRAGGING SOLDIER, 1915

Soft pencil on paper, $9 \times 10\frac{3}{4}$ *(22·8 × 32·4)*

Signed 'John' bottom right

Miss Amaryllis Fleming

An unpublished and interestingly uncharacteristic drawing, 'The Bragging Soldier' (with its provincial air) belongs almost certainly to the Irish visit of 1915. The men, John explains in his correspondence, were going away 'to fight England's battles', and there was a great wailing on the platforms as the women saw them off. Most of the women, having men in the Army and Navy, received Government pay: 'the consequence is an unusually heavy traffic in stout'. There seem to be no references to such military matters from Wales.

[33]

vi A CLASSICAL SUBJECT, ? 1915

Pen and blue-black ink on Lady Gregory's grey, embossed writing-paper, $4\frac{7}{16} \times 7$ (11·4 × 17·8)

The John Estate

John paid his first visit to Coole Park in 1907; but the style of the drawing suggests a later date, which could be 1915 (provided the paper was not purloined and put to this use after his return to England). With Keats, one inquires, 'Who are these coming to the sacrifice?' The composition does not seem to have been carried further, and the question remains unanswered. Though he must have been a keen admirer of Ingres, John rarely ventured into the world of classical mythology.

vii ENTRANCE TO A BROTHEL, 1917

Pen-and-ink and wash or watercolour: from a photograph
(original untraced)

Signed and dated 'John 1917' bottom right

The John Estate

The theme of prostitute and procuress may have come to John by way of the Venetian School and Caravaggio and the Caravaggesque. In pen-and-ink, it harks back to Guys. Or is it a memory of old Marseille? The seated hag crops up perennially in John's work, expressing her displeasure wherever the joys of youth are celebrated. In December 1917 the artist arrived in France for his brief tour of duty as war artist, but the sketch hardly suggests Canadian Corps H.Q.

viii PLAISIRS ET MISERES DES COURTISANES, ? *c.* 1920

Crayon, pen and black ink, $14\frac{5}{8} \times 10\frac{1}{2}$ (37·1 × 26·7)

The John Estate

We have chosen a title which would equally suit a multitude of sketches thrown off by John over the years. If the atmosphere is Balzacien, this would be in keeping with the literary taste of the artist and his friends about the close of the nineteenth century. Charles Conder (1868–1909) produced a series of lithographic illustrations to the *Comédie humaine*. For a portrait of Alick Schepeler John chose the title 'Séraphita', one of Balzac's stories from the *Etudes philosophiques*. The drawing is a flight of fancy offering no blandishments. But this deliberate clumsiness matched a recurrent mood in John. Here, we believe, he returns quite late to the old topic.

Augustus John : Chronology

1878	4th January, born at Tenby, Pembrokeshire, Wales.	1902	6th January, David born. Autumn, meets Dorothy McNeill in London.
1884	August, mother dies. Family move from Haverfordwest to Tenby.	1903	Elected to N.E.A.C. March, Carfax Gallery. Paintings (3), Pastels (8), Drawings (21) and Etchings (13) by Augustus E. John. Paintings (3) by Gwen John. 22nd March, Caspar born. August, Gwen and Dorelia's 'walk to Rome', via Toulouse. Augustus and Ida move to Elm House, Matching Green, Essex.
1894–8	Slade School of Fine Art, London.
1897	Bathing accident.
1898	'Moses and the Brazen Serpent' wins the Summer Composition Prize. Visits Holland with Ambrose McEvoy.
1899	First one-man show at Carfax Gallery. Makes £30 and goes to Vattetot-sur-mer with William Rothenstein, William Orpen, Charles Conder. Meets Oscar Wilde in Paris. Begins exhibiting at New English Art Club.	1903–7	Involved with Orpen and Knewstub in the Chelsea Art School, Rossetti Studios.
		1904	Gwen and Dorelia arrive in Paris. Dorelia elopes to Bruges. August, Dorelia returns and lives at Elm House. Augustus elected to membership of the Society of Twelve. 23rd October, Ida's Robin born.
1900	Goes to Swanage with Conder. 'Walpurgis Night'. Visits Le Puy-en-Velay with the Rothensteins and Michel Salaman. Painted by Orpen.	1905	April–May, on Dartmoor. Dorelia's Pyramus born. September, emigration to rue Monsieur-le-Prince, Paris. November, Chenil Gallery. Drawings by Aug. E. John (42) and William Orpen (22). 27th November, Ida's Edwin born.
1901	12th January, marries Ida Nettleship. Moves into 18 Fitzroy Street, London.
1901–2	Art instructor at Liverpool. Meets John Sampson and the Dowdalls. Etchings.

1906   January, move to 77 rue Dareau, Paris.
May, Chenil Gallery. Eighty-Two Etchings. Alick Schepeler.
August, at Ste-Honorine-des-Pertes with Wyndham Lewis.
Dorelia's Romilly born.
November, Dorelia detaches herself and moves to 48 rue du Château.

1907   February, Augustus and Ida move to 3 Cour-de-Rohan.
9th March, Ida's Henry born.
14th March, Ida dies.
Summer, at Equihen with Dorelia.
September, visits Lady Gregory at Coole, Ireland. Paints W. B. Yeats.
Moves to 8 Fitzroy Street, London.
November, Carfax Gallery.
Eighty-one Drawings.

1908   Gets to know Lady Ottoline Morrell.
Starts off for Spain, via Paris.
July–September, at Dielette with Dorelia and children. Visited by Mrs Nettleship.
Autumn, moves into 153 Church Street with Dorelia and families.

1909   January, paints William Nicholson.
Takes studio at 181a King's Road.
July, caravans to Cambridge.
Paints Jane Harrison.
August, paints His Worship the Lord Mayor of Liverpool, and Smith.
Meets John Quinn in London.
September, agrees to decorate Hugh Lane's house.

1910   January–September, travels, at Quinn's expense, to Italy and Provence. Visits Frank Harris at Nice.
April, Villa Ste Anne, Martigues.
November–December, Chenil Gallery. Provençal Studies (48) and

Other Works (35 drawings). Begins working with J. D. Innes.

1911   Elected to the Camden Town Group.
May, rents cottage with Innes in North Wales.
July, paints Kuno Meyer in Liverpool.
August, moves to Alderney Manor.
September, in France with Quinn.
October, in Wales.
December, Chenil Gallery. Paintings, Drawings and Etchings.

1912   March, Pyramus dies. Poppet is born.
Summer, West Coast of Ireland with Francis Macnamara and Oliver St John Gogarty.
September, stays at Chirk Castle with the Howard de Waldens.

1913   January, in South of France with Innes.
February, Armory Show, New York (23 paintings, 14 drawings).
Spring, Madam Strindberg's Cabaret Club opens.
July, North Wales with Holbrooke and Sime.
August, visits Modigliani in Paris.
September, North Wales.
November, Goupil Gallery. Fifteen Panels.

1914   February, elected President of the National Portrait Society.
In Cornwall with Laura Knight.
April, Crab Tree Club opens.
May, Cardiganshire.
Gives up studio at 181a King's Road, moves into 28 Mallord Street.
June, one week in Boulogne.
August, Eilean Shona, Acharcle, Argyleshire.
Last visits to Innes at Brighton and Swanley in Kent before his death.
October–November, drilling with

Wadsworth in the courtyard of the
Royal Academy.
December, sees Gwen John in Paris.
Fails to persuade her to return to
England.

1915   March, Vivien born.
June, at Coole. Paints three portraits
of Bernard Shaw.
Hugh Lane sunk in Lusitania.
October, Aran Islands and Galway.

1916   February, Chenil Gallery. Paintings
(21) and Drawings (41).
Portrait of Lloyd George.
May, Chenil Gallery. Etchings by
Augustus E. John.
July, goes to Herbert Barker for
knee operation.
August, rejected for military service.
'Galway' shown at Arts and Crafts
Exhibition, Burlington House.

1916   Starts experiments in lithography.
Bust by Jacob Epstein.

1917   20th March, Monster Matinée at
Chelsea Palace Theatre.
27th April, meets Lady Cynthia
Asquith.
August, portrait of Oliver St John
Gogarty.
9th October, begins portrait of
Lady Cynthia Asquith ('Lady in
Black').
November–February (1918),
Alpine Club. Pictures and
Decorations (67 exhibits).
December, advances to Aubigny as
a Canadian major.

1918   March, retires from France after
knocking out Captain Wright.
May, starts Canadian cartoon.
'Fraternity'.
8th–28th August, represented at
Englische Moderne Malerei, an
exhibition organized by the
Contemporary Arts Society at the

Kunsthaus, Zürich.

1919   February–May, in Paris as official
war artist.
Paints Marchesa Casati and
duchesse de Gramont.
First drawing of T. E. Lawrence.
March, Chenil Gallery. One
hundred and twenty-five etchings.
September, at Deauville with
Lloyd George.

1920   *Augustus John* by Charles Marriott
published by John Lane in the
'Masters of Modern Art' series.
Elected Fellow of University
College, London.
March, Alpine Club. War, Peace
Conference and Other Portraits
(39 exhibits).
April, Sister Carline Hospital.
Operation on nose.
May, Rouen and Dieppe.
October, rumpus over Lord
Leverhulme's decapitated portrait.
John retreats to Broadstairs.
Campbell Dodgson's *Catalogue of
Etchings by A. E. John* published.

1921   22nd April, elected Associate of the
Royal Academy.
Begins painting Mme Suggia.
June, portrait of Herbert Barker.

1922   March, the Sculptors' Gallery,
New York. Works by Epstein,
Gaudier-Brzeska, Innes, Augustus
John and Wyndham Lewis from
Quinn Collection. (7 Paintings,
7 Drawings).
April, Paris.
May, arrives in Spain.

1923   March, Alpine Club Gallery.
Paintings and Drawings. First
showing of 'Mme Suggia'.
28th March–23rd June, America.

June, Beaux Arts Gallery.
Paintings (29).
Augustus John by A.B. [Anthony Bertram] published by Benn.
21st September, meets Thomas Hardy at Kingston Maurward. Completes portrait at Max Gate in October.

1924
'Mme Suggia' wins first prize at International Exhibition, Carnegie Institute, Pittsburgh.
April–June, America.
July, in Dublin for Taillteann Games. Stays with Lord Dunsany.
September–October, Paris.

1925
February, Lord Duveen gives 'Mme Suggia' to the Tate Gallery.
March–April, in Berlin. Paints Gustav Stresemann and Lali Horstmann.
May–June, Ischia with T. W. Earp. Italy.
Starts flower painting.

1926
February–March, Albright Art Gallery, Buffalo Fine Arts Academy. Drawings.
February–April, France.
April, Norfolk.
May, New Chenil Gallery.
Paintings (47) and drawings (35).
Gwen John paintings (44) and 4 albums of drawings.
17th June, begins portrait of Hugh Walpole.
9th July, 'Art and the Public' B.B.C. talk.
Meets and paints Sean O'Casey.
October, walks from Avignon to Marseille with Horace de Vere Cole and A. R. Thomson.
December (till February 1928), at Villa Ste Anne.

1927
Begins portrait of Lord D'Abernon.
March, moves from Alderney Manor to Fryern Court.

June–July, at Château de Missery.
July, helps Gwen John buy Yew Tree Cottage, Burgate Cross, Fordingbridge.
December (till January 1928), South of France.

1928
14th January–4th February, Anderson Gallery, New York, Paintings and Drawings.
April, Villa Ste Anne sold.
August–December, in America. Portrait of Governor Fuller.
5th December, elected Royal Academician.
Meets James Dunn and family.

1929
February, at Cap Ferrat with James Dunn.
4th April–17th May, Tooth's Gallery. Recent Paintings (27).
May–June, designs sets for Act II of Sean O'Casey's *The Silver Tassie*.
July, Château de Missery.
September, Rheims.
October, paints T. E. Lawrence at Fryern Court.
November, drawing of Delius.
December, designs Noah's Ark for Chelsea Arts Club Ball at Albert Hall.

1930
April, Harlow, McDonald & Co, New York. Etchings and Drawings.
1st April, begins portrait of Montagu Norman.
April–May, in hospital. Preston Dennery Hall, Northampton.
July–August, Ireland. Portraits of W. B. Yeats and Brenda Gogarty.
September, Galway.
October, Kiddalton Castle, Port Ellen, Isle of Islay.
To Antwerp with Dorelia.
November, Paris, James Joyce drawings.
December (till February 1931), Cap Ferrat.

1931   July, Montagu Norman's hair changes from grey to white.
21st November, funeral of John Sampson who bequeaths John, under Clause 8 of his Will, 'my Smith and Wesson Revolver No. 239892'.

1932   February–March, in Jersey with Sir Herbert Barker. More attention to knee.
Lord D'Abernon's portrait signed.
May, portraits of Joe Hone and T. W. Earp.
June, represented at XVIII Biennial International Art Exhibition, Venice.
July, France.
August, Cornwall.
December, Majorca.
Death of Mrs Nettleship.

1933   January, Leicester Galleries. Sixty Etchings.
LL.D Cardiff University.
August, appointed trustee of the Tate Gallery (to 1941).
Venice.

1934   *Augustus John* by T. W. Earp published by Nelson.
21st May, elected President of Royal Cambrian Academy of Art.
September, Paris.
October, Etchings at the National Museum of Wales.
Mallord Street sold to Gracie Fields.
New studio built at Fryern Court.

1935   30th April, 'La Séraphita' and other paintings destroyed in fire at Fryern.
14th May, letter to *The Times* about Stanley Spencer's works.
June, borrows Vanessa Bell's studio for one month.
22nd June, Henry John missing. Body found drowned on 6th July.
November, takes studio at 49 Glebe Place.

1936   5th–29th February, Adams Gallery. Forty Etchings.
April, Paris.
25th April, Laugharne Castle, Carmarthen.
Portrait of Dylan Thomas.
26th May, fined £5 for drinking after hours at the Old Mill Club, Salisbury.
June, represented at XX Biennial International Art Exhibition (4 paintings).
Autumn, British Empire Exhibition, Johannesburg.
Works (later with Ernst Stern) on designs for costumes and scenery for C. B. Cochran's production of J. M. Barrie's *The Boy David* which opens on 14th December.

1937   Elected President of the Gypsy Lore Society.
March, Wildenstein Gallery, London. Thirty Drawings.
February–May, Jamaica. Travels back on a banana boat via Rotterdam.

1937   September, rents Mas de Galeron, St-Rémy-de-Provence.
Visits Matthew Smith at Aix-en-Provence.

1938   February, one of three British artists (with Sickert and Steer) represented at Exhibition of British Art at the Louvre, Paris.
March, Leicester Galleries. Drawings.
Takes Park Studio, Pelham Street, London.
7th April, father dies in Tenby.
28th April, resigns from Royal Academy following its rejection of Wyndham Lewis' portrait of T. S. Eliot.
19th May–11th June, Tooth's Gallery. Latest Paintings (32) including Jamaican pictures.

18th June, Dorelia's mother dies following a fall from the balcony of her bedroom at Fryern Court on 20th May.
4th July, opens Exhibition of Twentieth Century German Art at Burlington House.
July, signs contract with Jonathan Cape for autobiography.
August, at Laugharne.
27th August, goes to Mas de Galeron.

1939 February–March, Redfern Gallery. Exhibition of Paintings by John, Innes and Derwent Lees.
July–August, Mas de Galeron.
18th September, Gwen John dies at Dieppe.
Autumn, begins painting the Queen.
Represented at British Council Exhibition, New York.

1940 Honorary Member of the London Group.
16th February, re-elected to the Royal Academy.
July, moves to studio at 33 Tite Street, Chelsea.
November, National Gallery. *British Painting Since Whistler*. 'Drawings of Augustus John' (112).
December, exhibition at the Francis Taylor Gallery, Hollywood.

1941 February, starts writing for Cyril Connolly's *Horizon* (until April 1949).
June, Redfern Gallery. Drawings (40).
July, joins the Green Shirts and 'throws in his lot' with the Social Credit Party.
October, Augustus John *Drawings* edited by Lillian Browse published by Faber and Faber.

1942 March, etchings collected by Gerald Brockhurst shown at Boston Library, New England.

May, stays at Mousehole, Cornwall.
June, awarded Order of Merit.
31st June, writes to *The Times*, deploring the lack of interest shown by Press and public in Ethel Walker's exhibition at the Lefevre Gallery.

1943 January, elected Honorary Member, American National Institute of Arts and Letters.
Artists International Association (1 painting).
May, Leicester Galleries. Drawings by Augustus John, Paintings by Gilbert Spencer.

1944 Matthew Smith stays at Fryern; he and John paint each other.
14th March, Alfred Munnings 24 votes, John 17 in elections for the presidency of the Royal Academy.
7th June, in a light fawn tropical suit opens Exhibition of Indian Art for the Mayor of Culcutta's Relief Fund.
2nd August, appointed First President of the Central Institute of Art and Design.
October, *Augustus John* by John Rothenstein published by Phaidon and Allen & Unwin as Phaidon Press Art Books: British Artists Series No. 2.

1945 In Wales with the Howard de Waldens.
July–November, Tite Street studio under repair.

1946 Elected member of Académie Royale de Belgique.
Jeu de Paume, Paris. Represented in Exposition de peinture anglaise du XX siècle (portraits and a composition).
24th July–31st August, Temple Newsam House, Leeds. Exhibition of Paintings and Drawings (124 exhibits).
24th December, letter to *The Times*

about the dangers of picture
cleaning at the National Gallery.

1947   A long convalescence.
        September–October, Mousehole,
        Cornwall.

1948   May, Leicester Galleries.
        Exhibition of work from previous
        fifteen years (52 exhibits),
        including 12 foot canvas
        'The Little Concert' (*grisaille*).
        31st May, on the cover of *Time*
        magazine, New York.
        10th July, elected President of the
        Royal Society of Portrait Painters.
        30th July, Welsh National
        Eisteddfod, Bridgend. Arts Council
        Exhibition. Paintings (61) and
        Drawings (65).
        October, Drawings at the
        American-British Art Center.

1949   7th March, 'Engaged on a long and
        vast composition' (letter to
        Wyndham Lewis).
        21st March–12th April, Scott and
        Fowles, New York. Exhibition of
        Works in American Collections
        (23 paintings).
        9th September, radio talk, Far
        Eastern Service. 'I Speak for
        Myself'.
        November, Lefevre Gallery. Works
        by Augustus John and Ethel Walker.

1950   30th April, profile in London
        Observer.
        June–July, Mas de Galeron.
        July–August, Mas de Galeron given
        up.
        Castello San Peyre, Opio, France.
        October, Paris.

1951   15th January, Café Royal closes.
        Leaves Tite Street studio.

1952   28th January, on the cover of *Life*
        Magazine.

March, *Chiaroscuro* published by
Jonathan Cape (by Pellegrini and
Cudahy in America).
28th March, Guest of Honour at
Foyles Literary Lunch. 'I am two
people instead of one : the one you
see before you is the old painter. But
another one has just cropped up –
the young writer.'
October, Introduction to the
catalogue of Ulrica Forbes
exhibition, Walker Art Gallery,
Liverpool.

1953   Resigns as President of Royal Society
        of Portrait Painters.
        April, drawing of Walter de la Mare.
        Begins sculpture with Fiore de
        Henriques.

1954   March–April, Royal Academy,
        Diploma Gallery. 'Exhibition of
        Works by Augustus John
        O.M., R.A.' (460 exhibits).
        7th May, interviewed on Radio by
        A. Vaughan.
        November, Nuffield House, Guy's
        Hospital. Prostate gland operation.
        December (till March 1955), Spain.

1955   March, bronze head of Yeats
        purchased for the Abbey Theatre,
        Dublin.
        November, Wales. Drawings of
        John Cowper Powys.

1956   August, France.
        September, Graves Art Gallery,
        Sheffield. Paintings (43), Drawings
        (88) and Prints (15).

1957   4th November, interviewed by
        Malcolm Muggeridge on television
        'Panorama': 'Have you always
        wanted to be a painter?' 'Give me
        another hundred years and I would
        become a very good one.'
        December, *Fifty-two Drawings*, with
        an Introduction by Lord David
        Cecil, published by Rainbird.

1958   Asks Russians to stop testing nuclear weapons.
Campaigns against capital punishment. Joins British Peace Committee.

1959   22nd May, interviewed on radio by Bill Duncalf about his work.
29th October, given the Honorary Freedom of Tenby.

1960   4th January, eighty-second birthday. 'Work as usual' (*Daily Telegraph*).
3rd February, interviewed by A. Vaughan on radio.
15th March–30th March, Tooth's Gallery. Paintings and Drawings not previously exhibited.
20th April, interviewed on B.B.C. radio.
12th May, 'Face to Face'. Interviewed by John Freeman on television.
14th October, letter praising Matthew Smith in *The Daily Telegraph*.

1961   15th March–30th March, Tooth's Gallery. Paintings and Drawings not previously illustrated.
31st October, dies at Fryern Court.
5th November, Television Obituary Programme, B.B.C. 'Monitor'.

1962   20th July, Christie's. First Studio Sale (115 drawings, 70 paintings). £99,645.
Augustus John by John Rothenstein published by Beaverbrook Newspapers Ltd.

1963   21st June, Christie's. Second Studio Sale (103 drawings, 62 paintings). £33,405.

1964   November, *Finishing Touches* published by Jonathan Cape.

1967   *The Drawings of Augustus John*, with an Introduction by Stephen Longstreet, published by the Borden Publishing Company, California.
1st October, memorial statue by Ivor Roberts-Jones unveiled by Lord Mountbatten at Fordingbridge.

1968   18th July, Harlech Television. Augustus John programme.

1970   25th October–14th November, The University of Hull. Augustus John: Portraits of the Artist's Family.

1972   Over 1,000 drawings, 110 paintings and 3 bronzes, the last remains of the artist's studio, purchased by The National Museum of Wales.

Plates

Guide to the notes on the plates

Dimensions are given in inches and centimetres, height preceding width. Paintings have been measured to the nearest quarter-inch and 0·5 of a centimetre; drawings and etchings with greater exactness. '*S*' signifies a sight-measurement.

References to exhibitions are selective and abbreviated. Details will normally be found in the Chronology against the year quoted. Where this is not so, the following list should be consulted:

Pittsburgh, 1910: Carnegie Institute, International Exhibition

Rome, 1911: International Fine Arts Exhibition

Pittsburgh, 1933: International Exhibition

N.G., 1945: 'Some Acquisitions of the Walker Art Gallery, Liverpool, 1935–1945' ('N.G.' always denotes National Gallery, London)

Arts Council, 1945–6: 'Portraits' (tour)

Arts Council, 1946: 'British Painters. 1939–1945'

Exeter, 1946: 'Works of Art from the Ford Collection'

Birmingham, 1952: City Museum and Art Gallery, 'Early Years of the New English Art Club'

Liverpool, 1955: Walker Art Gallery, 'Augustus John. An Exhibition of Paintings, Drawings and Lithographs from the Collection of Mr and Mrs Peter Harris'

Sheffield, 1956: Graves Art Gallery, 'Augustus John, O.M., R.A.'

King's Lynn, 1959: The King's Lynn Museum, 'Augustus John, O.M., R.A. Drawings, Lithographs and Paintings from the Collection of Peter Harris, Esq.'

Goldsmiths' Hall, 1959: 'Treasures of Cambridge'

Upper Grosvenor Galleries, 1965: 'A Loan Exhibition of Drawings and Murals by Augustus John, O.M., R.A.'

R.A., 1968: Royal Academy, London, Bicentenary Exhibition

R.A., 1971: Royal Academy, London, 'The Slade, 1871–1971'

Pierpont Morgan Library, New York, 1971: 'Artists and Writers. Nineteenth and Twentieth Century Portrait Drawings from the Collection of Benjamin Sonnenberg'

Halifax, Nova Scotia, etc., 1972–3: Dalhousie Art Gallery, 'Augustus John' and tour, organized by the National Gallery of Canada

'R.A., summer' indicates the annual summer exhibition as distinct from a supplementary Academy exhibition during the same year. 'N.E.A.C.' = New English Art Club, the April–May exhibitions of which were sometimes confusingly called 'spring' instead of 'summer'. In the Notes on etchings, 'Campbell Dodgson', or 'C.D.', stands for Campbell Dodgson's *A Catalogue of Etchings by Augustus John, 1901–1914* (1920).

As every item is illustrated, it has not been thought necessary to list plates in other publications. For *Literature* the reader is referred to the official biography by Michael Holroyd.

Though John modelled some portrait heads in clay, afterwards cast in bronze, during the 1950s, we have not thought them important enough to reproduce here in the very limited space at our disposal. Our attitude has been the same towards the lithographs which he produced from time to time. One of the best of these, a self-portrait, appeared late in the artist's life as a frontispiece to *Augustus John. Fifty-Two Drawings. With an Introduction by Lord David Cecil* (1957). It was drawn on zinc specially for that compilation. But John himself did not like it, quibbled about 'lithography' on metal and would rather it had been withheld. We have respected his wishes.

Mention is made of the artist's two volumes of autobiography, *Chiaroscuro* (1952) and *Finishing Touches* (1964, posthumous). They can be found described more fully, along with the series of short studies by other authors (of which Sir John Rothenstein's are the most important), in our Chronology.

Description of frontispiece

DORELIA STANDING BEFORE A FENCE, *c.* 1903–4

Oil on canvas, $79\frac{1}{2} \times 48$ (202×122)

Signed 'John' lower right

Exhibited Temple Newsam, 1946 (No. 13); R.A., 1954 (No. 119); University of Hull, 1970 (No. 5)

Collection: Hugo Pitman; Mrs Reine Pitman
Miss Jemima Pitman

To judge by the costume, this is of about the same period as Manchester's 'Ardor' (Pl. 5); and the late Hugo Pitman connected it with Mr Peter Harris' 'Dorelia in a feathered hat' for the same reason. But while both of those paintings are studies from life, 'Dorelia standing before a fence' is an ideal work, and we have Dorelia's own word for it. The clothes, however, accurately convey those designed by their wearer. Mme Poppet Pol, the artist's elder daughter, suggests that her mother has trimmed her hat with a complete cock's tail. It is worn with a long green skirt and a three-quarter length jacket of black *cotton*-velvet: Dorelia did not like velvet.

There are a number of monumental, ideal portraits of the same subject standing, the most remarkable, perhaps, being that in the National Gallery of Victoria, Melbourne, but none has succeeded quite as well as this in conveying the hypnotic power Dorelia exercised over the artist. John early conceived an admiration for the Spanish School and there is more than a touch of Goya here.

[45]

1 AN OLD LADY, 1899

Oil on canvas, $26\frac{3}{4} \times 22$ (68×56)

Exhibited Arts Council, 1945–6 (No. 91)

The Tate Gallery

When Sir John Rothenstein discovered this painting at the Leger Galleries in 1941 and bought it for the Tate, he was informed by the artist that the sitter had given him his very first commission in portraiture. The old lady, her name later forgotten, lived in Eaton Terrace. 'The fee was fixed at forty pounds,' John recalled, 'of which half was paid in advance.' But mutual dislike resulted in his abandoning the picture and forgoing the balance. None of this comes through in the work, which is fresh and sympathetic, except that he was unable to finish the right hand. The head is modelled in the yellow-brown-against-darker-brown of Rembrandt: whose influence, however, would not be paramount for much longer.

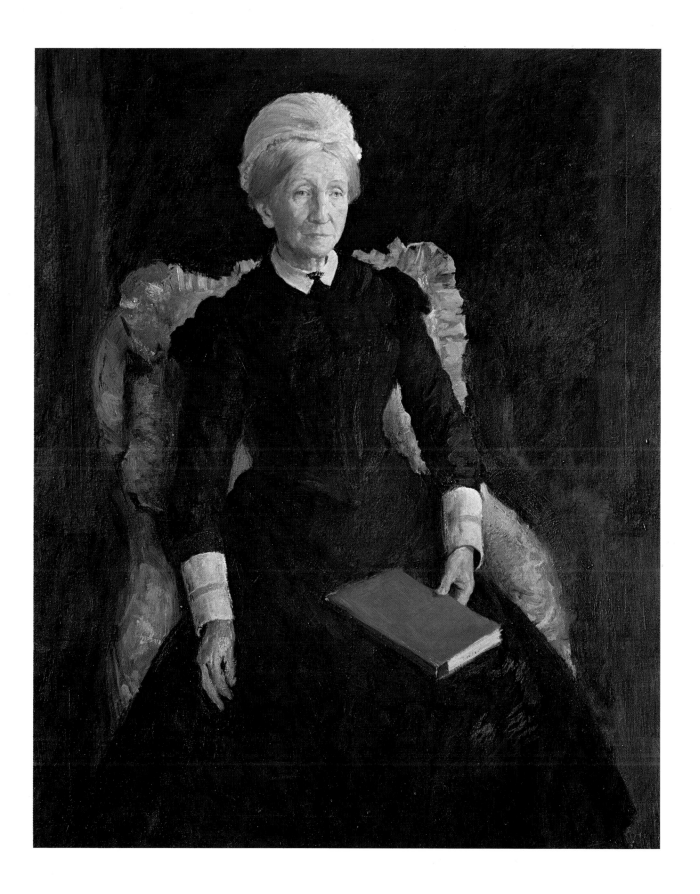

2　IDA, *c.* 1901–2

Oil on canvas, 24 × 18 (70 × 45·5)

Exhibited Broadway Art Gallery, spring 1962 (No. 5)

Collection: the artist's father, Edwin William John
Mr and Mrs John Gardner

Another painting, showing Ida in an identical dress and having the same provenance, was entitled 'A Sketch near Tenby'. Ida and Augustus married on 12th January 1901, and paid a duty visit to the artist's father later that year and again in 1902. Augustus disliked Tenby. On either occasion he could have cut short his stay, leaving this portrait behind. It remained forgotten till old Mr John's death in 1938, when the attic at 5 Lexden Terrace was cleared out by the housekeeper, a member of whose family sold the picture to the present owner (Augustus having expressly refused to bother himself with such lumber). The wedding-ring rules out, of course, a date earlier than 1901. If Ida's glance conveys a certain apprehension, this would not be extraordinary in one struggling to keep pace with her husband's swift changes of mood even during the initial period of the marriage. The portrait was restored in 1962 and the paint is now very thin.

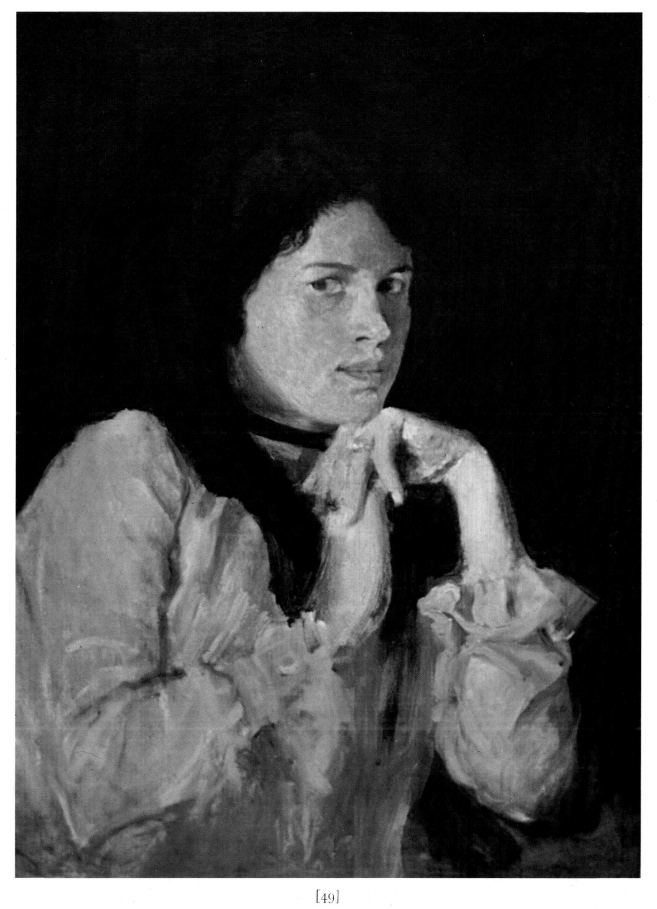

3 IDA PREGNANT, ? 1901

Oil on canvas, 60 × 40 (152·5 × 101·5)

Collection: Michel Salaman
The National Museum of Wales

Together with that picture of his future wife which, John tells Michel
Salaman in February 1900, 'has clothed itself in scarlet', this is one of the
very few full-length oil portraits of Ida which have survived. It remained
for several decades in the Salaman home, Michel himself having been a
contender for Ida's hand, and his brother Clement actually engaged to
her. 'Ida pregnant' was not seen by the general public till put on view in
the National Museum of Wales in 1972. In spite of the colour, there is a
striking dependence upon Hals.

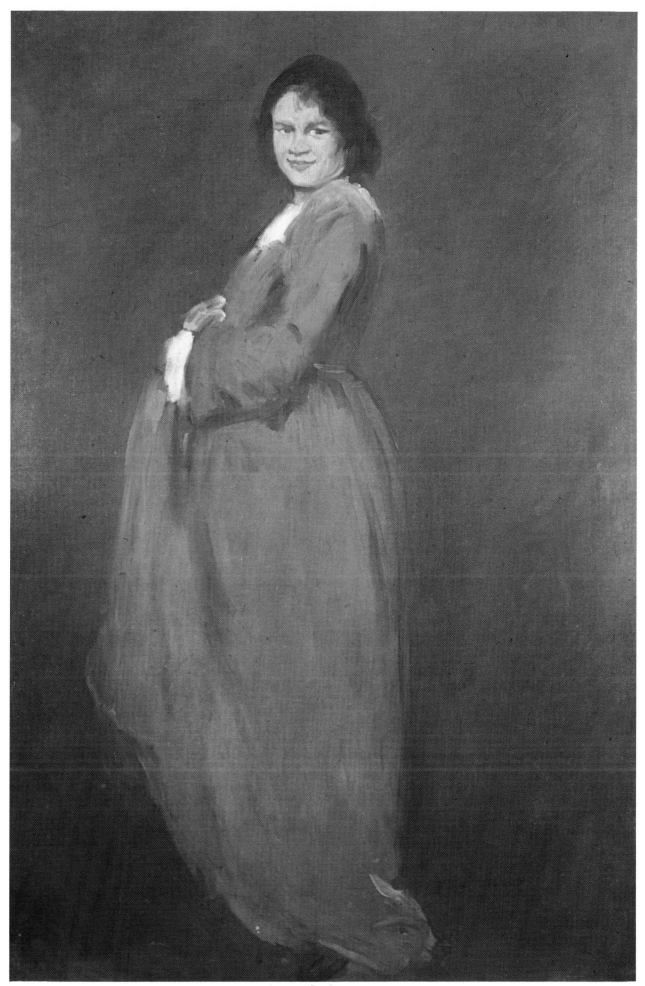

4   SIGNORINA ESTELLA CERUTTI, 1902

Oil on canvas, 36 × 28 (91·5 × 71)

Signed 'Augustus John' on back of canvas

Exhibited N.E.A.C., winter 1902 (No. 63); Temple Newsam,
1946 (No. 3); R.A., 1954 (No. 343)

Collection: Judge William Evans
The City Art Gallery, Manchester

The Italian girl whom the artist called 'Esther' Cerutti lived in rooms
below the Johns at 18 Fitzroy Street, their earliest London home. Augustus
made a number of studies of her in various media. Ida, having a baby –
and then babies – to look after, could feel outshone at times by the buxom,
well-groomed model: 'for how can one wear grey linen by her silks and
laces?' (letter to Alice Rothenstein). But Esther's reign proved transient
enough.

   This is an extremely important work, by which (as Sir John Rothenstein
has pointed out) John's stature can be judged for the first time. Here is
Olympian drawing with the brush, supplying marvels of supple, sinuous
edge. As to colour, the artist never bettered the peach-like bloom of the lit
flesh and the reflections in the shadowed areas. The hands' pose recalls
that in a Velázquez Infanta, but the closest parallel of the whole is to be
found in Ingres' copies of his 'Duc d'Orléans', one of which is now (but
was not then) in the National Gallery. After the Cerutti portrait, John for
the most part abandoned such finely adjusted contours. Whether he
regretted it or not, he felt obliged to leave the nineteenth century behind.

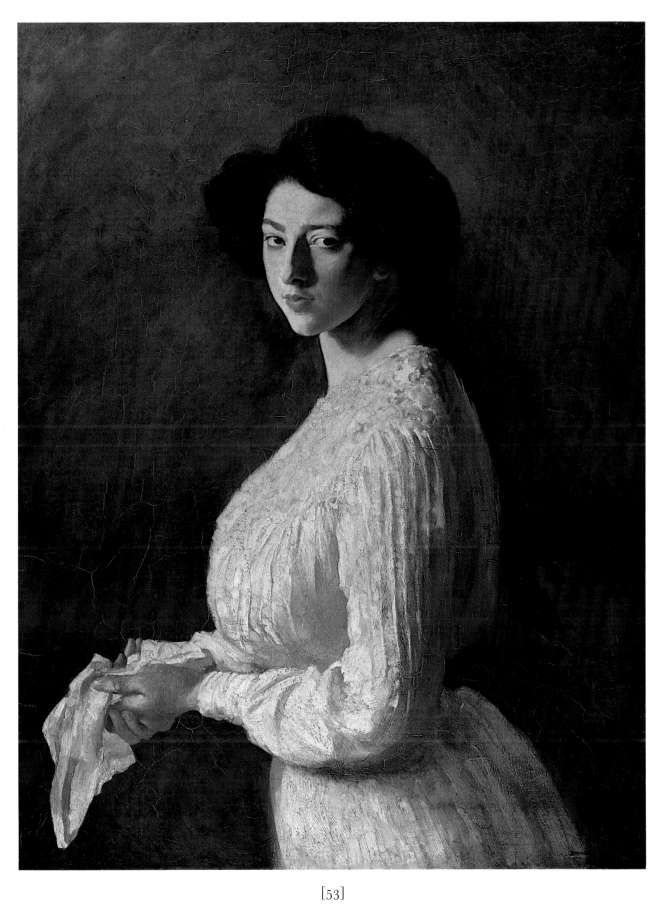

5 ARDOR, *c.* 1903

Oil on canvas, $18\frac{1}{4} \times 14$ (46·5 × 35·5)

Exhibited N.E.A.C., winter 1904 (No. 45); R.A., 1954 (No. 135)

Collection: C. L. Rutherston
The City Art Gallery, Manchester

'Ardor' was the first of several pet-names given by John to the exquisitely
beautiful girl who entered his life early in 1903. Dorothy McNeill's origins
have become obscured, not without her admirer's complicity, in a
romantic mist. She was born at 97 Bellenden Road, Camberwell, on
19th December 1881, and had found employment as a secretary in
Basinghall Street when, attracted by art and artists, she began to attend
evening classes at the Westminster school. By the summer of 1903, John
was enslaved. Dorothy, or most often 'Dorelia', was his 'dear sweetheart'
and he her 'Gustavus Janik': for under his guidance she was learning
Romani. Indeed, she seemed made to share the para-Gypsy existence he
had adopted for himself. A letter he wrote to her in the summer of 1903,
shortly after their meeting, is very close in spirit to this picture: 'Ardor my
little girl, my love, my spouse whose smile opens infinite vistas to me . . .'
It is, of all his early works, the most Halsian, faithfully reproducing not
only the smile, but the exact range of blacks, greys and pinks employed by
the Dutch master.

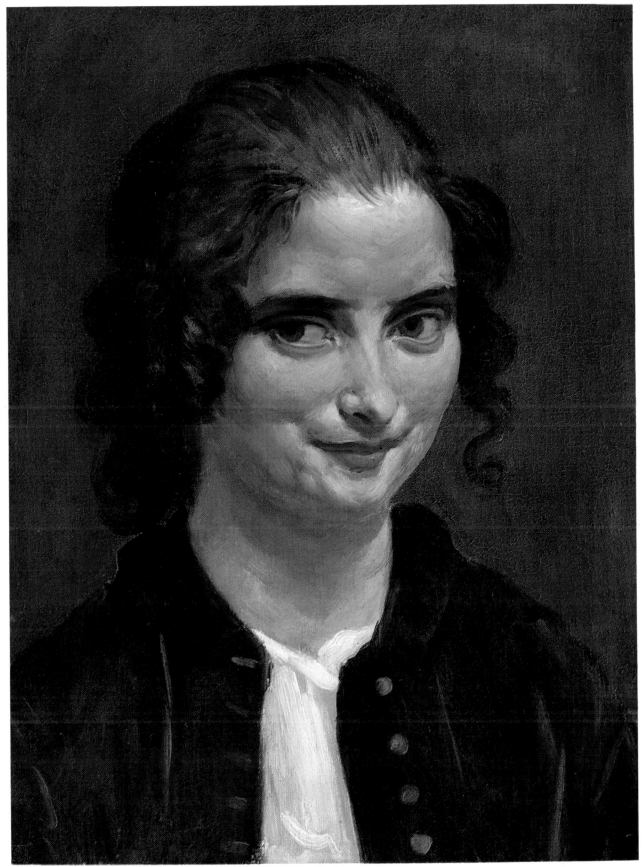

6 GYPSY ENCAMPMENT, 1905

Oil on canvas, $12\frac{1}{2} \times 18\frac{1}{2}$ (32×47)

Exhibited Arts Council, 1948 (No. 6); R.A., 1954 (No. 331);
Sheffield, 1956 (No. 17)

Collection: Morton Sands
Private Collection

This connects closely with Pl. 35, for the striped tent is the same: from
which we now look out on the rest of the party, that early summer in
newly-discovered Devon. John himself is clearly the bearded man
leaning over the half-door of the caravan. Of the children in 1905,
David would have been a little over three; Caspar a little over two; while
Robin, born the previous October, was not yet toddling. No doubt, it is he
whom Ida nurses on the right of the group, Dorelia being the standing
figure in the hat. The latter reappears on the extreme left, briefly sketched
in the tent with the new baby, Pyramus. In the N.E.A.C. winter exhibition
of 1905, John showed a painting called 'Bohemians'; in the summer of
1906, another, 'Van Dwellers'; and, in the winter of the latter year, a
further painting called 'The Camp': any of which might have been the
present work. It is interesting to note how much later are the Romany
subjects of Sir Alfred Munnings (born in the same year as John and his
successful rival for the presidency of the R.A. in 1944). The best known of
these, 'Gypsy Life' and 'Arrival at Epsom Downs for Derby Week' were
not painted till 1920.

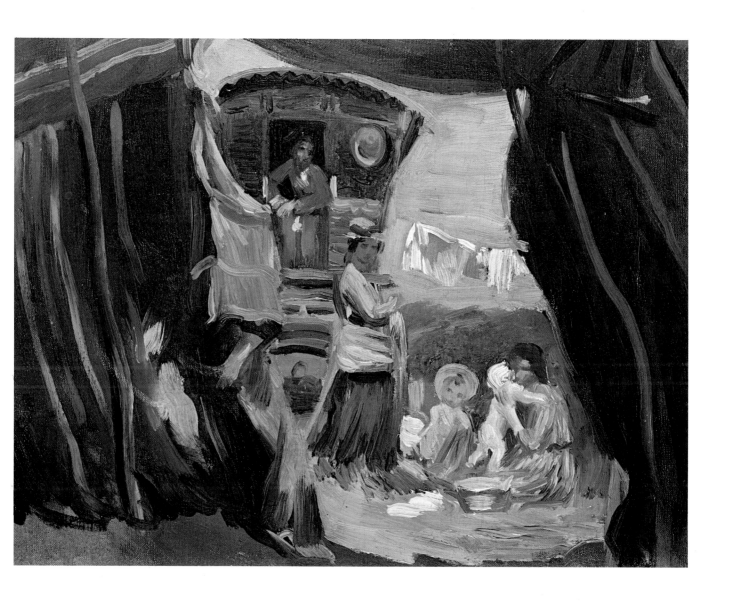

7 FRENCH FISHER-BOY, 1907

Oil on canvas, $86 \times 35\frac{1}{2}$ $(218 \cdot 5 \times 90)$

Collection: John Estate
Mr and Mrs Stephen Tumim

After Ida's death on 13th March 1907, John's art, as well as his domestic
life, took various turnings, first in one direction, then another. 'I should
like to work for a few years entirely "out of my head", perhaps for ever,'
he wrote in April to Will Rothenstein. Paris distracted him. In the same
month he set out to explore the 'top of France', soon discovering Equihen,
suitably off the beaten track on the north coast near Condette. The
fisher-folk, both men and women, reminded him of a similar community
near Haverfordwest in childhood days. The boy he paints on this occasion
is very much *out of John's head*: though an admiration for Gauguin makes
itself felt – and, more, for Picasso. We assume that John knew the 'Blue
Period' Picassos (he had certainly seen the historically all-important
'Les Demoiselles d'Avignon' in the same studio) before he wrote that letter
to Henry Lamb, of 5th August, describing the Spaniard's work as
'wonderful'. He was, as a matter of fact, once again at Equihen in August.

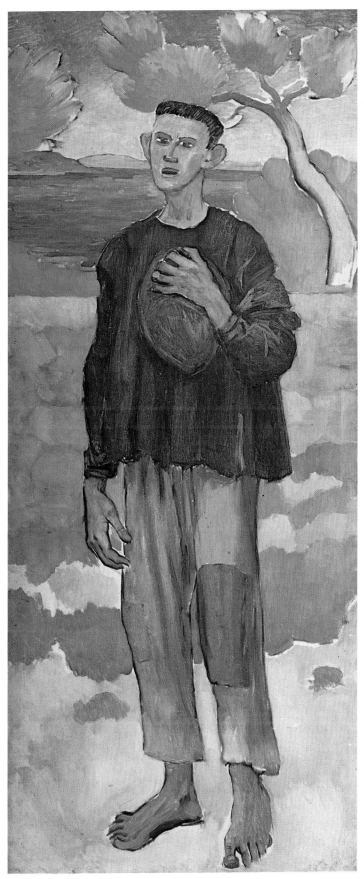

[59]

8 W. B. YEATS, 1907

Oil on canvas, $29\frac{1}{2} \times 19\frac{1}{2}$ (75 × 49·5)

Exhibited Birmingham, 1952 (No. 35); R.A., 1954 (No. 345);
Sheffield, 1956 (No. 22)

The City Art Gallery, Manchester

Lady Gregory's son Robert suggested that John should undertake the
portrait of William Butler Yeats (1865–1939) required as a frontispiece
for A. H. Bullen's 1908 edition of the *Collected Works*. It was to be an
etching. But, as other artists' have been, John's preliminary sketches were
paintings, the one shown here and another in the Tate Gallery, besides
additional studies. It is difficult to think of a better realization of the
leader of the Celtic Revival in literature, dark and dreamy against a
brilliant, emblematic green. John admired the gift of tongues; a writer
always drew from him his best work. Yeats, however, complained bitterly
to Quinn, particularly of the etching, which made him, he felt, 'a sheer
tinker, drunken, unpleasant and disreputable'. Lady Gregory held up her
hands in horror, too. Looking now at the Manchester painting, of which
the etching is a transcription in reverse, we are astonished at all the fuss.
But this was John's universal reputation: everything he touched seemed to
his contemporaries to have been deliberately coarsened, if not caricatured.

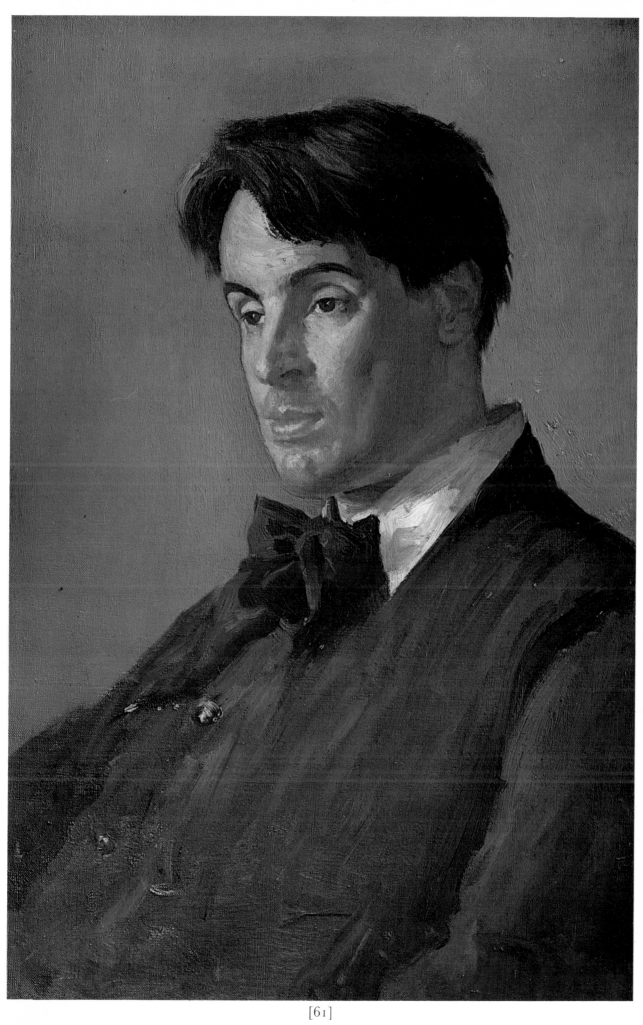

9 THE SMILING WOMAN, 1909

Oil on canvas, 77 × 38 (195·5 × 96·5)

Exhibited New Gallery, 1909 (No. 181); and in a series of
Contemporary Art Society exhibitions in Newcastle, 1912
(No. 158), at the Goupil Gallery, 1913 (No. 21), at 53 Grosvenor
Street, and in Belfast, 1914 (No. 13)

Collection: Dr C. Bakker; Contemporary Art Society
The Tate Gallery

This portrait of Dorelia found its way to the International Society's
exhibition, 'Fair Women', at the New Gallery in Regent Street, and made
John's name. His first idea had been on the lines of the later 'Lyric
Fantasy', of a group of pixie-ish beauties dominated by Euphemia Lamb.
Euphemia failed him. A barmaid called Bertha did not come up to scratch.
Alick Schepeler faded out. Finally Dorelia, unhappy about this constant
change of plans, agreed to sit solo. Roger Fry (in *The Burlington Magazine*
of May 1909) can be forgiven for not recognizing in the model a Miss
Dorothy McNeill of respectable urban origins. 'The vitality of this gypsy
Gioconda,' he wrote, 'is fierce, disquieting, emphatic': and he was quite
right. Between them, John and Dorelia had affected an ethnic change of
the most startling order. Fry proved extremely fair in his appraisal of a
work by no means up Bloomsbury's street. 'The very swiftness of the
handling,' he continues, 'the summary strokes with which the swift play of
the features and the defiant poise of the hands are suggested heightens this
effect of intense life, just as the large, simple massing of the colours
accentuates the dominant rhythm of the design.' And the inevitable sting
in the tail was not as deadly as it might have been: 'Yet this intensity has
not been obtained without some sacrifice. Even among other modern
pictures the work looks bare, for all its dignity: in more weighty company
this bareness might become baldness. The very haste which has
contributed so much to the spirit of the piece has brought with it an
undeniable loss of that shapely and pleasant handling of material which
has been an aim, if not the supreme aim, of so many other generations of
great artists . . . Fortunately there are many mansions in the house of Art;
and if a remarkable talent chooses one of them we should be content to let
him have his place there, even if we think he might be better
accommodated elsewhere.' The picture was presented to the Tate in 1917
by the Contemporary Art Society.

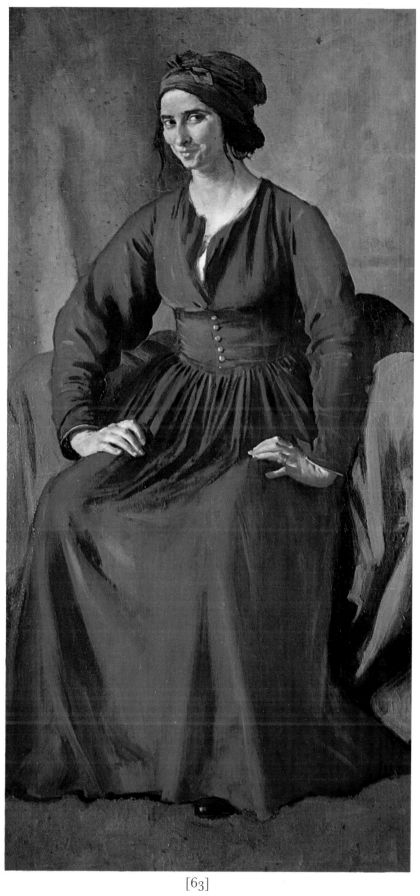

10 NEAR THE VILLA STE ANNE, 1910

Oil on canvas, $10\frac{3}{4} \times 18\frac{1}{2}$ (27×32)

Private Collection

Without doubt, John was never more in his element than in Martigues, first spied from the train as he crossed into Italy during his 1910 travels under Quinn's aegis. By April of that year, the date of the painting of this picture, the family was established at the Villa Ste Anne, with its views of the Etang de Berre, the little town of Martigues and a not so distant Mont Ste-Victoire. The un-English brilliance of sky and inland sea was joyously recorded by John as a background for the velvety grey of the olives and the vividly-dressed Dorelia and assorted children. Painted just before Fry's first Post-Impressionist exhibition, such a study explains John's avant-garde standing, though he gradually thereafter retired into a haughty and self-sufficient isolation.

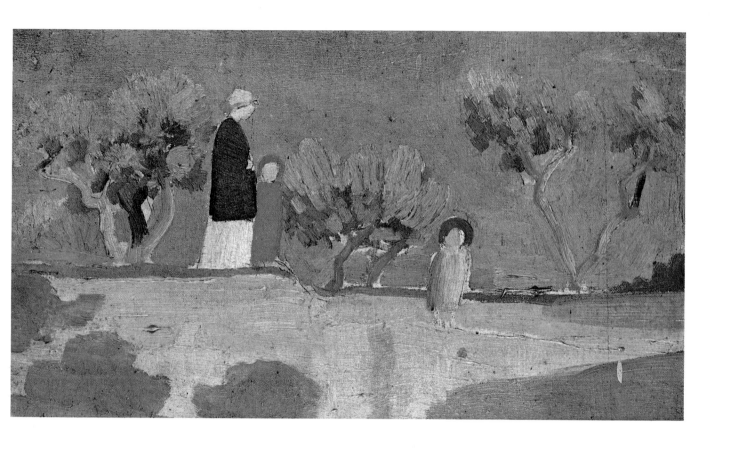

11 DORELIA WITH THREE CHILDREN, 1910

Oil on panel, $9\frac{1}{4} \times 12\frac{3}{4}$ $(23 \cdot 5 \times 32 \cdot 5)$

Signed 'John' bottom right

Exhibited R.A., 1954 (No. 211); Liverpool, 1955 (No. 22);
King's Lynn, 1959 (No. 25); University of Hull, 1970 (No. 26)

Mr Peter Harris

The picture belongs to the period of John's initial discovery of Martigues during the prolonged stay abroad in 1910. The young boy on the left, one may presume, is David (his entitlement to the 'large hat' is discussed in the note to Pl. 38). The child to the right suggests Pyramus, but either of the little ones could be Romilly, who gives a particularly vivid picture of Martigues in his *The Seventh Child*. What we see here is the fifteen-foot bank looking out on the blue lagoon called the Etang de Berre. Close at hand was the Villa Ste Anne, a house retained by John for family holidays until as late as 1928. 'Wherever my larger half-brothers went,' records Romilly, 'whether up cliffs or down ravines, there I was always to be found, panting in the rear.' To read some accounts of contemporary British painting, one might suppose that it was Gore and Gilman who lightened our native palette and Sickert who first insisted that the model must be observed in a natural context. John's blues and greens and crushed-strawberry pinks qualify the first assumption, while the French and (soon) the Dorset settings with which Dorelia is invariably united lead us to question the second.

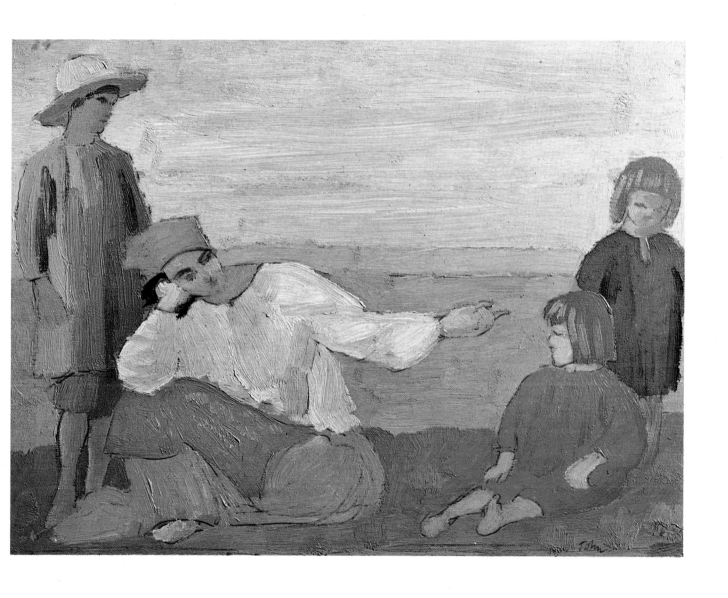

12 PYRAMUS, *c.* 1910

Oil on panel, $15\frac{1}{4} \times 12\frac{1}{2}$ (38·5 × 31·5)

Exhibited University of Hull, 1970 (No. 20)

Private Collection

Born in 1905, Pyramus was Dorelia's elder son and eldest child, the others being Romilly and the two girls, Poppet and Vivien. John Knewstub, who ran the Chenil Gallery, described Pyramus as the 'most lovable' of all the artist's sons. The corn-coloured hair may seem surprising, but Romilly recalls that, like his half-brothers, both he and his full-brother were fair as young children. If the type of bust-portrait suggests Tuscan work of the late fifteenth century, this is what we might expect: for in 1910, on a first trip to Italy, John was reporting to Quinn, his American patron, how greatly he admired Luca Signorelli. Pyramus had been born in a caravan, and shared to the full his parents' wanderings and his brothers' barefoot existence. He does not seem to have suffered for roughing it; but in his seventh year he fell ill with meningitis. He died in the early summer of 1912.

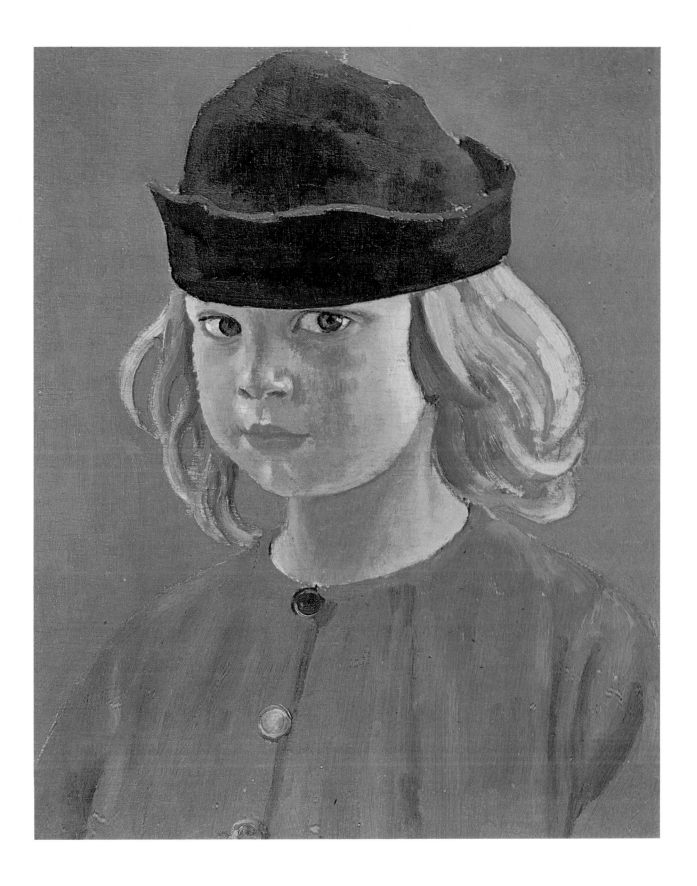

[69]

13 LLYN TREWERYN, 1911

Oil on panel, 12½ × 16 (31·5 × 40·5)

Collection: Antonio Gandarillas
The Tate Gallery

John had been searching for an ideal landscape long before he met John Dickson Innes (1887–1914), at the same time employing a flat-colour simplification which, if reminiscent of the younger man's approach, certainly did not derive from it. Yet, suspicious of alliances in general, John found in Innes the perfect companion in wanderings far afield. Both had been brought up in Wales, both felt especially at home among the peaks and tarns of the Welsh highlands. Enjoying Innes' company, John shared a cottage with him near Rhyd-y-fen (Merionethshire) on the slopes of the Migneint during the summer of 1911. They filled panel after panel with views of this district, returning regularly, sometimes with Derwent Lees (1885–1931), in the few years still left to Innes. John's painting of Llyn Treweryn, a diminutive stretch of water sparkling under kaleidoscope mountains and a brilliant blue sky is at the very opposite pole from Innes' savage renderings of Mount Arenig nearby. The picture was on view at the Chenil Gallery under the title of 'The Blue Pool' in 1917.

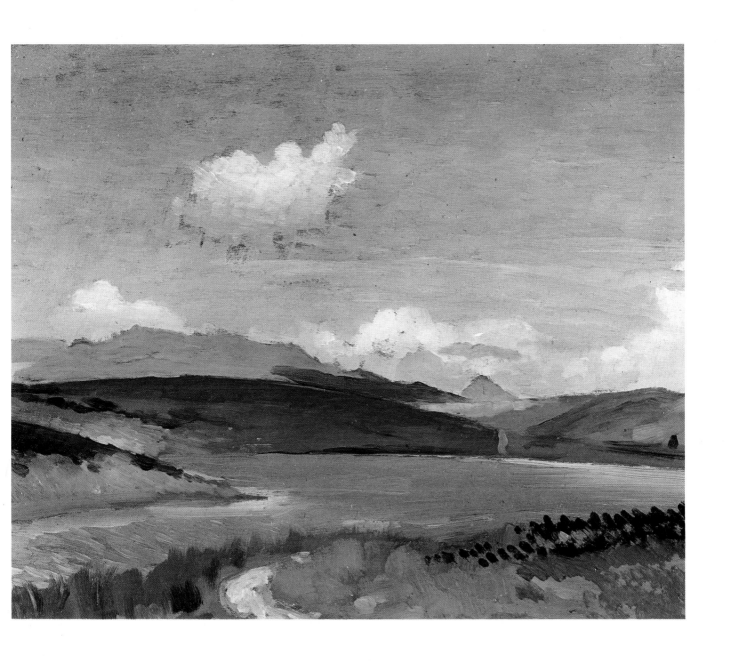

14 ROMILLY, ROBIN AND EDWIN, 1911

Oil on panel, 16 × 13 (40·5 × 33)

Signed 'John' top left on the bare wood

Exhibited Temple Newsam, 1946 (No. 21); R.A., 1954 (No. 210);
University of Hull (No. 28)

Lady Kleinwort

An old label on the back establishes, no doubt correctly, the identities of
the children, together with the date and place: the latter, the county of
Dorset. It was in 1911 that the Johns moved from Chelsea to Parkstone,
near Poole, to the 'Gothick' bungalow set in its wild garden and romantic
heathland. Here Robin would be about seven; Romilly and Edwin, five
and six. The sunlight flooding the scene suggests what Romilly long
afterwards called the 'glorious summer of our installation'.

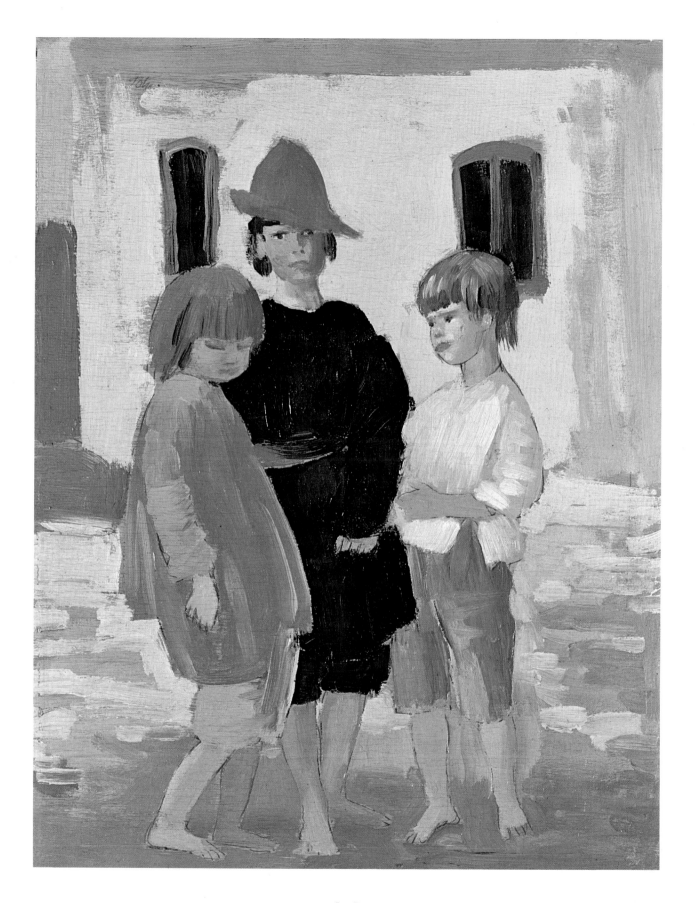

15 THE MUMPER'S CHILD, *c.* 1912

Oil on panel, $22\frac{1}{2} \times 19$ (57 × 48)

Signed 'John' bottom right

Exhibited R.A., 1954 (No. 366); Liverpool, 1955 (No. 27);
King's Lynn, 1959 (No. 33)

Mr Peter Harris

In Henry Lamb's words, Alderney Manor, to which the Johns moved in
June 1911, was an 'amazing place – a vast secluded park of prairies,
pinewoods, birchwoods, dells and moors' as well as a house where lived
the Wimbornes' eccentric tenant with Dorelia and her raggletaggle
charges. When the lunch bell sounded, Romilly tells us, and the family
trooped back into the house, the grounds filled up with poachers and
marauders, a gang of thieves (their progeny trundling piratical soapboxes
on wheels), whom the gypsies themselves declined to regard as equals.
Inheriting an old English title meaning 'beggars'*, they made themselves
at home in John's unfenced territory, establishing their claim to rabbits
and firewood, and finally conquering his good opinion. These *mumpers*,
like the artists themselves, were but part of the great consortium of
outcasts. The portrait known as 'The Mumper's Child' is splendid in
colour, and one of John's finest evocations of the wild earthiness he loved
so well.

* Or, in modern times, to use Mr Rupert Croft-Cooke's definition, 'non-gypsy
travellers', i.e. tramps.

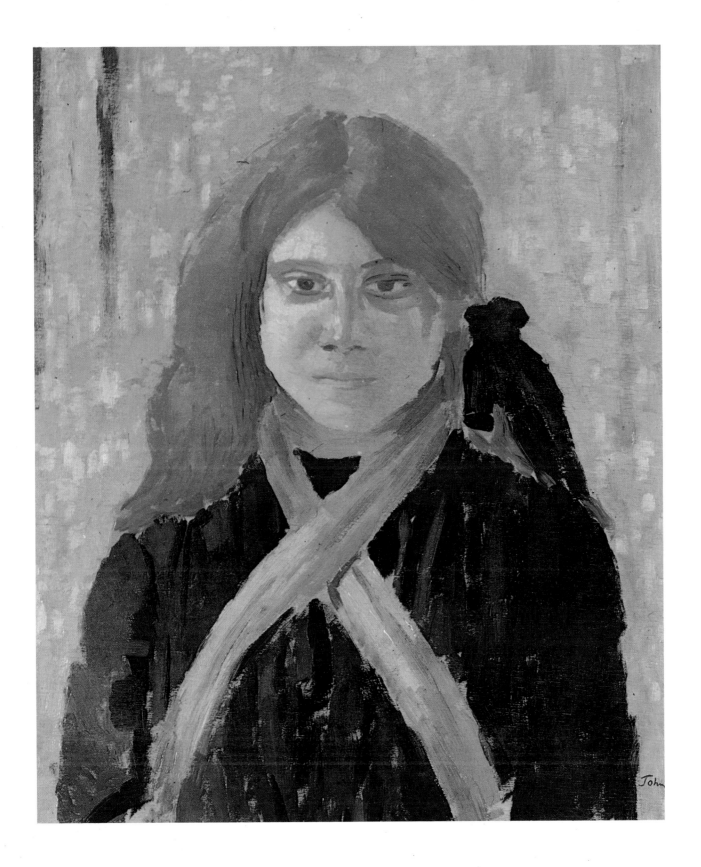

16 LYRIC FANTASY, 1911–1915

Oil on canvas, 92 × 185 (234 × 470)

Exhibited N.G., 1940, 'British Painting since Whistler' (No. 183);
R.A., 1954 (No. 37); and – as 'The Blue Lake' – R.A., summer 1962
(No. 124)

Collection: Hugo Pitman; Mrs Reine Pitman
The Tate Gallery

In a letter, undated but certainly of 1907, to John Fothergill, the artist
wrote: 'I am about to paint a picture which will prove conclusively that
the finest decoration can be produced without *any* direct reference to
visual "Nature" – that is it will be as it were a natural growth itself –
coming unbidden and self-sufficient like any flower and not at all
concerned to imitate other flowers.' 'Lyric Fantasy', though later, is the
supreme example among John's works of this large-scale improvisation.
The world transferred on to the canvas is an imaginary one; uncomfortably
so, since Ida herself (extreme right) reappears like Proserpine from the
Underworld to part two quarrelling boys. Seeing the picture again quite
recently, Romilly thought these two might be Caspar and himself, just as
he might also be portrayed – as a much younger child – in the arms of the
unknown woman in the centre. The two women to the left cannot be
identified. There is no doubt, of course, that the guitar-player is Dorelia
herself. Its unfinished state is a further proof that, the picture having
'taken charge', problems arose which improvisation could not solve.
Much as John may have regretted the death of Sir Hugh Lane in the
Lusitania disaster, and the end of Lane's Cheyne Walk murals, he seems to
have been glad to throw his hand in. 'Lyric Fantasy' remained rolled up
in the smaller Fryern Court studio till Hugo Pitman discovered it by
chance nearly twenty years later. Though freely interpreted, the setting
owes much to Wareham Heath, Dorset, where there are a number of small
lakes occupying the site of old claypits. The largest and best known is the
Blue Pool, Furzebrook, its colour determined by finely suspended clay
particles and enhanced by the surrounding yellow sandhills.

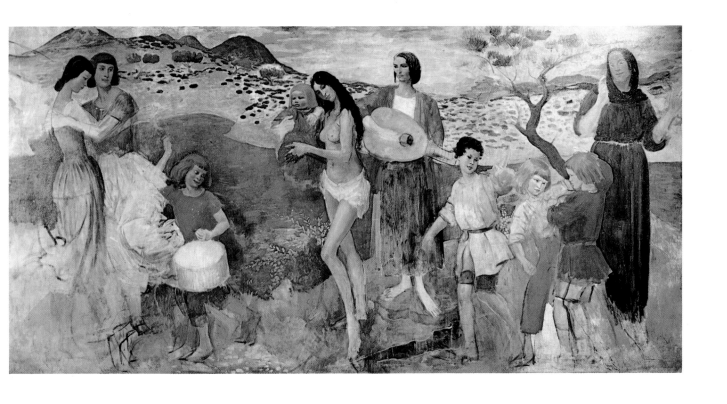

17 GALWAY SUBJECT, 1916

Charcoal and bodycolour on paper laid upon canvas,
105 × 142 (266·5 × 366)

Exhibited Upper Grosvenor Galleries, 1965 (No. 66)

Gwen Lady Melchett

In addition to these two panels which form a single composition, the present owner acquired a further panel in the same series, its dimensions some ten inches greater both vertically and horizontally. The three panels, in spite of many fine qualities, are evidence of John's regrettable tendency to theatricalize the proletariat. Some pull seems to be exerted back to the noble peasants of Puvis de Chavannes, but these stereotypes are then, in a disconcerting – and artistically distracting – manner, made fun of. The fact is that John was looking for peasants when the peasantry had ceased to exist. 'Their drapery is often very pleasing – one generally sees one good thing a day at least – but the population is greatly spoilt now – 20 years ago it must have been astonishing,' he wrote to Dorelia. The lower orders in Russia, symbolized by a Grigori Rasputin capable of praying, tippling and dancing a *komorinskaya* to the phonograph at the same time, might have suited him better. But the October Revolution of 1917, if not the Easter Rising of 1916, revealed the essential artificiality of Chelsea-style celebrations of the Simple Life.

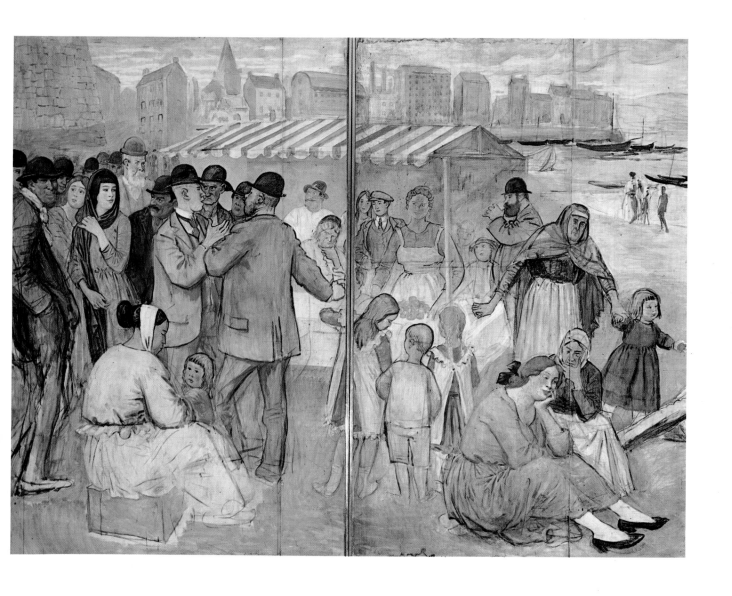

18 THE MARCHESA CASATI, 1919

Oil on canvas, 38 × 27 (96·5 × 68·5)

Exhibited Toledo and Toronto, 1948 (No. 18); Halifax, Nova
Scotia, etc., 1972–3 (No. 29)

Collection: Sir Evan Charteris
The Art Gallery of Ontario

Still sartorially a Major attached to the Canadians, John was invited to
Paris in 1919 to paint pictures commemorating the Peace Conference.
This meant a series of portraits, by no means exclusively of ministers and
generals. Through a Chelsea friend, Gandarillas, he was able to establish
himself in an apartment in the fashionable Avenue Montaigne; during
the day he frequented the Hôtel Majestic, where many of the Allied
delegates were staying; and leisure intervals were partly spent at the
Gramont mansion on the Champs Elysées. It was on a short stay in
Deauville, that summer, that he first encountered what Cole Porter
(moving currently in the same set) called the 'rich rich'. It seems likely,
however, that John would have wanted to paint the Marchesa, and
somehow have seized the opportunity, whether she had been rich or poor,
an aristocrat of the Faubourg or a barmaid in the Tottenham Court Road.
All the same, the two celebrated portraits he painted of this lady (the other
belongs to the Hon. Mrs Mary Anna Marten) have tended to give the
wrong impression: that John toadied to titled wealth. In fact, the artist
could take only a little of this rarefied existence before stripping off his
Sam Browne and seeking relief among the artists and writers of
Montparnasse. It is altogether typical of the concealed philanthropist in
John that, the Marchesa having lost every penny of two fortunes, he made
a permanent contribution to her wants by banker's order. According to
Sir Evan Charteris, the portrait was originally a full-length in pyjamas.
Described by Lord Duveen as an 'outstanding masterpiece of our time',
it passed to the Art Gallery of Ontario in 1934 for £1500. 'The Marchesa
Casati' had been painted in April 1919: after some lapse of time, John
himself misdated it 1918.

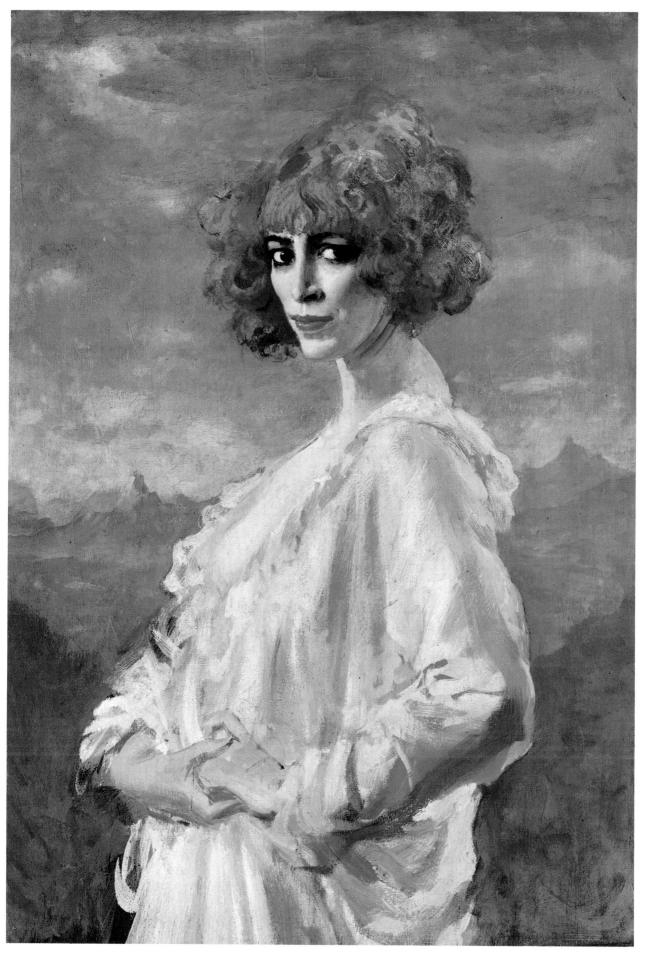

19 LADY OTTOLINE MORRELL, *c.* 1919

Oil on canvas, 26 × 19 (66 × 48·5)

Exhibited R.A., 1954 (No. 354) ; Sheffield, 1956 (No. 26)

Collection : Lady Ottoline Morrell
Mrs Julian Vinogradoff

This portrait shocked both those who knew the sitter and those who
admired the artist. And Lady Ottoline, even more perceptive than
Viscount D'Abernon (see No. 67a), well understood that what John
regarded as a friendly likeness might seem to friends and relations, as well
as to strangers, a malicious caricature. Press reaction, this time, finally
succeeded in alarming John himself. 'I would like you to have that
portrait,' he told Lady Ottoline, 'but I don't think it's one you would like
to hand down to posterity as a complete representation of you.' Far from
taking his advice, she hung it over the mantelpiece in her much frequented
drawing-room at Garsington Manor. 'Whatever she may have lacked,'
the artist observed, after her death, 'it wasn't courage.'

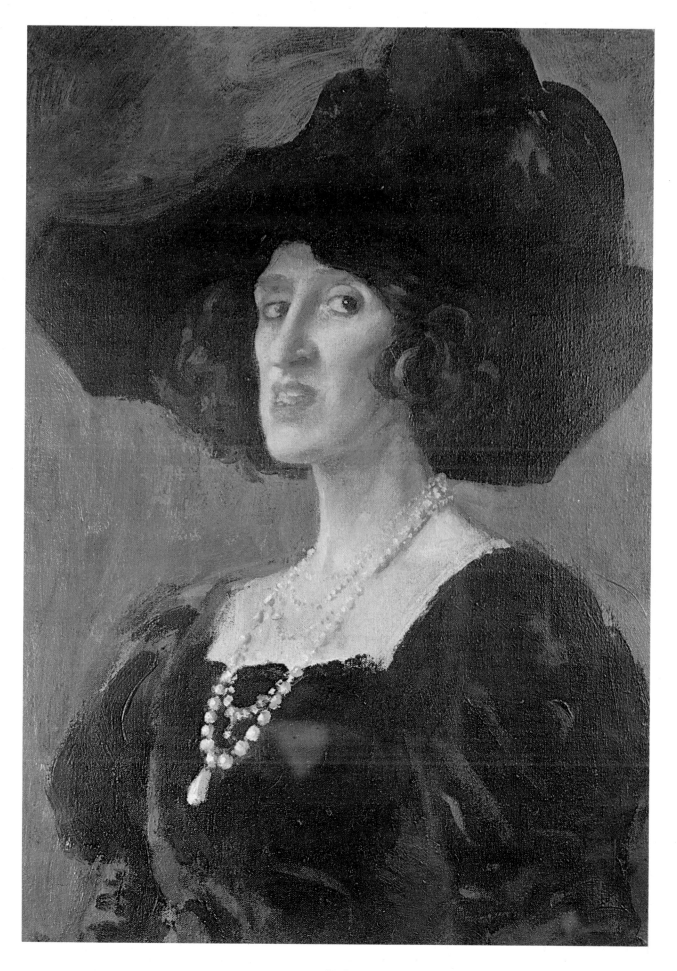

20 MADAME SUGGIA, 1923

Oil on canvas, $73\frac{1}{2} \times 65$ (186×165)

Exhibited Alpine Club Gallery, 1923 (No. 12); International
Exhibition, Carnegie Institute, Pittsburgh, 1924 (No. 224)

Collection: William P. Clyde, Jr
The Tate Gallery

Guilhermina Suggia (1888–1950) studied at Leipzig and under Casals,
whom she was believed to have married in 1906. Portuguese in origin, from
1914 she lived in England, giving her last concert at the Edinburgh
Festival of 1949. John seems to have embarked upon the portrait with
more than usual enthusiasm, and Mme Suggia to have been an unusually
privileged sitter: 'John,' she related afterwards, 'does not only allow his
sitters to view the unfinished portrait, but encourages criticisms.'
Obviously, all went well to begin with, for Mme Suggia continues: 'On my
first view of the picture, I was surprised to see how swiftly it had already
progressed.' Soon, however, the artist ran into trouble, not so much over
the position of the bow and the instrument itself as over the colour of the
dress, which was more than once dramatically altered. Begun in 1920, the
work dragged on beyond sending-in time for the R.A. summer show of
1922 and was only completed by 1923. Suggia played Bach throughout the
sittings; by contrast, Miss Amaryllis Fleming, another distinguished cellist
whom John painted with her instrument (though a young girl as yet and
little known), remembers having the pose constantly 'frozen', and neither
from her nor from any other sitters we have encountered were any
criticisms invited! The grandeur of this portrait made a deep impression
on the public, and Lord Duveen was felt to have performed an important
service to the nation in buying it back from its American owner and
presenting it to the Tate. For some years now, it has been on loan to the
British Embassy in Athens.

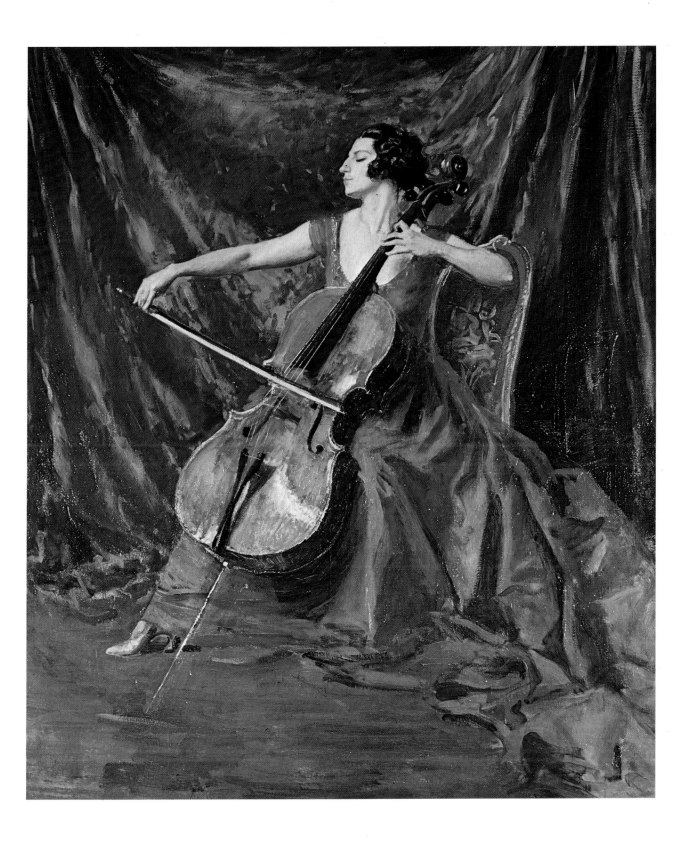

21 PEONIES IN A JUG, after 1925

Oil on canvas, 25 × 21 (63·5 × 53·5)

Signed 'John' top right

Exhibited R.A., 1954 (No. 421)

Mrs Thelma Cazalet-Keir

It was not till the mid-1920s that the artist began to devote some part of his energies to flower-painting. A number of examples appeared at an exhibition held at Messrs Tooth's in April–May 1929. Flowers were an alternative to, and in some respects (at least from Dorelia's point of view) preferable to, models. 'There's nothing much in the way of flowers here and I have no models,' John wrote to Dorelia from the Villa Ste Anne on 6th April 1928, 'I might as well be dead.' According to Dorelia, the very first flower picture – now owned by Admiral Sir Caspar John – was painted during the visit to Ischia in the early summer of 1925.

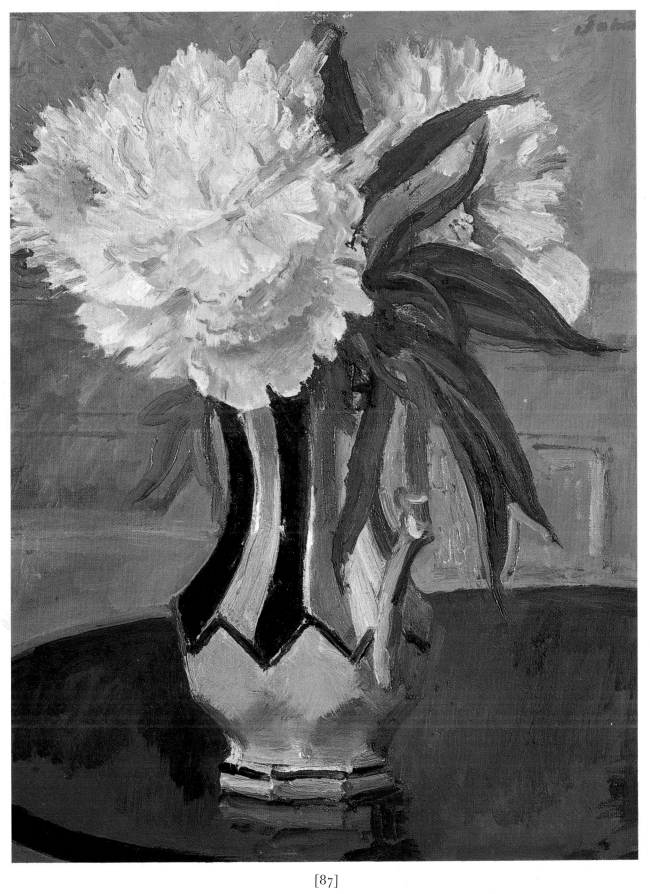

22 THE LATE LADY ADEANE, 1929

Oil on canvas, 74 × 38 (188 × 96·5)

Exhibited R.A., summer 1951 (No. 132)

Sir Robert Adeane

Sir Robert Adeane's first wife was Miss Kit Dunn, daughter of Sir James
Dunn and sister of the present Baronet. Fifteen sittings took place. John
wanted more, but (as with the portrait of Joseph Hone and the majority of
his more successful commissions during the last half of his life) it was
smuggled away 'unfinished'. It appeared at the summer exhibition at
Burlington House in 1951 and created a considerable stir: John had
produced here, it was felt, the quintessential spirit of the Twenties.

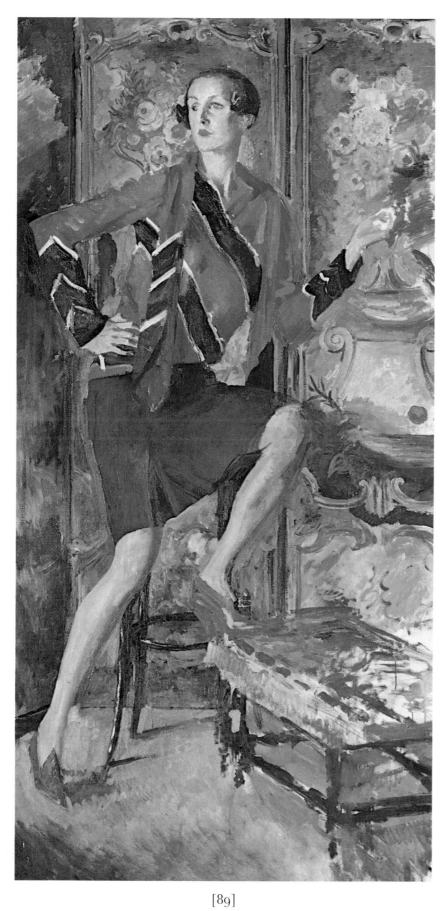

23 HEAD OF A JAMAICAN GIRL, probably 1937

Oil on canvas, $15\frac{1}{2} \times 12\frac{3}{4}$ (39·5 × 35)

Exhibited Temple Newsam, 1946 (No. 56) ; R.A., 1954 (No. 450) ;
R.A., 1963 (No. 117)

Collection : Edward Le Bas
Mr Richard Burrows

This painting, some say, does not belong to the Jamaican series, but was
painted in New York. The girl has even been described as 'East Indian'.
Without doubt, portraits of coloured models constitute John's most
successful *genre* during his later years and not all are Jamaicans. Here we
keep the title accepted by the late Edward Le Bas, a distinguished painter
himself and active in organizing the 1954 John retrospective. Thus we
regard the picture as a likely product of 1937.

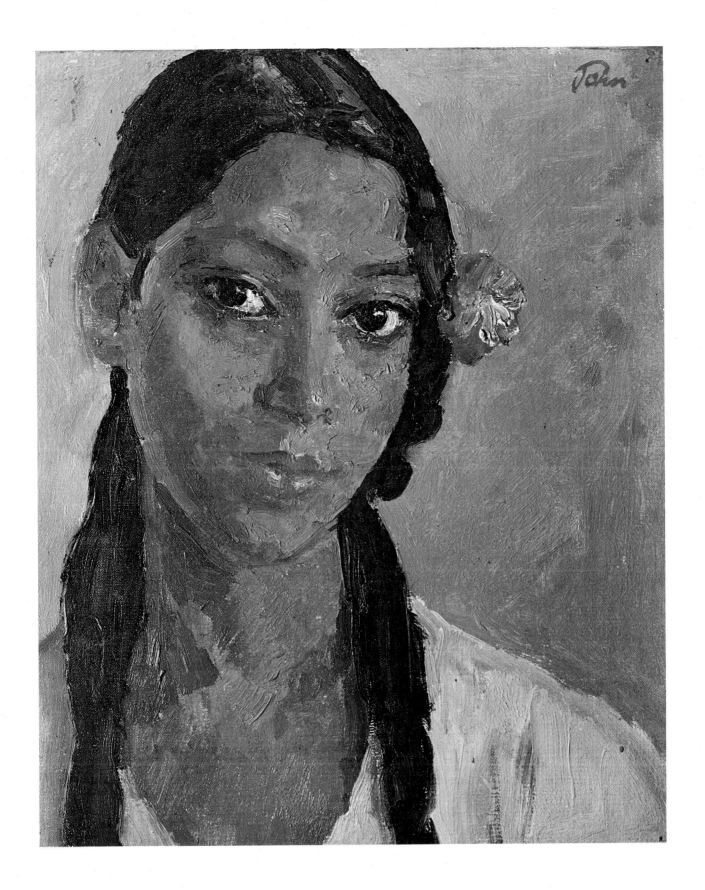

24 MIXED FLOWERS IN A GLASS JAR, *c.* 1938

Oil on canvas, 31 × 25 (78·5 × 63·5)

Signed 'John' bottom right

Exhibited Leicester Galleries, 1948 (No. 18)

Private Collection

The flower-painting reproduced here is unusually ambitious and seems to
have brought the artist himself some satisfaction, since it hung in the
drawing-room at Fryern Court for eight years. The signature was added
later, at the present owner's request and through the good offices of John's
daughter Poppet.

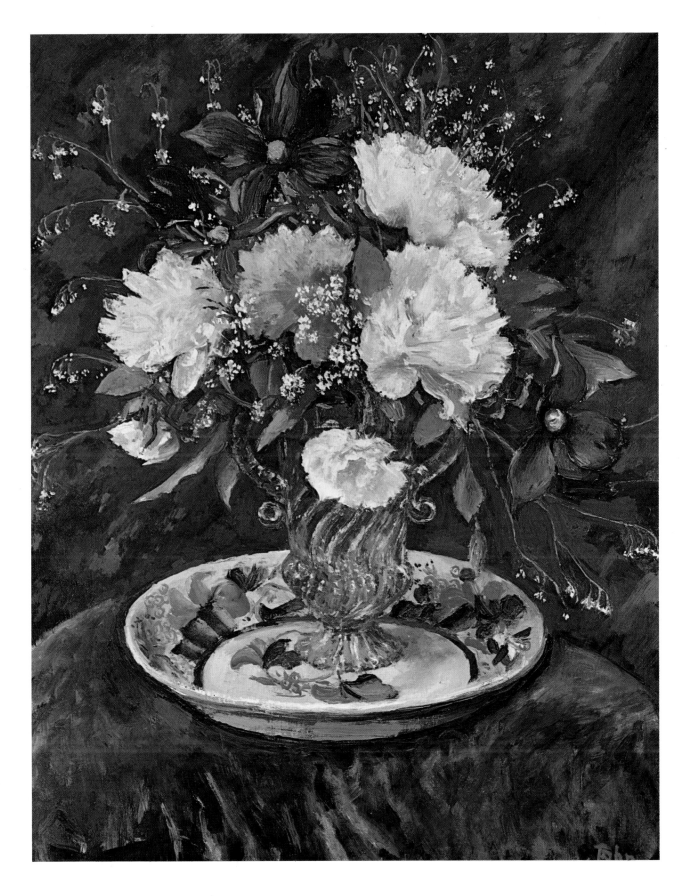

[93]

25 STUDIES OF A MALE NUDE WITH A STAFF, *c.* 1897

Charcoal on paper, 24 × 18¼ (60·9 × 46·3), *S*

Signed 'John' bottom left
Stamped on verso 'A. E. John Studio, July 1962' (this stamp appeared on all drawings in Messrs Christie's John Studio Sale of 20th July 1962)

Gwen Lady Melchett

As John's tribute to him in 'A Note on Drawing' long afterwards records, it was Fred Brown, the Slade Principal, as much as Tonks who inculcated this 'method of rendering the human form by a succession of rhythmical lines following the surface and explaining its structure'. No doubt, Brown himself had been brought up on the life-studies of Alfred Stevens (1817–1875), of the English school; but there existed throughout Europe many venerable precedents for the all-over linear mesh – going back at least as far as Dürer.

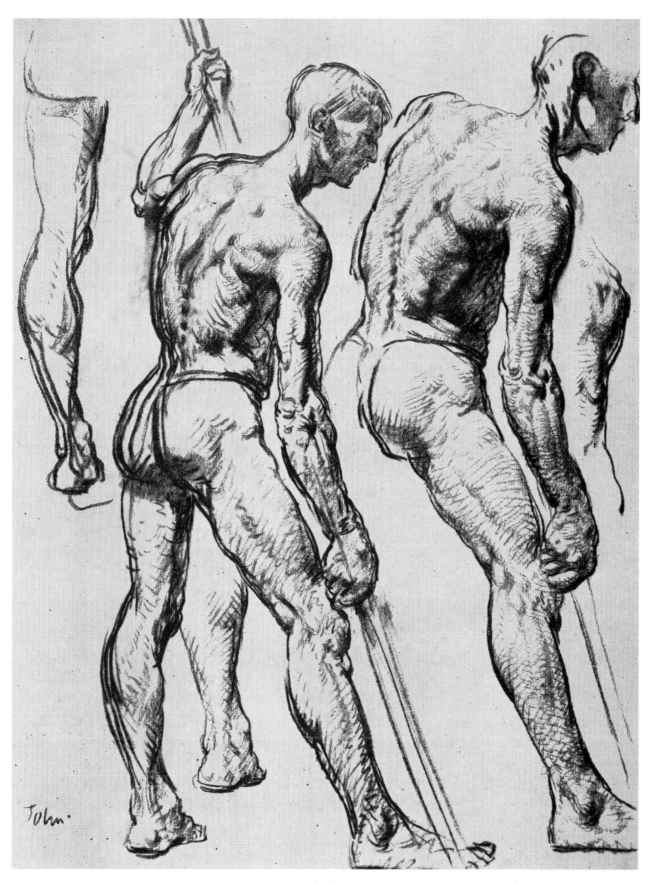

26 IDA NETTLESHIP, URSULA TYRWHITT AND GWEN JOHN, *c*. 1897

Pencil on paper, 12×9 ($30 \cdot 5 \times 22 \cdot 8$)

Exhibited R.A., 1954 (No. 11)

Private Collection

Before Ida's ascendancy, and particularly in 1897, Ursula Tyrwhitt dominated John's affections. It was through his sister Gwen that he became close friends with a number of contemporary girl students at the Slade, where Ida had arrived as early as 1892. Gwen (1876–1939) herself registered in 1895, a year after her brother. Though neither Ida nor Ursula shared Gwen's remarkable genius, both continued to paint after leaving art school. The short pencil-strokes, often cross-hatched, show that the Brown–Tonks method could be abandoned at will. They resemble the scratches of an etching-needle. A large number of drawings of about this date are carried out in the same, anything but conventionally elegant, manner, and might be cited as evidence that John embarked upon the etching process rather earlier than the experts have supposed.

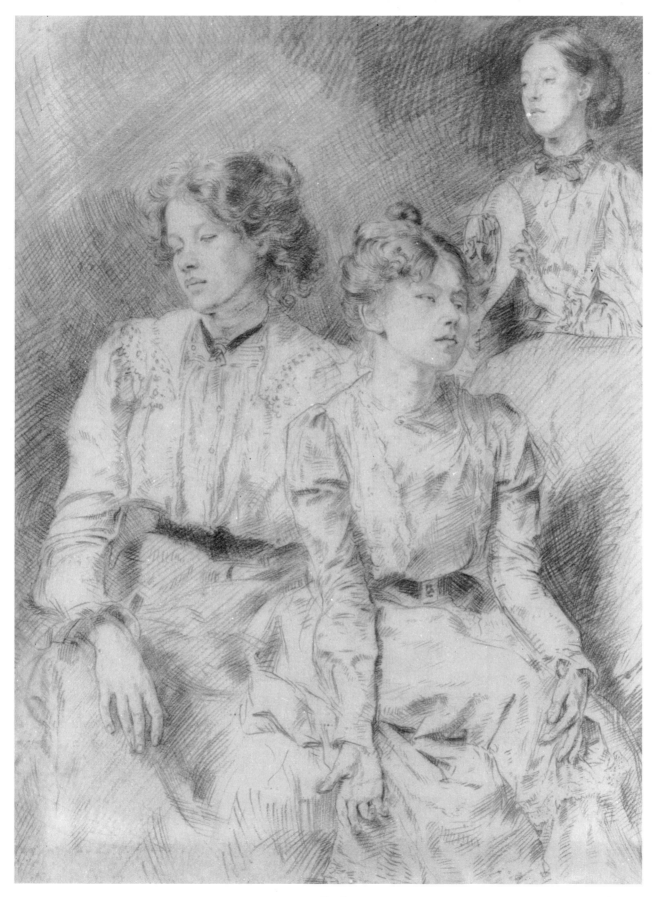

27 BENJAMIN EVANS, ? 1897–8

Etching, 5 × 4 (12·7 × 10·1)

Signed 'A. E. John' bottom right on plate, and 'Augustus John' in pencil below

Listed in Campbell Dodgson as 14 I/4; now accepted as II/5
Messrs P. and D. Colnaghi

This is the rare, lightly etched state of the plate, which was heavily reworked in later states. The year scratched on the copper after the signature, while largely illegible, has '9' as third digit. We may suppose, therefore, a date of 1897 or 1898, since that would tally with the specific references to Evans and this plate in *Chiaroscuro* and account, at least partly, for the etching's strongly Rembrandtesque character. 'Benjamin Evans, a Welshman whom I had met at school at Clifton, made a third party in the trio we formed [of fellow-students, including McEvoy, at the Slade],' John writes. 'Evans was an original and witty draughtsman, well versed in Rembrandt. At his suggestion I attempted etching: my first plate was a portrait of him.' The trio embarked on a donkey-cart expedition through Pembrokeshire in 1897; and perhaps Evans' Romany-style hat indicates a shared enthusiasm for the open road and the wind on the heath. In the year following, the trio visited Amsterdam, again at the suggestion of Evans, to see a Rembrandt exhibition held at the Stedelijk Museum between 8th September and 31st October. The sitter finally gave up art to become a sanitary engineer (*Chiaroscuro*, pp. 43–6). We ought to add that Dodgson, who ascribed the earliest etchings to 1901, would have regarded a date in the 1890s for this plate as an error on the part of the artist. This opinion is respected in our own queried dating here.

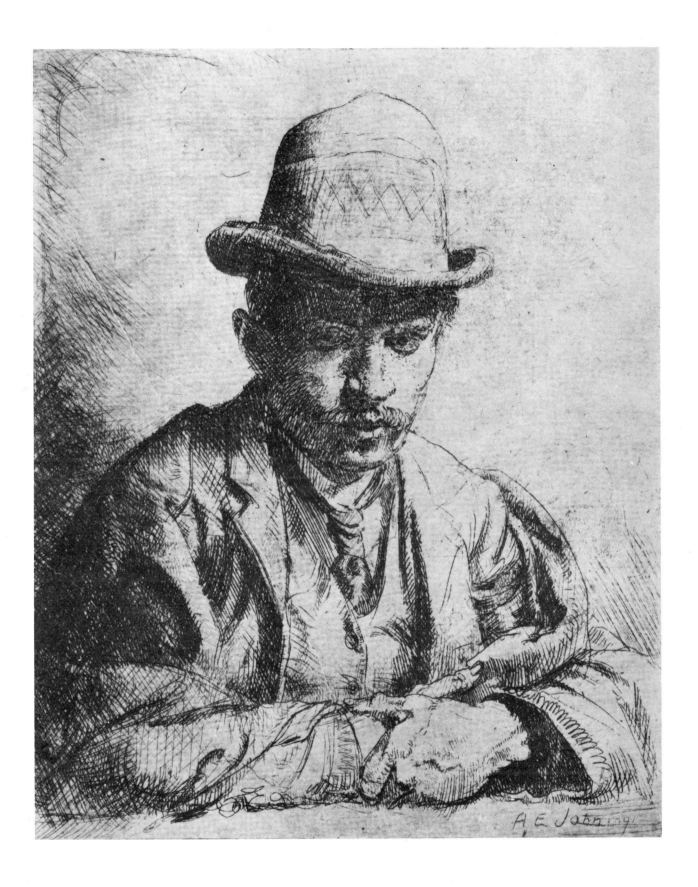

28 MOSES AND THE BRAZEN SERPENT, 1898

Oil on canvas, 60 × 84 (152·5 × 101·5)

Exhibited Birmingham, 1952 (No. 34); R.A., 1971 (No. 11)

The Slade School of Fine Art, University College, London

'And Moses made a serpent of brass, and put it upon a pole; and it came to pass, that if a serpent had bitten any man, when he beheld the serpent of brass, he lived' (*Numbers*, XXI, 9). Such was the solemn and rather intimidating subject set for the Summer Composition at the Slade which won for John the First Prize in 1898. While not much to the modern taste, this represents a concentrated study of the Old Masters wholly laudable in a beginner, and a most courageous attempt to work out his ideas on the grand scale. Rembrandt and El Greco form an uneasy partnership in what the artist described – with proper zest – as his 'Holy Moses treat' (letter to Michel Salaman, of June 1898). The influence of other great forebears is also evident, though in places it is difficult to distinguish between Mannerism and mannerisms.

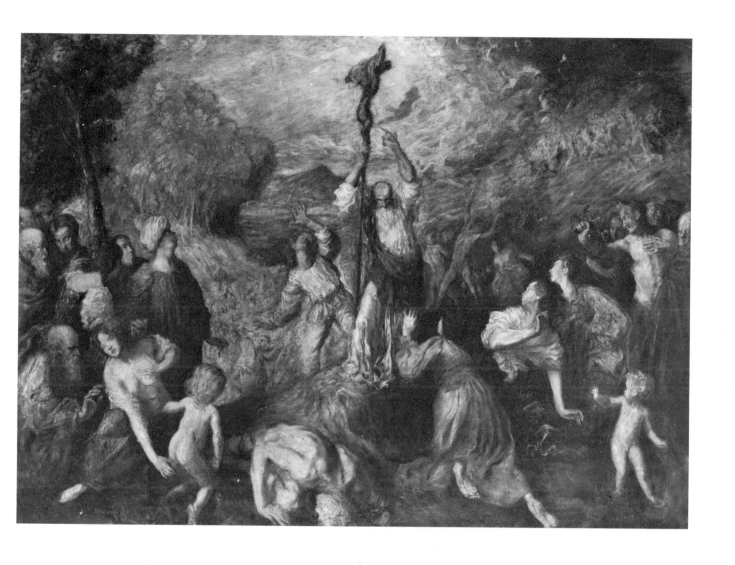

29 TETE FAROUCHE (PORTRAIT OF THE ARTIST), ? 1899–1900

Etching, $8\frac{1}{4} \times 6\frac{5}{8}$ (21·3 × 14·3)

Listed in Campbell Dodgson as 10, second state

The National Museum of Wales

One of the most remarkable features of John's output is the very large proportion of self-portraits. This holds good for the etchings, too, where a long series of mirrored heads and busts seems deliberately to invite comparison with Rembrandt. If the title 'Tête farouche' means, as it should, 'Head of a Rebel', then it could hardly have been better chosen for the years immediately succeeding 1898, when John left the Slade. Both Michel Salaman and John Everett testify to the change in their friend's character. Removed from Tonks' daily supervision, John was at his wildest, his most 'farouche', precisely during 1899–1900, when, among other escapades, he led the police a dance across the flower-beds of Hyde Park and himself danced on the roof of St John's Church, Charlotte Street. Dodgson would, one presumes, have assigned this print, though undated, to 1901. The impression reproduced has been clean-wiped; others carry a great deal of plate-tone, with enhanced dramatic effect.

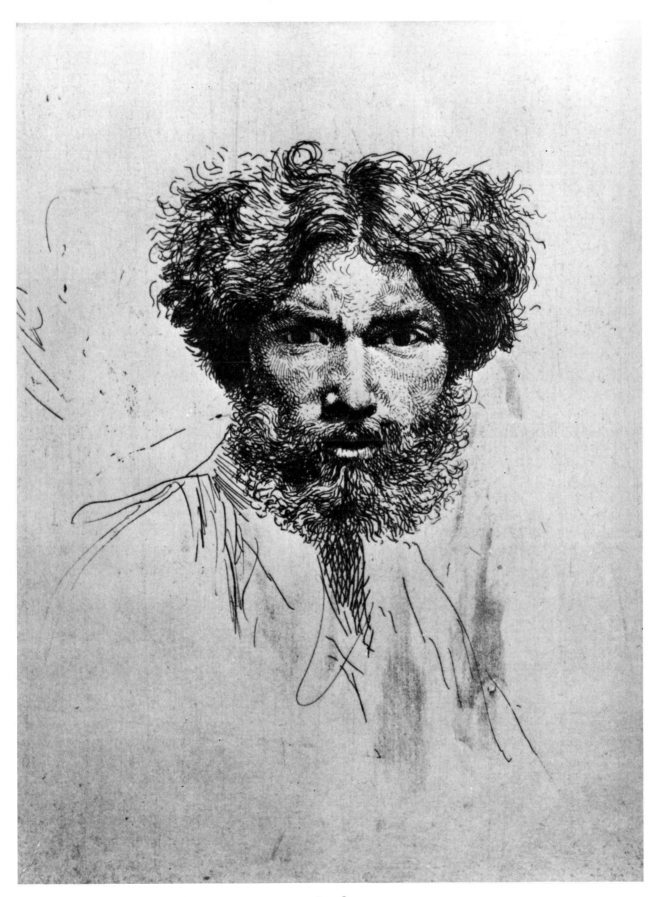

30 MERIKLI, 1901–2

Oil on canvas, 30 × 25 (76 × 63·5)

Exhibited N.E.A.C., winter 1902 (No. 111); Temple Newsam, 1946 (No. 4); R.A., 1954 (No. 330)

Collection: C. L. Rutherston

The City Art Gallery, Manchester

Though paintings of Ida are rare compared with the very great number of Dorelia portraits, there must be at least a dozen, not counting the posthumous and group pictures in which she appears. 'Merikli' comes nearest to the various versions of 'Ida with a Scarab', one of which, belonging to Sir Caspar John, was shown at the University of Hull (No. 3) in 1970. It has the same Rembrandtesque lighting and colour-range. The meaning of the word *merikli* would have been made plain to John by his friend Sampson, in whose later publication, *The Dialect of the Gypsies of Wales*, it is defined as: 'Connected with the Sanscript "pearl", "gem", or "jewel", *i.e.*, "ornament worn round the neck". Gem, bead, especially coral.' In fact, Ida is wearing a coral necklace. The basket may suggest another Gypsy connection, since basket-making is a home industry among the caravan-dwellers. Any symbolism intended by the proffered daisy is not immediately obvious. 'Merikli' was voted the New English Art Club's 'Picture of the Year' when shown in 1902.

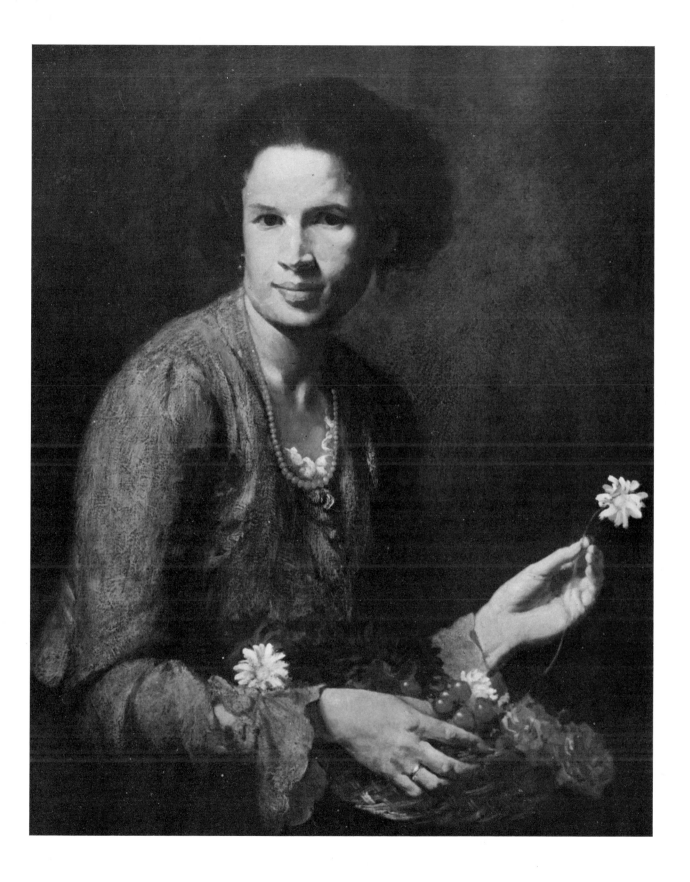

31 JOHN SAMPSON, ? 1903

Chalk on paper

Signed and dated 'John f. 03 [?]' bottom right

Exhibited N.E.A.C., winter 1903 (No. 132)

Present owner untraced

John Sampson (1862–1931), Liverpool University College Librarian when John arrived there in 1901, introduced the artist to Gypsy modes and manners. John proving an apt pupil in the study of Romani, they visited encampments together and shared longer journeys into Wales by horse-and-van. Later, John sent back notes of Gypsy dialect made during his wanderings in Provence. Sampson was a strange mixture of sound scholar and sentimental Romantic. His Romani poems (translated by himself) suggest that any influence he exerted over John was an unfortunate one. In his 'The Apotheosis of Augustus John', God appoints the artist Grand Vizier of Heaven, 'for I must really have a little amusement', a choice of court comic which would certainly have turned out disastrously. Altogether, Sampson encouraged the stage Gypsy in John, and helped to promote an image of larger-than-life, amorous, wine-bibbing jollity little to the taste of post-Georgian connoisseurs. For the best side of Sampson, we need to consult, *The Dialect of the Gypsies of Wales*, first published in 1926, a work of fascinating erudition. We have assumed that this, the only known (though unlocated) drawing of Sampson, must be that recorded as exhibited at the N.E.A.C. in 1903. A reproduction of it can be found, facing p. 58, in *Chiaroscuro*.

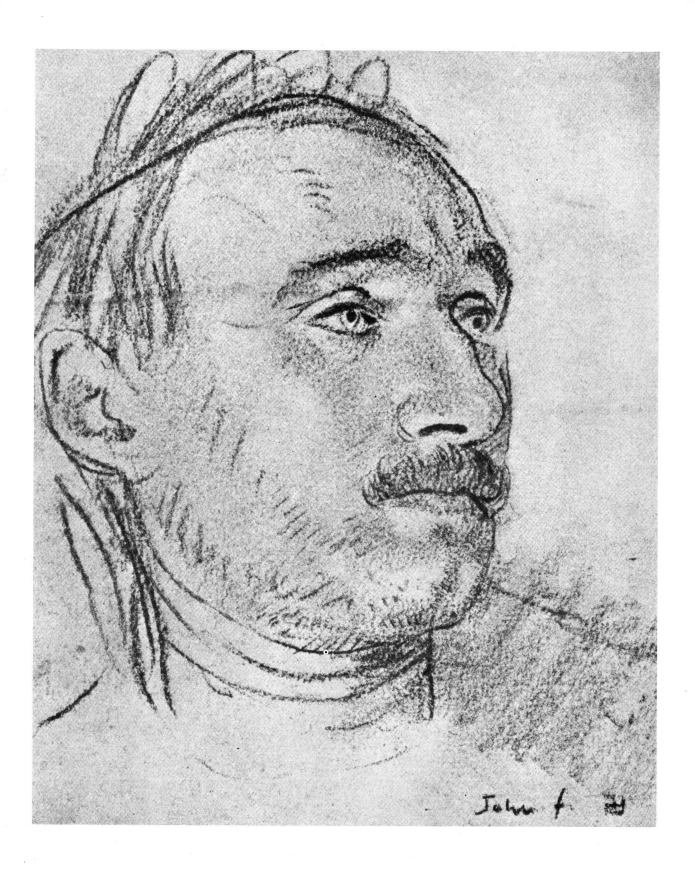

32 WYNDHAM LEWIS, *c*. 1903

Etching and drypoint, $6\frac{15}{16} \times 5\frac{1}{2}$ (17·7 × 13·9)

Listed in Campbell Dodgson as 19, fourth state
Signed 'John' and dated (erroneously) '1893' bottom right on plate

Messrs Thos Agnew and Sons

It was William Rothenstein who introduced Wyndham Lewis (1882–1957) to his older friend Augustus, probably in the summer of 1902. Lewis, shy and ambitious, at first revelled in John's careless brilliance. On his side, John envied Lewis' literary gifts. Mutual admiration, however, could give place to frequent disagreements, which continued throughout their lives. In 1938, John resigned from the Royal Academy, ostensibly on account of its rejection of Lewis' portrait of T. S. Eliot – then later, when he saw the picture, announced that his sympathies were after all with the hanging-committee. John did another etching of the same sitter (C.D., 18). By common consent, that reproduced is the more sharply observed of the two and, indeed, one of his very finest plates. Though John may have made mistakes in dating, as here, on a particular plate, it is difficult to understand his attributing plates to the 1890s if he never touched a needle till 1901. One's first introduction to the novel paraphernalia of etching is not so easily forgotten.

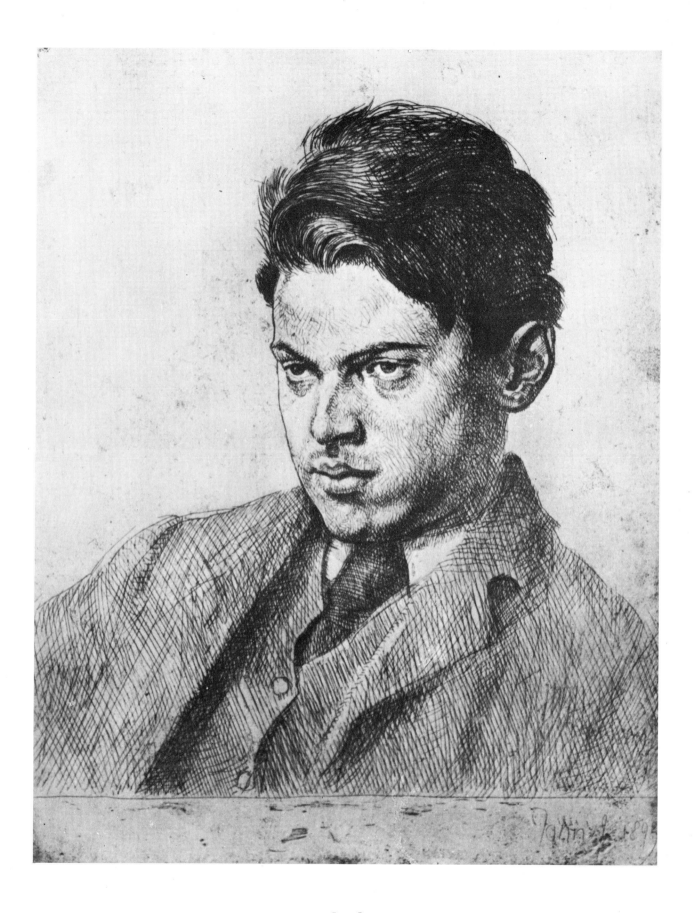

33 STUDIES OF YOUNG CHILDREN, *c.* 1904

Pencil on paper, $9\frac{1}{2} \times 13$ $(24\cdot1 \times 33)$

Private Collection

The children are David and Caspar, aged about three and two respectively. The 'location' could be the house at Matching Green, Essex, with large garden, orchard and stables, which Augustus and Ida took on a two-year lease in November 1903. The drawing is interesting in showing that from the beginning the boys' home-designed clothes were more picturesque than convention approved. One can also take it as a very early manifestation of the use made of David and Caspar (then Robin, Edwin, Pyramus and Romilly) as – after their mothers – John's favourite models. Though charcoal had been the main vehicle of drawing at the Slade, John seems to have been most at home with a lead pencil during the years immediately following.

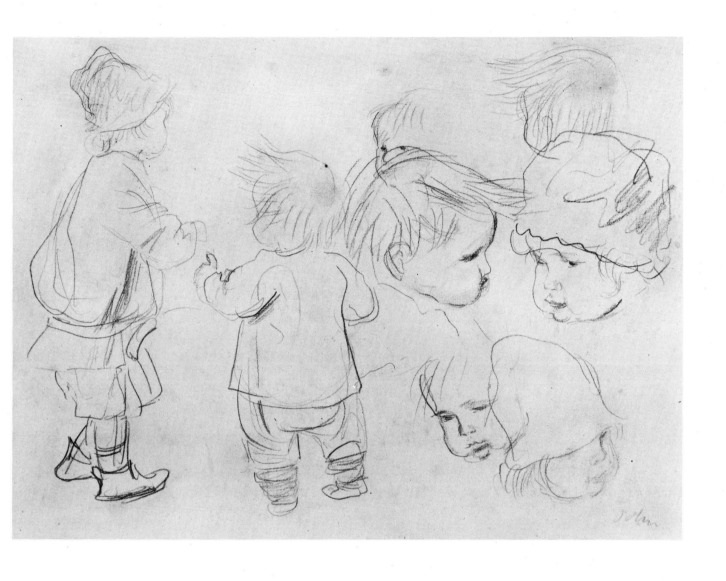

34 CARAVAN AT DUSK, 1905

Oil on canvas, $32 \times 35\frac{3}{4}$ $(81 \cdot 5 \times 91)$

Exhibited Temple Newsam, 1946 (No. 12)

Collection: The John Estate; with the Piccadilly Gallery and the
Tib Lane Gallery, Manchester
Mr Richard Driver

One of the most striking of the early landscapes, it includes the caravan
acquired from Salaman on the 'never-never' and a Gypsy tent of
traditional hazel-rod construction. It was on this stretch of moorland (still
bleak enough) in the straggling parish of Lydford, that Dorelia's son
Pyramus was born as early summer approached. 'It is adorable and
terrible here,' wrote Ida, who came down with her sons to assist: and we
can feel John's appreciation of these qualities. When not painting, he read
or played with a toy boat in the stream where Ida washed the family
linen, seen here drying on the grass. The Dartmoor experience, after a
short interval, inspired the artist to take even more ambitiously to the
road. A new celebration of the beauties of the English countryside was
initiated among painters, by Innes, Derwent Lees and John himself;
among writers, by W. H. Davies and Ralph Hodgson. The picture's fine
colour has been re-established after a recent cleaning.

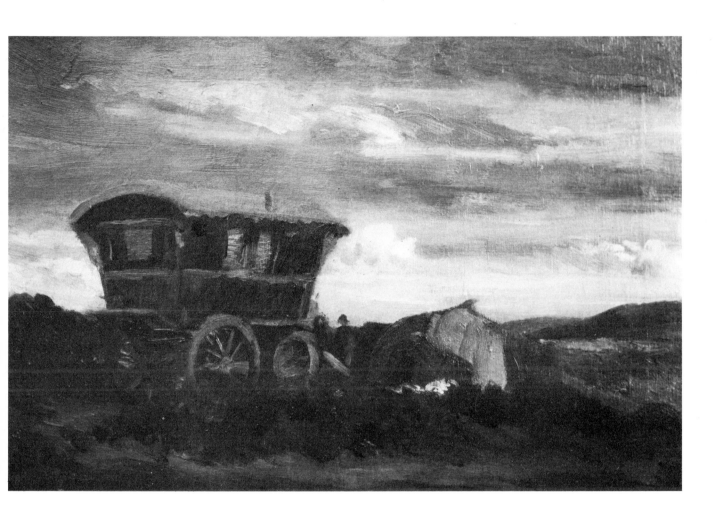

35   THE WOMAN IN THE TENT, 1905

Oil on canvas, $14\frac{1}{2} \times 17\frac{3}{4}$ (37×45), *S*

Signed 'John' top centre

Collection: Arthur Crossland; with Adams Brothers
Mr Peter Harris

John wrote to the Hon. Evan Morgan on one occasion (no year given):
'You know very well I think your "Woman in the Tent" is the best
example of my work at that period.' There are, of course, several
paintings by John of women (that is, Ida and Dorelia) in tents, and the
Morgan picture entitled 'The Woman in the Tent', shown at the R.A. in
1954, measured $21\frac{1}{4} \times 17$, a very different format. All the same, Mr Harris'
version is exquisite enough to deserve its author's highest praise. An
'In the Tent', without dimensions given and therefore unidentifiable, can
be found in the catalogue for the N.E.A.C.'s 1906 winter exhibition.

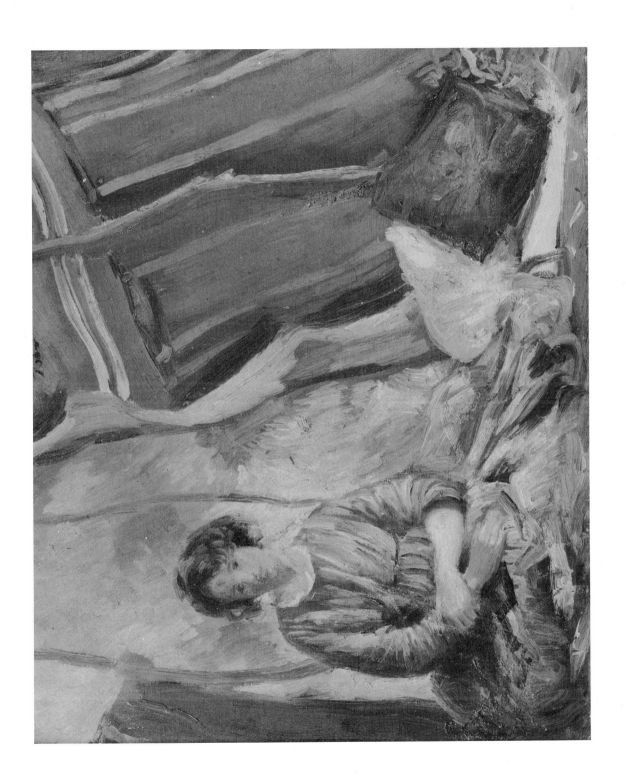

36 WYNDHAM LEWIS, *c.* 1905

Oil on canvas, $31\frac{1}{2} \times 24$ (80×61)

Signed 'John' top right

Collection: The John Estate
Mr Anthony Speelman

This fine painting sums up very well what Sir Osbert Sitwell referred to as
Lewis' 'lean Spanish elegance' (to be followed, in middle life, by a 'robust
and rather jocose Dutch convexity'). In an interesting letter published in
The Listener of 13th July 1972, Mr Geoffrey Grigson expressed his
astonishment that Lewis could have tolerated so 'academic' an artist as
John. Mr Grigson went out of his way to prompt Lewis to speak
disparagingly of John, but without success. This distressing loyalty (as
some may see it) was built upon a strong foundation which widely
differing creeds could not shatter, even at the instigation of his most
earnest disciples. In *Rude Assignment*, Lewis remembers how, four years
before their actual meeting, John came to draw from the model in the
life-class at the Slade on a brief visit to the school as an ex-student: 'I
joined the group behind this redoubtable personage. John left us as
abruptly as he had arrived. We watched in silence this mythological
figure depart.' By the time the portrait reproduced here was painted,
Lewis had already become John's assiduous, if not always faithful,
shadow, topped by the same 'enormous black Paris hat'.

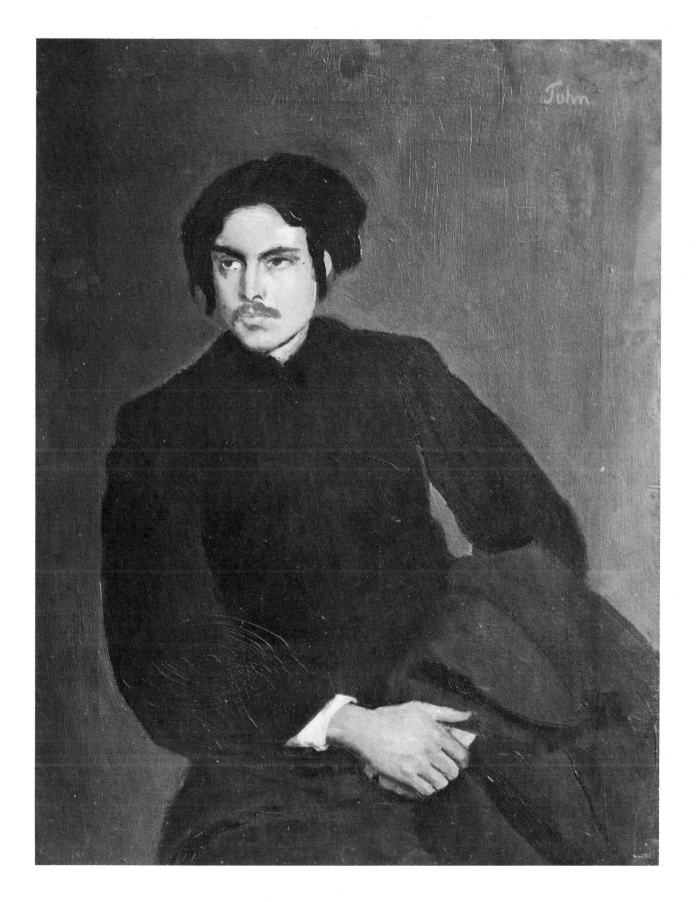

37 ALICK SCHEPELER, 1906

Pencil on paper, $8\frac{1}{2} \times 8\frac{1}{2}$ $(21 \cdot 6 \times 21 \cdot 6)$

Signed and dated 'John 1906' within the hair-strands, lower right

Exhibited N.G., 1940 (No. 92); R.A., 1954 (No. 76);
Sheffield, 1956 (No. 70)

Collection: Dr Louis Clarke
The Fitzwilliam Museum, Cambridge

John was most himself when under the influence of a new passion; that is, most surely himself as an artist. In 1906 he met Alick Schepeler, a secretary employed by *The Illustrated London News*, and the drawings he made of her form a unique yet highly characteristic section of his *oeuvre*. Always concerned to wrap in mystery the women he loved, John claimed a 'Slavonic origin' for Alick (baptised Alexandra), who was in truth of mixed Irish and German parentage, though born near Minsk in 1882. Some of the drawings are given the title of the water-sprite, Undine. There were paintings, too: 'La Séraphita', reputedly the finest, having suffered destruction in one of the artist's cigarette-fires in the 1930s. Technically, the Alick Schepeler drawings display, more than any other group (including the studies of Euphemia Lamb), the use of oblique-stroke shading. It is this stroke, moving downward from right to left, that reminds one of Leonardo silverpoints, despite the directional difference caused by Leonardo's left-handedness. The Slade life-school method seems to have remained an exclusively anatomical exercise.

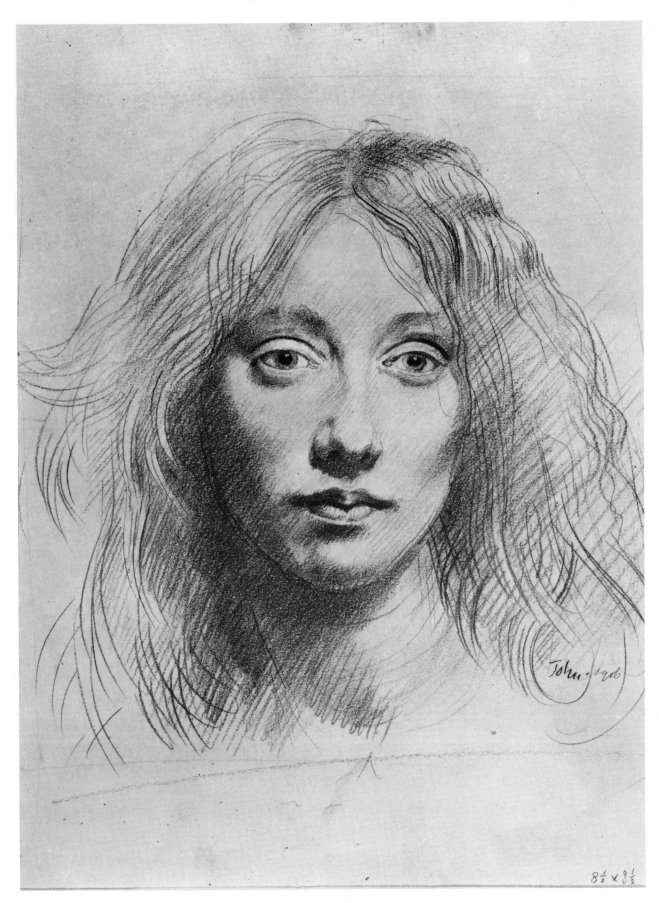

8½ × 8½

38 DAVID IN A LARGE HAT, *c.* 1906

Pencil on paper, $5\frac{1}{2} \times 5\frac{1}{2}$ (14×14)

Signed 'John' bottom right corner

Exhibited Venice Biennale, 1932; N.G., 1940 (No. 28); Arts
Council, 1948 (No. 116); R.A., 1954 (No. 35)

Collection: Morton Sands
Private Collection

In Romilly John's *The Seventh Child* there are also glimpses of the eldest
child. We see David, at Alderney, as 'lord' of the great rhododendron-
bush. Whenever the boys 'sighted anything peculiarly dilapidated – a boat
half under water or a house in ruins, or, even better, a bicycle with only one
wheel – it was immediately said to belong to David – being
thenceforward referred to as *David's* boat, or *David's* bicycle, with much
stress on the name.' David has several times figured in his father's drawings
and paintings wearing the same 'large hat', to which seniority rather than
settled ownership seems to have entitled him. The late Morton Sands,
brother of Ethel Sands (1873–1962), admirable painter and close friend of
Sickert, owned some of the finest John drawings, of which this is a
celebrated example.

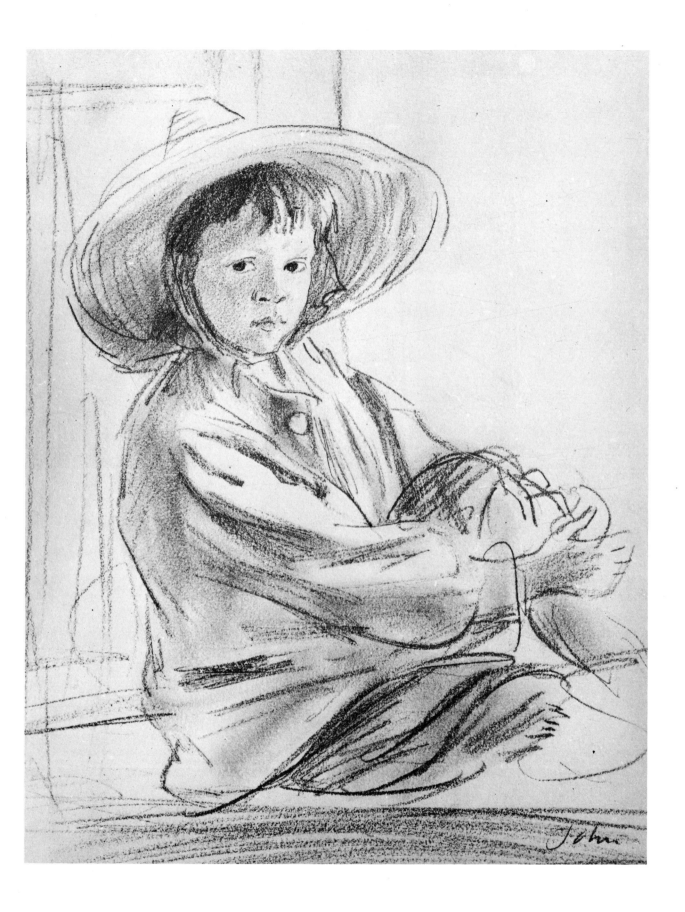

39 PYRAMUS ASLEEP, *c.* 1906

Pen and brown ink on paper, $4 \times 10\frac{3}{4}$ ($10 \cdot 2 \times 27 \cdot 3$)

Signed 'John' lower right

Exhibited N.G., 1940 (No. 4); R.A., 1954 (No. 43)

The John Estate

For biographical details, see note to Pl. 12. Perhaps twelve months after this drawing was made, John wrote to Will Rothenstein from Equihen: 'Pyramus grows more lyrically beautiful every day. He is like a little divine phrase from Shelley or Wordsworth.' The medium is an unusual one for John. There are plenty of reed-pen and fountain-pen drawings from his hand, but we know of no other important work produced with a steel nib and what looks like 'Prout's Brown'.

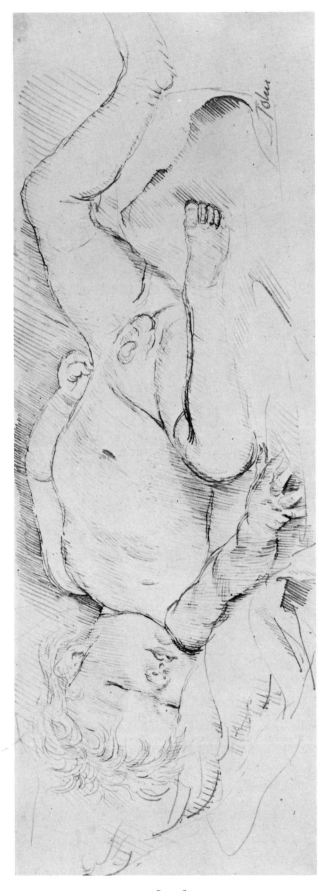

40 ALICK SCHEPELER, 1906–7

Pencil on paper, $12\frac{1}{4} \times 9\frac{1}{8}$ ($31{\cdot}1 \times 23{\cdot}2$)

Signed 'John' lower-middle right

Exhibited in the Wiggin Gallery, Boston Public Library, 1951

Collection: with the Childs Gallery, Boston
The Print Department, the Public Library, Boston, Massachusetts

The hat would be important. The one subject above all others upon which John and Alick tirelessly exchanged views was that of clothes. When they were separated, she had to describe for him in detail her dress of the day. 'Tell me, Undine,' he inquired, on one occasion, 'how are your shoes wearing? It seems so *fitting* that you – a soulless, naked, immortal creature, come straight out of the water – should take to *shoes* with such a passion!'

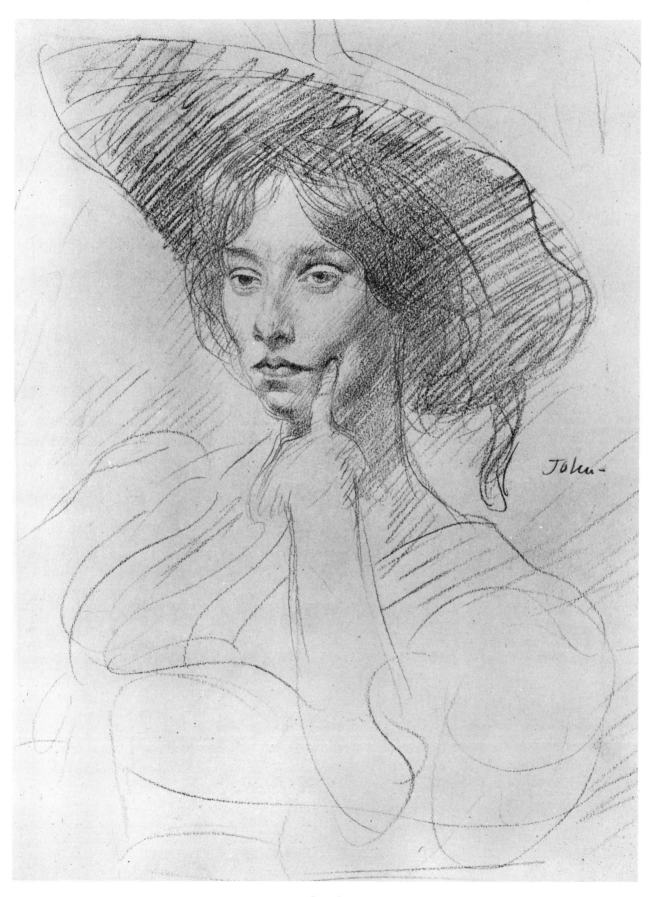

41 DAVID AND DORELIA IN NORMANDY, ? 1907

Oil on canvas laid upon millboard, $14\frac{1}{2} \times 18$ ($37 \times 45\cdot5$)

Signed 'John' bottom left corner

Exhibited Redfern Gallery, 1939 (No. 9); New York, 1939, British Pavilion (No. 49)

Collection: E. M. B. Ingram
The Fitzwilliam Museum, Cambridge

Idyllic as the subject seems, the John household was at its most topsyturvey during the summer months at Equihen in 1907 when, it is arguable, this exquisite study was painted. Ida's mother, Mrs Nettleship, felt very natural concern for her five grandsons. The baby, Henry, was passed over to the Nettleship family almost without argument, but there developed a determined battle between the widower and his mother-in-law for possession of the older boys. Dorelia, acting as resident mother (but resident for how long?), struck Mrs Nettleship as quite incompetent to manage six children, let alone her own unwashed, unbrushed Pyramus and Romilly. 'It is almost irritating that this place is so lovely,' she complained. And she scored a temporary success by taking David, Caspar and Robin with her when she returned to London in July. If the year is 1907, the month, therefore, can be no later than that. The David portrayed here is a rather uncertain guide to dating, since the clothes he wears (it greatly distressed John to think of this 'brave and beautiful attire' – mere rags to Mrs Nettleship – being exchanged for what was acceptable in Wigmore Street) do not in any recognizably Edwardian or early Georgian way fix a boy's age. David, in 1970, could not remember one of so many similar occasions, yet the traditional Normandy caption would seem to preclude any succeeding summer nearer, or during, his very early teens.

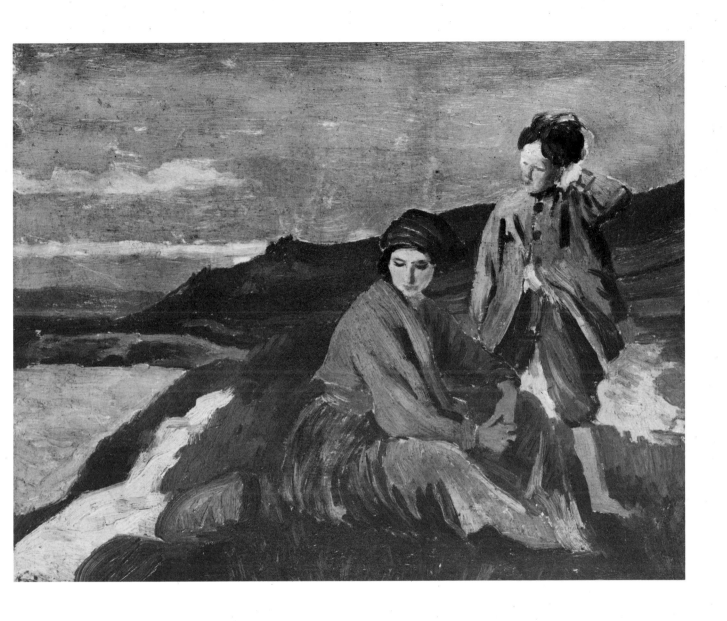

42   PEASANT WOMAN WITH BABY AND SMALL BOY, c. 1907

Charcoal and tempera on paper laid upon canvas, $71\frac{1}{4} \times 32$ $(181 \times 81\cdot5)$

Collection: The John Estate
Present owner untraced

About 1907, John began to find the atmosphere of the New English Art Club 'asphixiating'. Forced to exhibit there, he confessed: 'I always want to slough my skin after the bi-annual celebrations [the regular summer and winter show] and go into the wilderness to bewail my virginity.' Bewailing his virginity commonly took the form of painting large unsaleable canvases in which with a mischievous delight he abandoned every scrap of elegance, summoning up in its place 'elements drived from remote antiquity or the art forms of primitive peoples'. It is hardly surprising that the Picassos of the Blue and Rose Periods leave a mark on his paintings at this time. He recognized in Picasso, when the two artists met that summer, not only a co-disciple of Puvis de Chavannes but a fellow-sympathizer with the outcasts of society. Like Picasso's, John's noble vagrants are set symbolically on the barren shore of an inhospitable sea.

Something needs to be said about the medium here employed. The Birmingham artist, Joseph Southall (1861–1944), inspired by Eastlake and Cennino Cennini's treatise on painting, taught tempera to A. J. Gaskin and C. M. Gere. In 1901 the Society of Painters in Tempera was founded (for modern purposes, 'tempera' means pigment mixed with yolk of egg). John would seem to have little in common with the precise, almost Pre-Raphaelite Birmingham school; but no doubt the enhanced brilliance and purity of colour had attracted him to the method, and the Society later expanded its title to include Mural Decorators, a field in which John found himself increasingly interested. It was one of several societies of which he later became president.

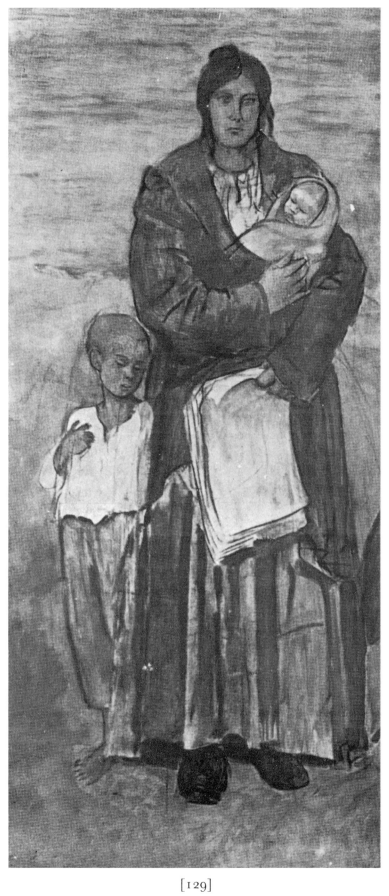

43 DORELIA STANDING, *c.* 1907–8

Pencil and watercolour on paper, $18 \times 10\frac{1}{2}$ (45·7 × 26·7)

Signed 'John' bottom left

Exhibited British Council, Empire Exhibition, 1936 (No. 503);
Arts Council, 1948–9 (No. 77); University of Hull, 1970 (No. 45)

Collection: Lord Henry Cavendish-Bentinck
The Tate Gallery

Though in Ronald Firbank's *Caprice*, Mrs Sixsmith 'placed a hand to her
hip in the style of an early John', and one often sees in one's mind's eye a
whole string of John models thus posed, the variety of stances adopted for
Dorelia is most remarkable. In fact, in none of the three examples chosen
here, does she rest a hand on her hip. More characteristic than any
particular placing of the hands (and this may not have been lost upon
Mrs Sixsmith) is John's insistence that the weight of the standing figure
be carried on one leg. While this is a traditional, and particularly
Renaissance, pose going back to the Antique, its significance for John
must have been connected with the emphasis given to the outthrust iliac
crest with its pad of fat and muscle, so much more prominent in a woman,
here further emphasized by the pleats springing away from the tight
bodice of the dress.

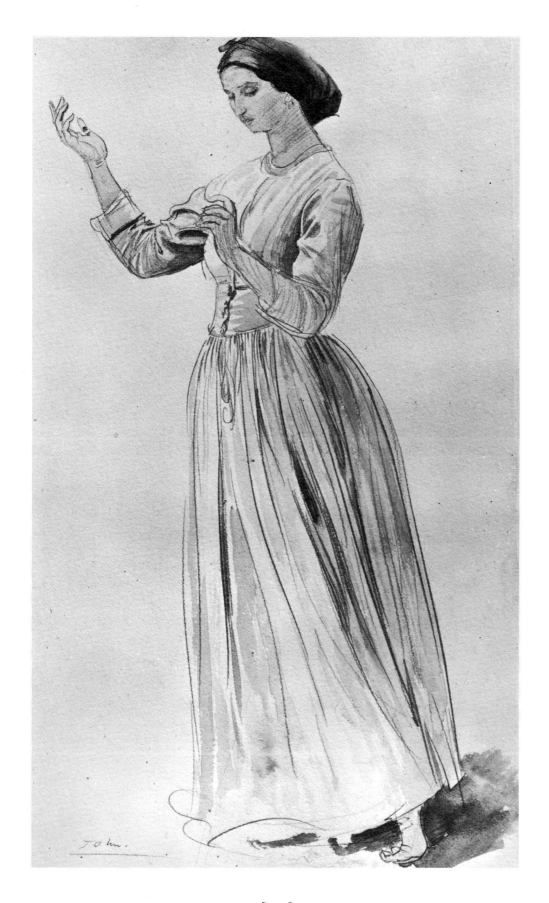

44 STUDIES OF DORELIA, *c.* 1907–8

Pencil on paper, $15\frac{3}{4} \times 9$ (40×23)

Signed 'John' low right, with further inscription: 'Augustus John to
Frank Harris Nov 24 1909'

Exhibited R.A., 1954 (No. 143); R.A., 1968 (No. 639)

Mrs Thelma Cazalet-Keir

Besides their intrinsic interest, these two studies arouse further attention
on account of the inscription. Most people succumbed momentarily to the
boisterous charm of Frank Harris (1856–1931), but in John's
recollection it was he himself – though unwillingly – who fascinated
Harris. The history of their relationship remains vague. We should like to
know more about the luncheon-party at which Lord Grimthorpe, Harris
and John were joined by Harris' protégé, the brilliant, tragical Richard
Middleton. But if John could still tolerate Harris in 1909, mutual
attraction had ceased to operate after 1910, when the artist was persuaded
to put up for a night or two with Frank and Nelly at their villa in Nice.
John, made uneasy by Mrs Harris' peculiar behaviour, fled at dawn. Even
this conjunction of Casanovas could not survive so flagrant a breach of
etiquette.

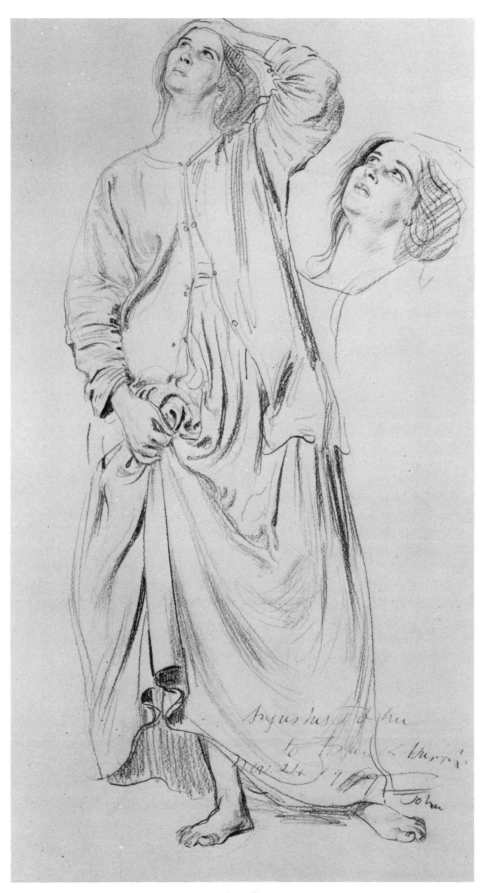

45 THE BLUE SHAWL (DORELIA), *c.* 1907–8

Pencil and watercolour (confined to shawl) on paper, 14 × 10 (35·5 × 25·3)

Signed 'John' below centre right

Exhibited R.A., 1954 (No. 132); Goldsmith's Hall, 1959 (No. 75); University of Hull, 1970 (No. 46)

Collection: with Goupil (William Marchant); A. E. Anderson
The Fitzwilliam Museum, Cambridge

John's watercolours are among his rarer productions. A more usual transition led from the pen-and-wash sketch to the oil-painting. The few tinted drawings, however, have a charm of their own. Among these, the Fitzwilliam's 'Blue Shawl' is not unique in the curious limitation of colour which accounts for its title: the Art Gallery of Ontario possesses a drawing called, in the same circumstances, 'The Blue Scarf'. The latter is dated 1908.

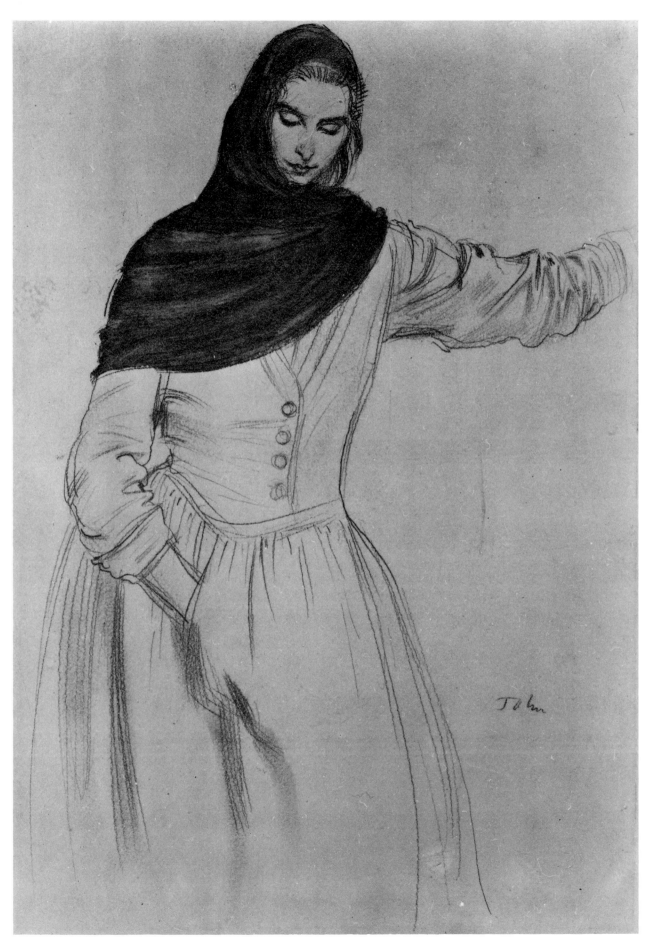

46 CASPAR, *c.* 1907–8

Pencil on paper, $9\frac{1}{4} \times 8\frac{1}{2}$ (23·5 × 21·6)

Signed 'John' bottom right

Exhibited Exeter, 1946 (No. 301); Australian and New Zealand
Galleries, 1958–9 (No. 9); University of Hull, 1970 (No. 53)

Mr Brinsley Ford

The owner was in John's studio at Fryern Court in 1941, when he
discovered this drawing torn into six pieces. Having fitted the pieces
together, he admired the drawing and was presented with it. By this happy
chance has been saved a particularly fine portrait of the second of Ida's
boys. Why had John intended to destroy it? Contrary to general
supposition, the artist was by no means easily pleased by his own efforts.
Unfortunately, he could be disastrously wrong, very often preferring an
inferior late work to one of his immaculate early records of his sons. In
June 1957, in a 'Note' prefacing the monumental *Fifty-Two Drawings*,
John wrote: 'Many of my drawings have been dispersed without trace . . .
not to speak of those I have myself sacrificed, perhaps too hurriedly, on the
altar of an imaginary perfection.'

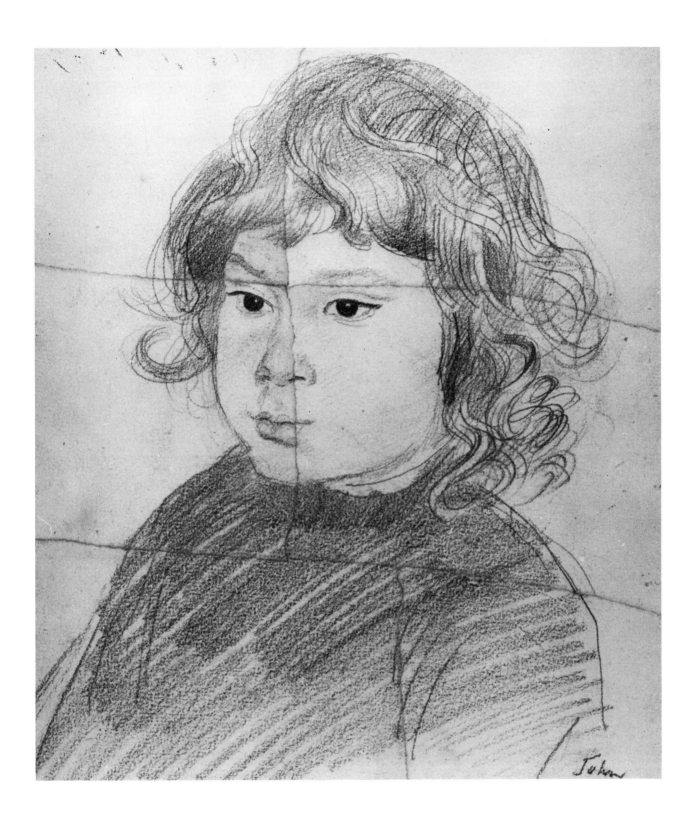

47 LADY OTTOLINE MORRELL, *c.* 1908

Pencil and gouache on paper, $11\frac{7}{8} \times 8\frac{3}{8}$ (30·1 × 23·8)

Signed 'John' bottom right

Exhibited Reid and Lefevre, 1949 (No. 55); Portraits, Inc.,
New York, 1966 (No. 71); Pierpont Morgan Library, New York,
1971 (No. 47)

Mr and Mrs Benjamin Sonnenberg

A very large number of John's pen-and-wash and watercolour drawings
of Lady Ottoline have come to light. Most of them were carried out during
the first months of their knowing each other. The model walked over daily
from Bedford Square to Fitzroy Street and inspired John to produce
endless sketches of the 'delicatest and noblest woman' he had known.
Though Ottoline might be thought to be of help to him professionally, he
was more concerned with petitioning her on behalf of his friends, in
particular Epstein and Henry Lamb. The latter, indeed, in some degree
replaced him. But the warm friendship continued till Lady Ottoline's
death in 1938. Lady Ottoline Morrell, who was married to Philip
Morrell, M.P., conducted one of the most celebrated salons of the day at
Garsington Manor, near Oxford – but in that area of her activities John
played little part.

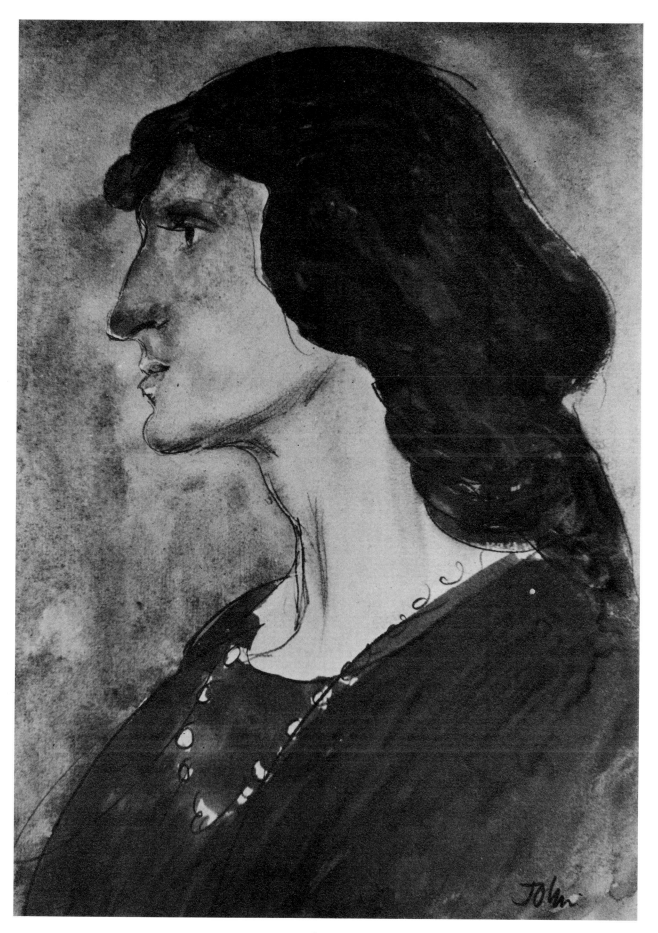

48 SIR WILLIAM NICHOLSON, 1909

Oil on canvas, $75 \times 56\frac{1}{2}$ (190×144)

Exhibited N.E.A.C., summer 1909 (No. 58); Pittsburgh, 1910 (No. 1666); Rome, 1911 (No. 227)

Collection: Sir William Nicholson
The Fitzwilliam Museum, Cambridge

The portrait was painted in the early months of 1909, and has some of the characteristics of Orpen in a genre in which the latter excelled. William Newzam Prior Nicholson, later Sir William (1872–1949), had joined forces with James Pryde to make a considerable reputation as 'J. and W. Beggarstaff', poster-designers. He did brilliant graphic work and décor for the theatre, but about this time was beginning to concentrate on still-life and portraiture. John wanted to paint Nicholson and Nicholson wanted to be painted by John. It was a gentleman's agreement: the small fee being neither paid nor pressed for. Nicholson, like Lovat Fraser, had a taste for the Regency. His air is impressively Corinthian; yet at first John thought some additional interest was necessary, and wrote to Lady Ottoline of a 'huge nude girl' that would help liven up the seated figure. The male portrait, however, even unattended, roused favourable comment at the International Exhibition held by the Carnegie Institute at Pittsburgh in 1910. As a result, American critics took early notice of John, and in the celebrated Armory Show, in 1913, he was the most strongly represented of all British artists.

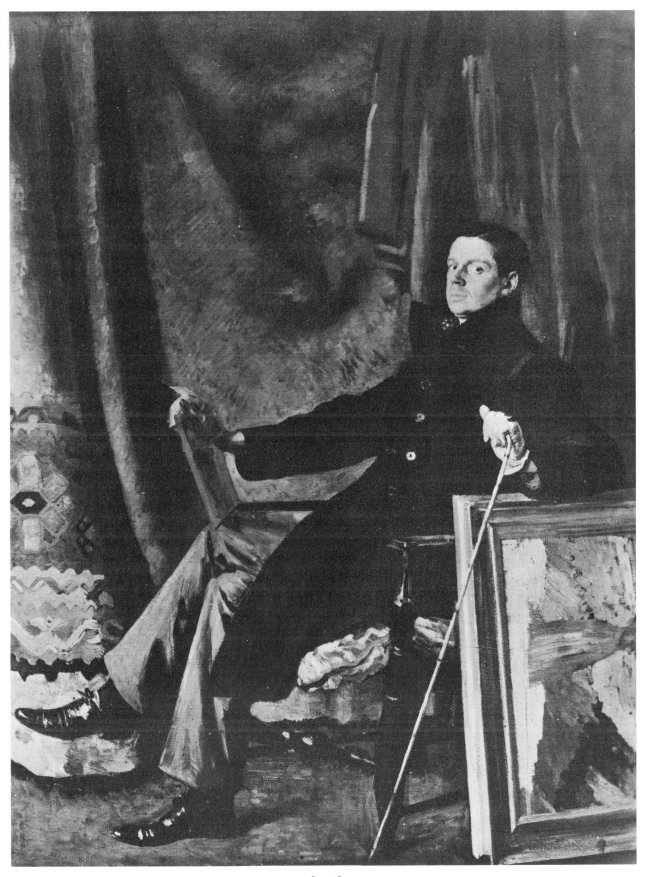

49 CHALONER DOWDALL AS LORD MAYOR OF LIVERPOOL, 1909

Oil on canvas, 81 × 54 (205·5 × 137)

Exhibited Walker Art Gallery, 1909 (No. 1044); N.E.A.C., winter 1911 (No. 33); R.A., 1954 (No. 337)

Collection: Judge Dowdall; E. P. Warren; H. Asa Thomas
The National Gallery of Victoria, Melbourne

H. C. Dowdall, K.C., husband of John's friend and confidante, the 'Rani', became Lord Mayor of Liverpool in 1908. In the following year, John cut short his caravan-trip with the family and returned to the scene of his University College activities to undertake this portrait. The grand dimensions were not of the subject's choosing, and, if John had had his way, would have been grander still. 'John liked the idea of doing it,' wrote Dowdall to Sydney Cockerell, in later days when he had been elevated to the Bench. 'We went to the colourman together and he wanted a vast canvas and I think had in mind a whole group of mace-bearers, etc, but I persuaded him to moderate the size.' It was a stroke of genius to have commandeered Smith, the Lord Mayor's footman, and success crowned a sharp struggle with problems largely self-imposed. Incredibly, one of the finest official portraits of modern times has been packed off to the other side of the world. But the picture's reception in its city of origin, in September 1909, reflects the great offence it gave: 'detestable'; 'crude'; 'unhealthy'; 'an insult'; and the 'greatest exhibition of bad and inartistic taste we have ever seen'. As late as 1932, the Director of the Walker Art Gallery had an opportunity of buying it back for Liverpool: he refused to do so. Thus, in 1938, Cockerell, as London Adviser to the Felton Trustees of the National Gallery of Victoria, was able to close with the then owner, Asa Thomas, for a sum of £2,400, twenty-four times John's original fee. 'The Thirty-Ninth Autumn Exhibition of Modern Art' at the Walker Art Gallery, Liverpool, in 1909, ran to no less than 2,300 items: hence the somewhat improbable catalogue-number of the Dowdall portrait.

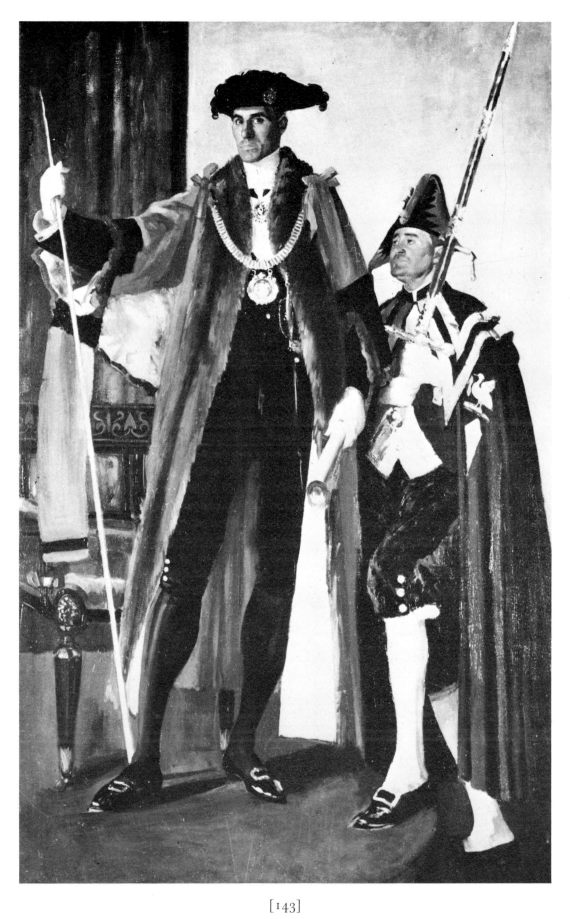

50 CASPAR, *c.* 1909

Oil on panel, 15¾ × 12¾ (40 × 32·5)

Signed 'John' top right corner

Exhibited R.A., 1954 (No. 363); Liverpool, 1955 (No.21); King's Lynn, 1959 (No. 30); University of Hull, 1970 (No. 14)

Collection: Mrs Otto Gutekunst; D. V. Shaw Kennedy
Mr Peter Harris

Caspar, Ida's second child, was born at 18 Fitzroy Street in 1903. He and his elder and immediately younger brothers, David and Robin (born in 1902 and 1904, respectively), formed a close-knit trio. From November 1903 till September 1905 the John home (studios apart) was Elm House, Matching Green, Essex. The family then moved to Paris, where Edwin was born, and after various adventures and changes of scene (a fifth son Henry having been born in 1907), Ida's sons, now motherless, returned to England in Dorelia's care. The Caspar shown here closely resembles the child to be seen in the caravan-holiday snapshots of 1909 and the picture has been given approximately the same date. It is close in feeling to the 'Pyramus', less colourful, but a good example of John's liking for the juxtaposition of light and dark blues. As is usual, a number of pencilled guide-lines, drawn direct on the wood, still remain visible. 'Caspar' first appeared at the Chenil Gallery in 1916.

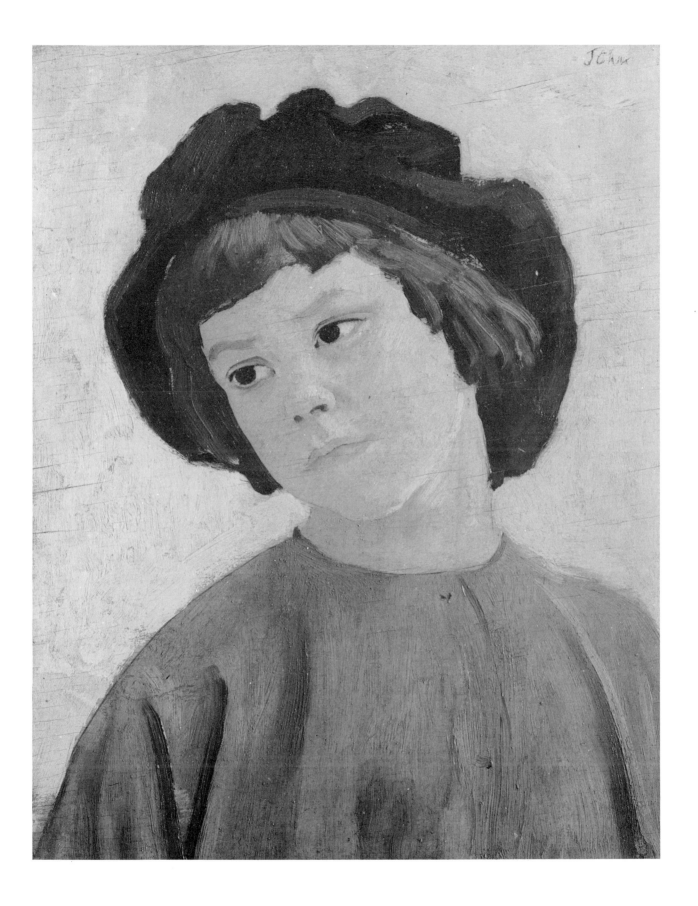

51 EDWIN AND ROMILLY, *c.* 1910

Oil on panel, $13 \times 9\frac{1}{4}$ $(33 \times 23 \cdot 5)$

Exhibited R.A., 1954; University of Hull, 1970 (No. 27)

Private Collection

A taste (in the artist's own words) for the 'fresh and raw' often took hold of the immensely sophisticated draughtsman. Long before Roger Fry introduced them to the great British public through the celebrated exhibitions of 1910 and 1912, Gauguin and Van Gogh had powerfully impressed John, who looked on life for a while, as Sir William Rothenstein recalled, with an '"early" eye'. This little work seems to emulate the naïve and photographic qualities of the Douanier Rousseau, Edwin and Romilly posing as if for a snapshot against a background of Martigues olive-trees. The two boys, one Ida's son, the other Dorelia's, were much in each other's company. They followed David, Caspar and Robin to lessons at Dane Court, Parkstone, on the same day. Later, they attended boarding-school in France together.

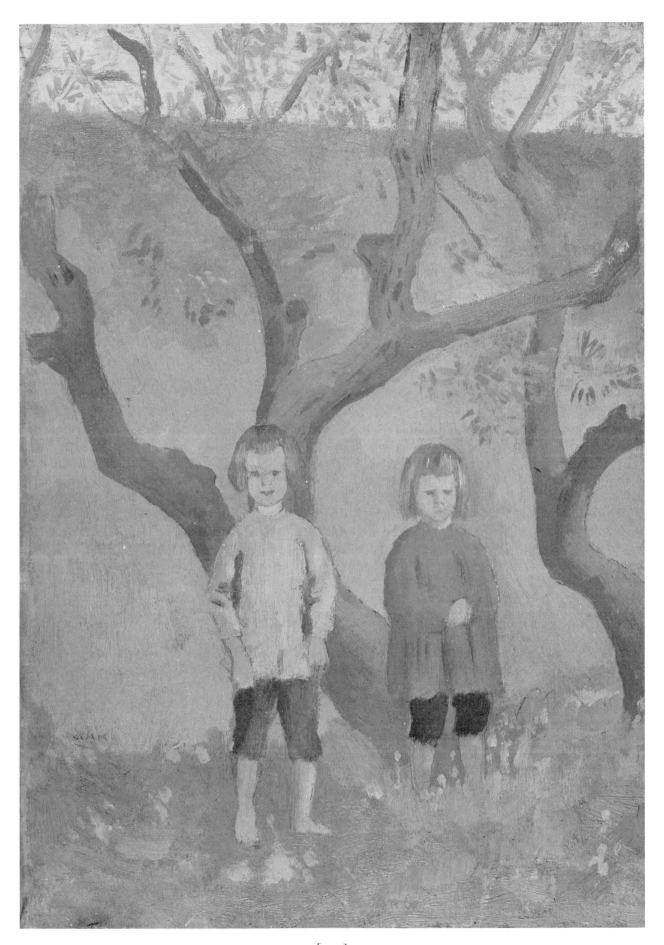

52 DR KUNO MEYER, 1911

Oil on canvas, 36 × 28 (91·5 × 71)

Exhibited N.E.A.C., winter 1911 (No. 19); R.A., 1954 (No. 342)

Collection: Dr Meyer; the Meyer family
The National Gallery of Ireland

This is one of John's most unexceptionable portraits, simple,
straightforward, forceful. To paint it, he left for Liverpool in July 1911,
when just about to move into Alderney Manor. The dignity and calm of
the picture are in strong contrast to the conditions under which it was
painted, the artist having been pursued to Liverpool by the redoubtable
Mme Strindberg. In 1912 Dr Meyer was appointed to the Chair of Celtic
Philology in the University of Berlin. During the First World War he
became a German agent. Other portraits of Liverpool University staff,
formerly belonging to the Club, are now the property of the University
and hang in the academic staff dining club known as Staff House.

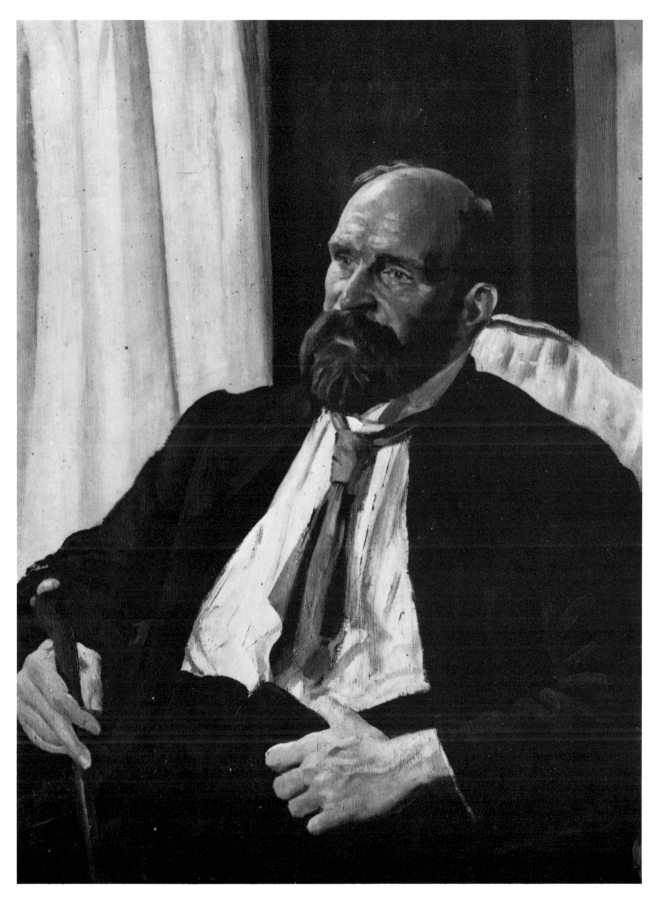

53 THE RED FEATHER, *c.* 1911

Oil on panel, $12\frac{3}{4} \times 16$ (32·5 × 40·5)

Signed 'John' bottom right

Exhibited R.A., 1954 (No. 206)

Collection: Mrs W. Murray
Private Collection

Sold at Sotheby's on 20th April 1972 for £4,500, this little panel set up a
new price record for the smaller paintings of the artist. A figure (Dorelia,
most often, as in the present example; but it might be her sister Edie or a
certain Lily, or Nora Brownsword) against the background of hilltop
or lakeside is one of the recurring themes in John's best work: and the lake,
or pool, seems, of all his backgrounds, the favourite. But background is the
wrong word. Whether grey stone-outcrop or dazzling blue water, model
and landscape are poetically inseparable. 'The Red Feather', remarkable,
too, for its perfect small-scale portrait of Dorelia, marks the high peak of
this integration with Nature.

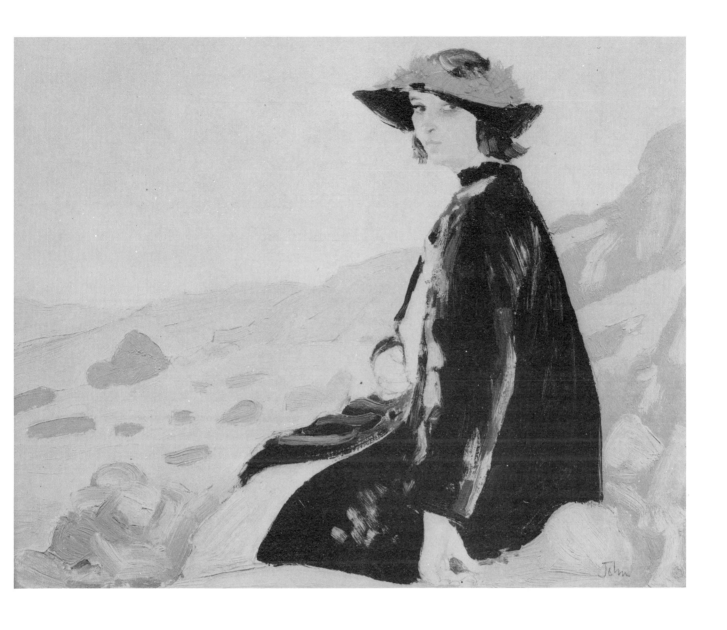

54 THE BLUE POOL, DORELIA STANDING, c. 1911

Oil on panel, 15 × 18 (38 × 45·5)

Signed 'John' bottom right corner

Exhibited R.A., 1954 (No. 203)

Collection: Mrs William Cazalet
Mrs Thelma Cazalet-Keir

If John's innate good sense failed him, it was when he felt obliged to build up mythological, quasi-moralistic compositions – small-scale or large-scale – from his superb on-the-spot drawings and swiftly captured poses in oils of Dorelia and his children. The Dorset 'Blue Pool' could have been inspiration enough: or any other stretch of water, brilliant in the sunlight. It must be said, however, that the particular stance adopted by Dorelia here can soon stale by repetition both in John's own figure compositions and those of a much less able imitator, Sir William Russell Flint.

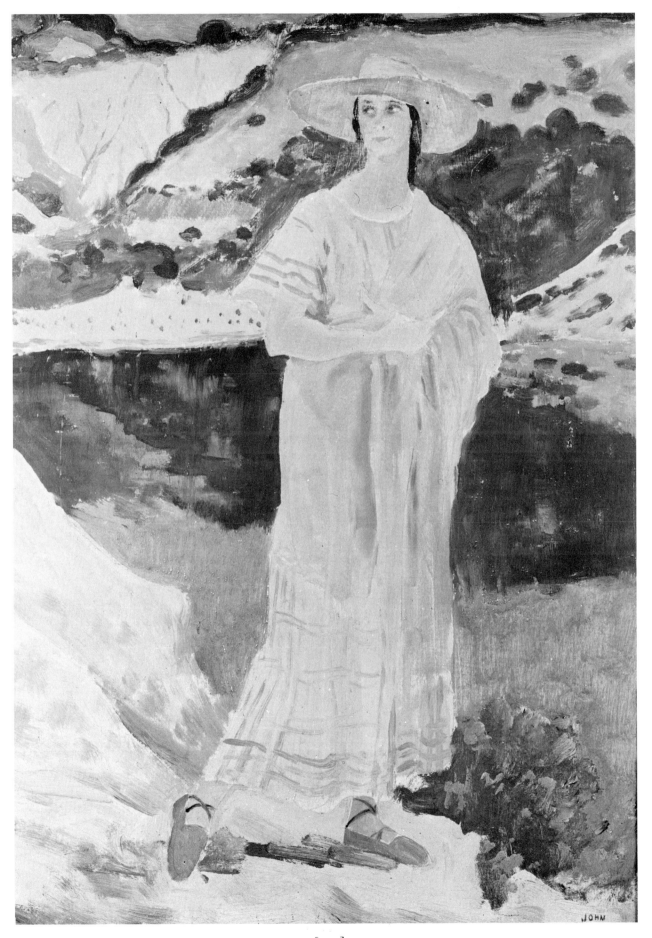

55 THE MUMPERS, 1912

Tempera on canvas, 108 × 228 (274·5 × 578)

Exhibited N.E.A.C., winter 1912 (No. 149)

Collection: The Hon. Kojiro Matsukata
The Detroit Institute of Arts

'The N.E.A.C. has just been hung,' John wrote to Hope-Johnstone (the boys' tutor) on 20th November 1912. 'I suddenly took and painted my cartoon of Mumpers – in tempera, finished it in $4\frac{1}{2}$ days, and sent it in.' He thought it might betray haste, yet not look so bad on the whole. Tempera can mean many things and has, in modern practice, little connection with the old craft of applying pigment to damp plaster. For those, like John, who adored the Italian fifteenth-century masters, there was a nostalgic charm and even a conscious sense of piety in using powdered, instead of tubed, colours. Alas, tempera also tends to lure the modern artist into an ill-judged archaism; and John himself recognised a certain uncouthness in the picture, 'but I may say I still like it . . .' Originally intended for Sir Hugh Lane's house in Cheyne Walk, 'The Mumpers' was dispatched to America late in 1915. For the significance of the title (mumpers = beggars), see the Note to Plate 15.

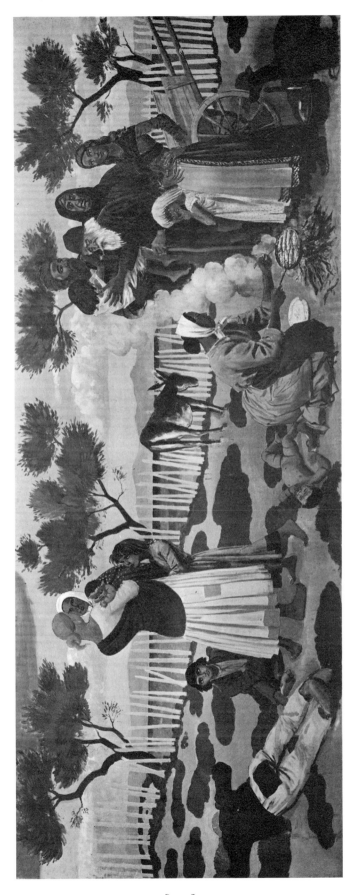

56 GEORGE BERNARD SHAW, 1915

Oil on canvas, 30 × 18 (76 × 45·5)

Signed 'John' top right

Exhibited R.A., summer 1922 (No. 675); R.A., 1968 (No. 488)

Collection: G. B. Shaw
The Fitzwilliam Museum, Cambridge

This was John's first 'celebrity portrait'. At the beginning of the century
C. W. Furse had seemed to represent the only serious rival to Sargent.
Then in 1904, when Furse died at the height of his skill, Orpen exhibited
his first Royal Academy picture, a portrait of Charles Wertheimer, and
Ambrose McEvoy and John himself attracted attention with further
portraits at the New English. But for a while it seemed as if the sitters
chosen by John would remain within his household circle. After
1910, Sargent having virtually given up his lucrative practice and a
somewhat compromised Orpen offering commercial rather than
aesthetic competition, John began to find himself, though still in the
estimation of a small circle only, the 'new man' of British portraiture.
During a stay at Coole Park, Lady Gregory's home at Gort, in 1915, he
produced three versions of Shaw. In one (now in the collection of Her
Majesty the Queen Mother), Shaw's eyes are shut. 'I think perhaps he had
taken too much cocoa for lunch,' John explained to a friend; and 'it may
be that he sleeps, if he ever does sleep, standing, like a horse.' A third
version is at Shaw's Corner, the property of the National Trust. The
painting-method employed for such portraits has been set down by the
artist on a scrap of paper. Here it is, verbatim: 'Make a puddle of paint on
your palette consisting of the predominant colour of your model's face
and ranging from dark to light. Having sketched the features, being most
careful of the proportions, apply a skin of paint from your preparation,
only varying the mixture with enough red for the lips and cheeks and grey
for the eyeballs. The latter will need touches of white and probably some
blue, black, brown or green. If you stick to your puddle (assuming that it
was correctly prepared), your portrait should be finished in an hour or so,
and be ready for obliteration before the paint dries, when you start afresh.' When we
sent a copy of this document to a friend of ours, a modern painter of
portraits whom long experience has made wise, he pointed out
immediately the link here with Hals. Soon afterwards we came across an
all-revealing phrase in a letter written to Lady Ottoline Morrell on
7th November 1931. Hals, John told her, was an 'old deity' of his, thus
confirming all we had assumed from works as early as 'Ardor' (Pl. 5) and
as important as 'The Smiling Woman' (Pl. 9). A *premier coup* method, then,
was what John habitually followed. It ensured 'vitality', but only too often
– without Hals' inspired brushwork and grasp of the third dimension –
little else. John himself seems to have felt some dissatisfaction with
his Shaw portraits: to Arnold Palmer, in 1938, he confessed he did not
think much of the version sometimes known as 'The Sleeping Philosopher'.

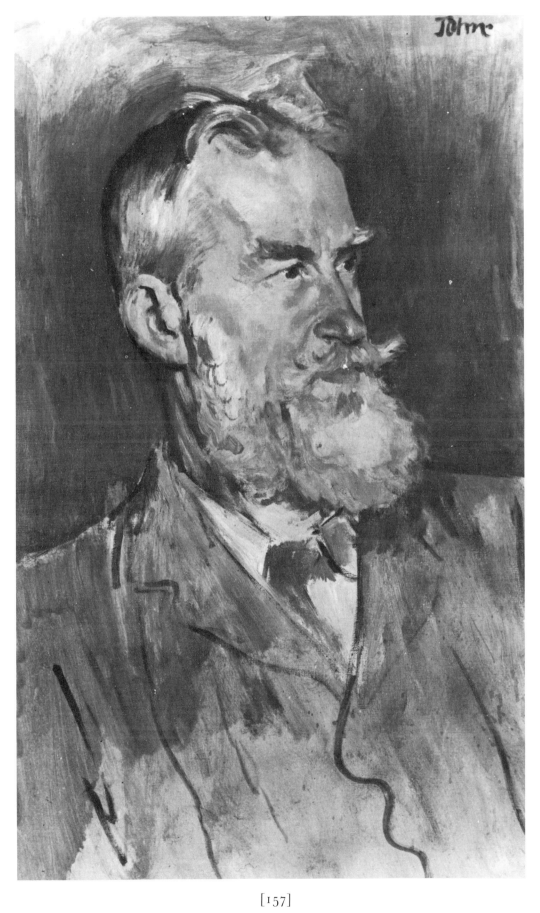

57 CARTOON FOR GALWAY (detail: left and central panels), 1916

Oil on canvas, $114\frac{1}{2} \times 472\frac{1}{2}$ (291×1200)

Exhibited R.A., 1916 (No. 541)

The Tate Gallery

Unfinished 'Galway' is: the suitably grand term *cartoon* insists upon this.
Yet one hesitates to describe it as incomplete. 'I'm thinking out a vast
picture synthesizing all that's fine and characteristic in Galway City – a
grand marshalling of the elements,' John wrote to Dorelia from Galway on
5th October 1915. 'It will have to be enormous to contain troops of women
and children, groups of fishermen, docks, wharves, the Church, mills,
constables, donkeys, widows, men from Aran, hookers [two-masted
fishing-boats of Dutch origin], etc, perhaps with a night sky and all
illuminated in the light of a dream. This will be worth while – worth the
delay and the misery that went before.' But when he went out into the
streets with his sketchbook he was at once identified as a German spy – 'so
that is another drawback, and a big one,' he told Dorelia. In a letter to
Ottoline Morrell, he complained: 'These are wonderful people and it is
beautiful about the harbour but if one starts sketching one is at once shot
by a policeman . . . It would be worth while passing 6 months here given
the right conditions.' The conditions being so bad, he decided to paint
from memory. 'Painting from nature *and* from imagination spells defeat I
see clearly,' he wrote to Dorelia. Much of the actual painting was done in
his studio at Alderney. His stay in Galway covered two autumn months of
1915 (he had also been in Ireland in June). 'Galway' was shown at the
Arts and Crafts Exhibition at Burlington House in 1916, as noted above.
John is said to have covered a hundred square feet in a single week,
working feverishly before his impressions clouded over: a miracle since
disputed. It may be noted that he was not a member of the Arts and
Crafts Society, which had nevertheless commissioned him to produce the
vast cartoon. To see it, the visitor ascended the Academy staircase,
reached a landing representing Trafalgar Square turned into a national
Campo Santo; passed through an 'Ecclesiastic' Section; then finally
entered the area entitled 'University', where 'Galway' somewhat
inappropriately shared the walls with William Rothenstein's 'Memorial
for Members of the English Universities Who have Served in the War'.

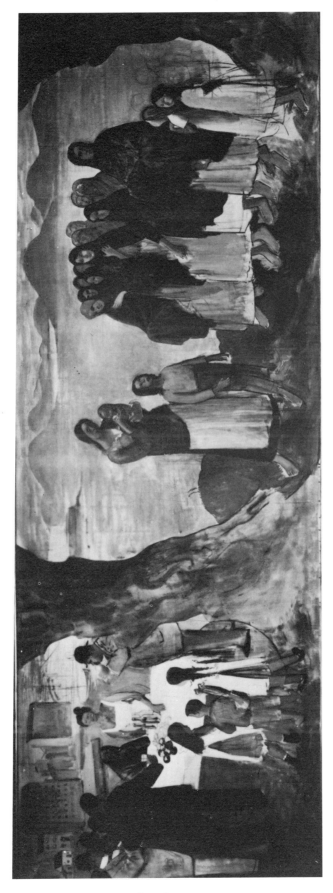

58 ARTHUR SYMONS, 1917

Oil on canvas, 34 × 25 (86·5 × 63·5)

Exhibited Scott and Fowles, New York, 1949; Albright Art
Gallery, Buffalo, 1949: no catalogue numbers.

Collection: John Quinn; Mrs Millicent A. Rogers
Mr Peter A. Salm

Arthur Symons (1865–1945), poet, essayist and critic, had been a leading
contributor to *The Yellow Book* and editor of *The Savoy*, a magazine made
unforgettable by Beardsley's drawings. Timidly in pursuit of riotous
living himself, Symons found a hero of the new century in John. He
pursued the artist with fulsome dedications from the year of their meeting,
1902. In return, John breathed some real life into an existence arid with
introspection and trembling always on and over the verge of insanity.
The strange relationship, encouraged for some years by John Quinn, who
was interested in both, continued till Symons' madness drove him into
necessary seclusion. This portrait was one of Quinn's last and most
grudging John purchases, and at £400 he considered it 'about £200 too
much'. It is now looked on as one of the artist's subtlest interpretations of
contemporary men of letters.

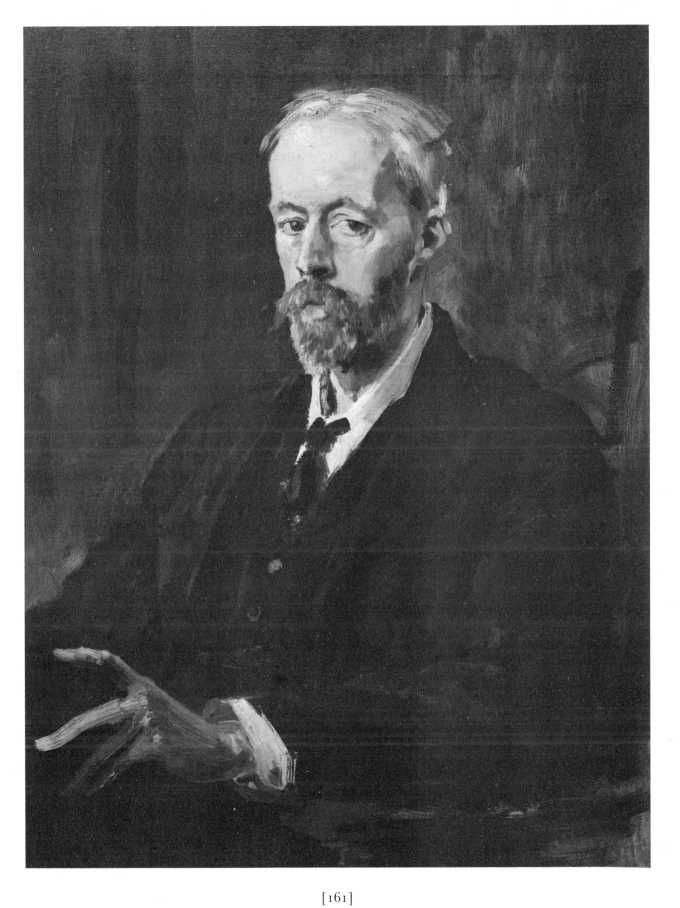

59 FRATERNITY, 1918

Oil on canvas, $93\frac{1}{2} \times 57$ ($237 \cdot 5 \times 145$)

Exhibited at the Tate Gallery, 1922–1924

The Imperial War Museum

John's early patron Quinn, busy making money on the safer shores of the
Atlantic, was alarmed lest the war should give a 'tremendous push to
sentimentality in art'. No doubt, his fears were often substantiated.
Though protected by an egocentricity almost as formidable in these
circumstances as the concrete honeycombing of Wytschaete Ridge, John
himself produced a tear-jerker or two (cf. the embarrassing lithograph,
'Britain's Ideals in the War: the Dawn'), but 'Fraternity' is not one of
them. It says its piece – and the brotherhood of arms is a risky subject –
with great dignity and restraint, and does not suffer in the least when
compared with the classic Nashes and Nevinsons.

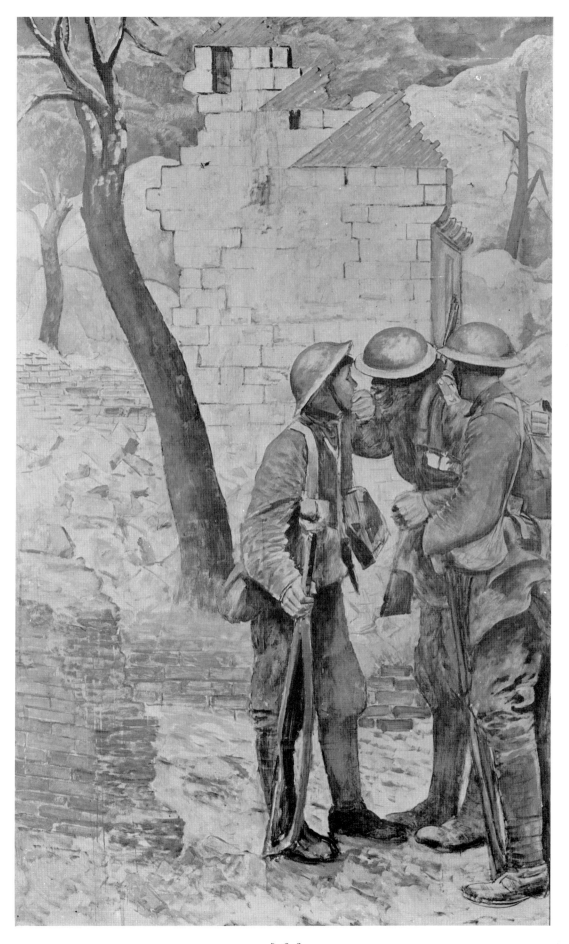

60 CANADIANS AT LIEVIN CASTLE, 1918

Oil on canvas, $14\frac{1}{2} \times 48$ (37×122)

Exhibited Halifax, Nova Scotia, etc., 1972–3 (No. 27)

The Beaverbrook Art Gallery, Fredericton, N.B.

The vast charcoal cartoon for this subject, commissioned for Canada by Lord Beaverbrook, was carried out in 1918, preceded by innumerable sketches of soldiers in ink, chalk and pencil now scattered throughout various public collections in the Dominion. It worked out at twelve by forty feet, of which the little oil here is an exact miniature version. Knewstub tried to tempt Quinn into buying the huge cartoon but the American collector having lost his first enthusiasm for the works of John, and now beginning to find the eighteen-foot long 'Mumpers' a sufficient embarrassment, cabled back: 'Not interested. Entirely too large'. Lord Beaverbrook, on the other hand, believed a full-scale painting was still owing to him. This John never produced, counter-arguing that Beaverbrook had no gallery as yet in which to display it. The charcoal cartoon was acquired for 550 gns at the first studio sale in 1962 by a collector from Chile. A further full-scale oil version, unfinished, also exists in a private collection in London.

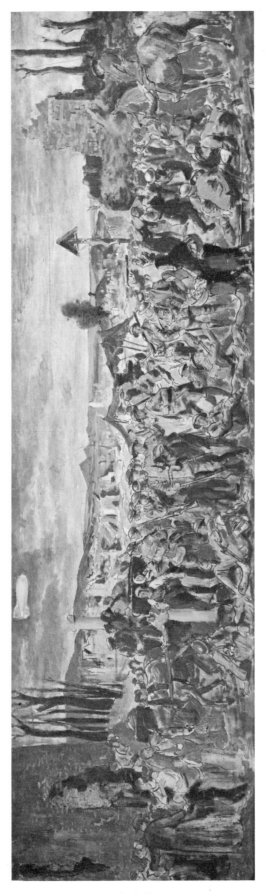

61 RONALD FIRBANK, *c.* 1917–1919

Pen and pencil (?) on paper

Signed 'John' bottom left

Present owner untraced

John's word for Arthur Annesley Ronald Firbank (1886–1926), witty author of *Caprice*, is 'evasive'; and, indeed, Firbank makes but one fleeting appearance in *Chiaroscuro*, where he is recalled 'struggling almost manfully with his asparagus and a bottle of wine' at the Eiffel Tower restaurant in Percy Street. In fact, John had parted with his sharpest observations of Firbank in a contribution to Kyrle Fletcher's *Memoir* of the writer, published back in 1930. This very short piece (two and a half pages) displays John the literary stylist at his ambitious best. For *Caprice* (1917), in which one of the characters bears the name Judy Johncock, John contributed designs for the frontispiece and dust-jacket. 'I spent a day or two over them and the design which in the end I destroyed,' he wrote from Renvyle. 'The best things just happen by themselves!' *Caprice*, he wrote, 'has its charming light quality', but he preferred *Vainglory* (1915) as being 'perhaps more idyllic – like a Fête galante'. On the other hand, 'I can only suggest that some of the names of the people are not pretty'. John's favourite among Firbank's novels was *Valmouth* (1919) – 'perfectly wonderful. Better than all the others' – which had as its jacket and frontispiece a black-and-white study by him of a lady in eighteenth-century dress. In the first edition of *The Flower beneath the Foot* (1923) Firbank included a portrait drawn spontaneously by John 'at 2 a.m. in the Café Royal'; while *Concerning the Eccentricities of Cardinal Pirelli* (1926) contains another drawing done in 1915 as its frontispiece. 'I wish I had kept some of the after-dinner sketches I made of R.F.,' John told Anthony Powell, 'they were much better than the more elaborate ones for which he used to squirm.'

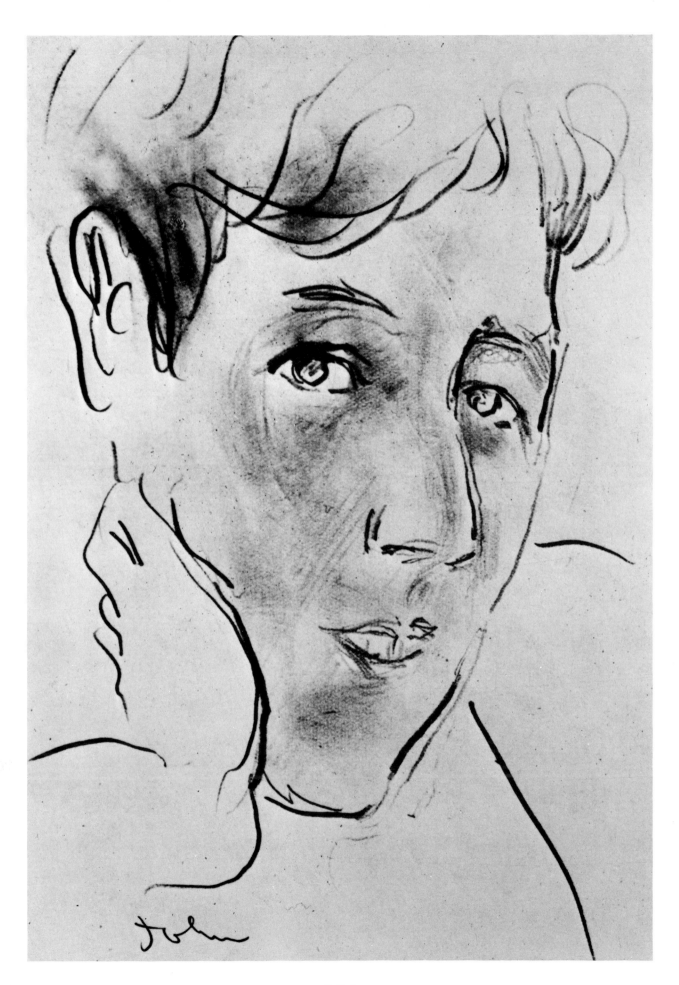

62　T. E. LAWRENCE, 1919

Pencil on paper, 14 × 10 (35·5 × 25·4)

Collection: G. B. Shaw
The National Portrait Gallery

Still in 'fancy-dress' as he described it, Lawrence was the most obviously
paintable guest John encountered at the Hôtel Majestic, Paris, in 1919.
There are several drawings which date from these first meetings, together
with the oil painting shown at the Alpine Club Gallery which was bought
by the Duke of Westminster for a thousand pounds and presented by him
to the Tate Gallery. Later, John produced further portraits of Lawrence as
Aircraftsman Shaw. Perhaps friendship is too strong a word to describe the
relations existing between the two men. In *Chiaroscuro* are printed some
fragments of letters from the sitter, recording his views on the
exhibition of the Peace Conference portraits. 'I never saw eye to eye with
him about pictures,' said John; though he seems to have been able to
tolerate Lawrence's hardworked facetiousness and the naïve pleasure he
took in being painted by every artist, good or bad. But Lawrence saw in
John the perfect 'image-maker'. On the other hand, it is worth noting that
John's portraits of Lawrence grow progressively more banal. Lawrence
got on best, perhaps, with Dorelia. Like other neurotics, he derived
comfort just from coming over and (having hidden his motor-cycle in case
it 'offended') being near her. By the 1950s, John was speaking with some
enthusiasm of Richard Aldington's biography of T.E.L.

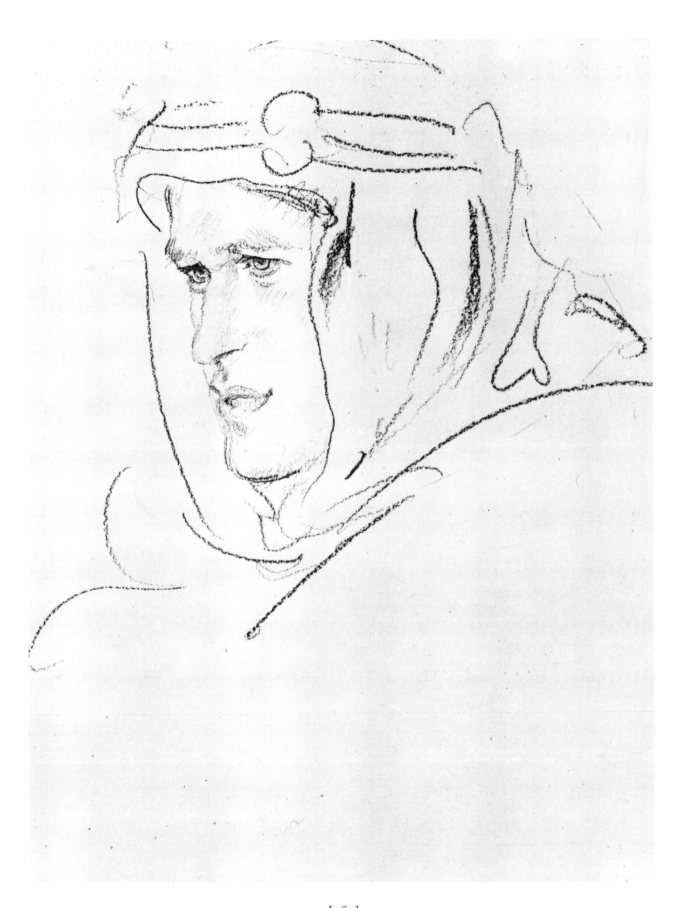

63 W. H. DAVIES, *c.* 1920

Oil on canvas, $29\frac{1}{2} \times 24\frac{1}{2}$ (75×62)

Exhibited Arts Council, 1948 (No. 33); R.A., 1954 (No. 349); Sheffield, 1956 (No. 25)

Collection: Miss Gwendoline E. Davies
The National Museum of Wales

John did not meet Davies (1871–1940) until long after the latter's book of verse, *A Soul's Destroyer*, and *The Autobiography of a Super-tramp* had made him famous. Davies' extolling of the simple life of the pedlar who is also a nature-lover precedes by only a year or two John's own caravanning days. The success of their ultimate meeting, and of the portrait which followed almost at once, was perhaps assured by their common cult of the open road. In *Chiaroscuro*, the artist assumed that the enraptured pose adopted by Davies, 'his hands clasped before him, his eyes focused, as it were, on Paradise, and his ears, it might be, intent on the song of an invisible bird', was perfectly natural to the sitter. Davies himself (in his own *Later Days*) explains it otherwise. Having wanted to sit quite still and not change his position, he concentrated his gaze on a 'little eye of light' in the curtain. After a while the round chink seemed to grow nearer and bigger. The trance was broken at length by the sound of John knocking the ashes out of his pipe: 'That I had almost hypnotized myself by looking so intently at that light is most certain.' Davies was a strict teetotaller and took it as a great compliment that John drank nothing during the six hard days' work he spent on the portrait.

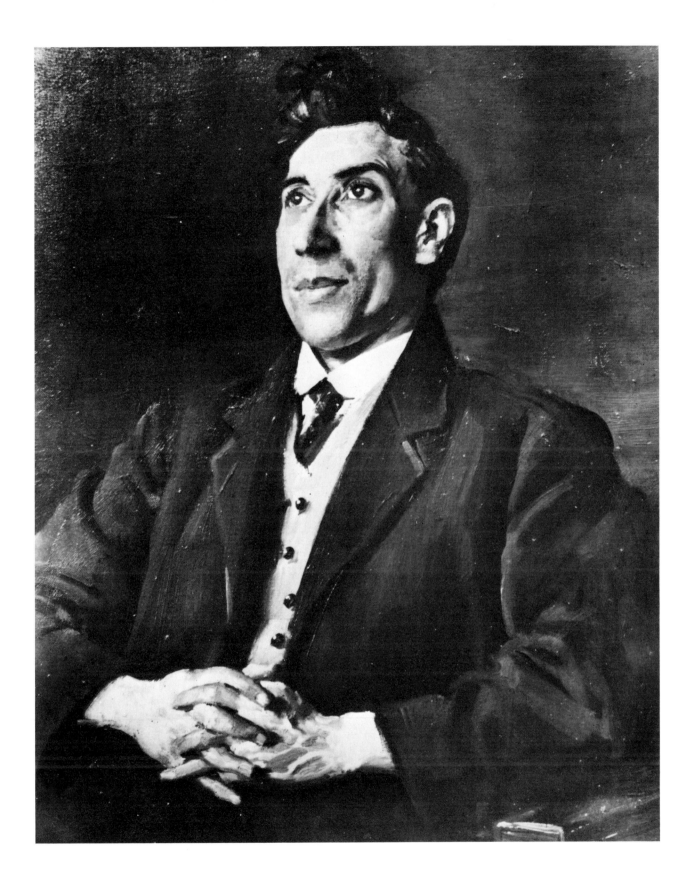

64 IN MEMORIAM AMEDEO MODIGLIANI, *c.* 1920

Oil on canvas, 50 × 40 (127 × 101·5)

Signed 'John' bottom right corner

Exhibited Temple Newsam, 1946 (No. 61); R.A., 1954 (No. 407)

The Executors of A. C. J. Wall

For John the primitive always exerted a strong fascination, whether the products of a genuine native culture, or their echoes in the work of Picasso and, somewhat later, in the sculptures of Modigliani. The stone head shown here was one of two which had struck his fancy in Modigliani's Montmartre studio during the summer of 1913. 'The floor was covered with them,' John recalled in *Chiaroscuro*, 'all much alike and prodigiously long and narrow.' It is not clear what the book is in this votive still-life, but it ought to have been Modi's 'bible', *Les Chants de Maldoror*.* To our regret, the Executors of the late Mr Wall's estate were not willing to give permission to re-photograph the picture. Its importance in the history of John's life and work has therefore obliged us to print from a reproduction approved by A. C. J. Wall during his lifetime.

* Since writing this, we have been able to consult a letter from John to D. S. MacColl, dated 27th December 1944, in which the symbolism is explained, as follows: 'The book represents his [Modigliani's] Bible – Les Chants de Maldoror; the cactus, Les Fleurs du Mal; the guitar, the deep chords he sometimes struck; the fallen tapestry, the ruins of time.'

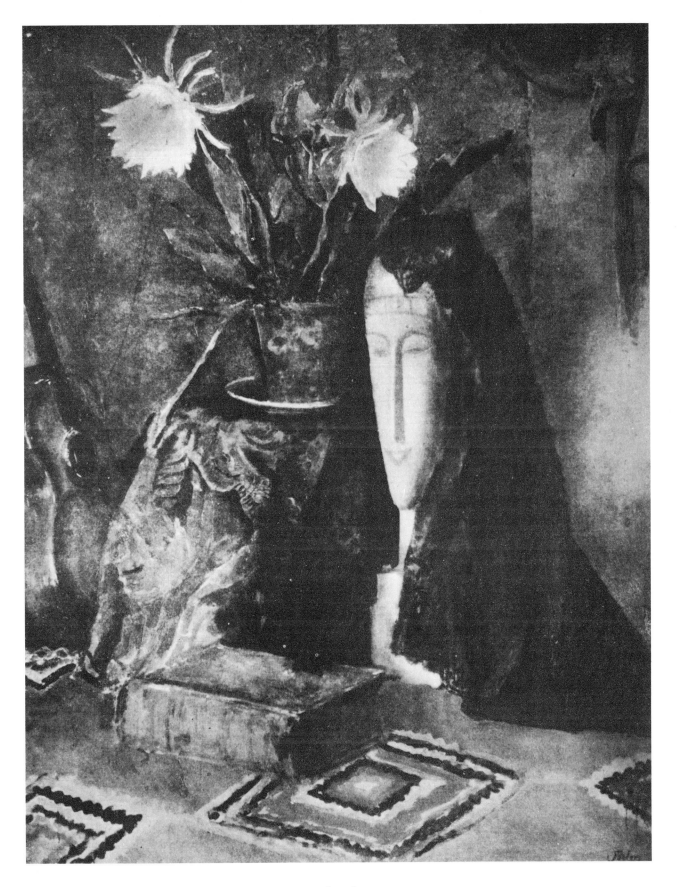

65 THE SPANISH GITANA, before 1921

Oil on canvas, 16 × 13 (40·5 × 33)

Signed 'John' top right corner

Exhibited R.A., 1954 (No. 431)

Collection : Mrs Valentine Fleming
Miss Amaryllis Fleming

The painting was presented to Mrs Fleming by the artist in 1921 : we have
no clue otherwise as to the date of execution. It might be connected with
one of the visits to Spain, if he had arrived there in time. But although he
actually set out for Spain early in 1908, he did not arrive until May 1922,
using it only once more as a convalescent post in the winter of 1954–5. If
Mrs Valentine Fleming was right about her date, then John must have
met this charming Spanish Gypsy through Fabian de Castro or in some
band travelling in France.

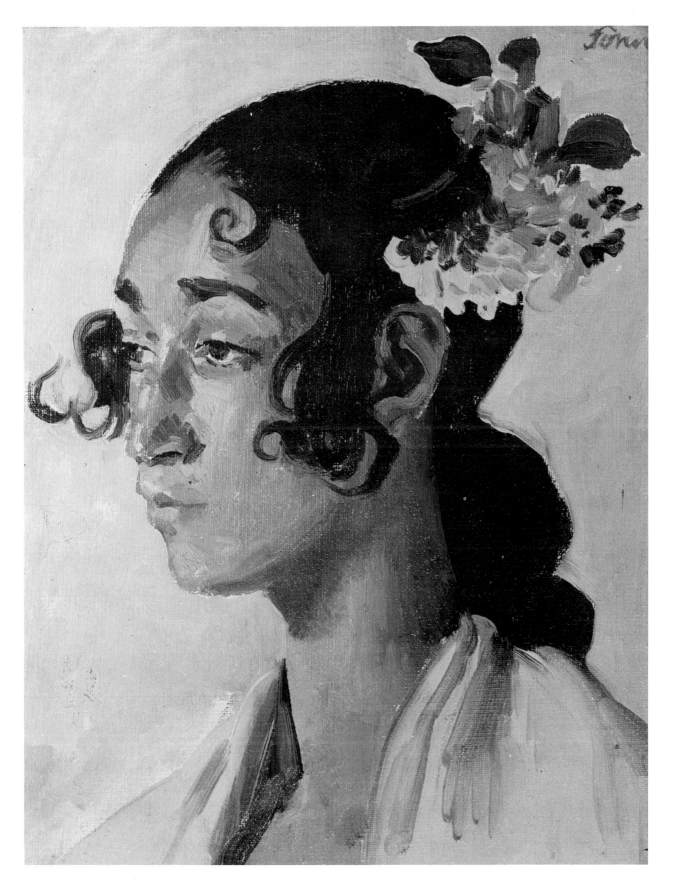

66　THOMAS HARDY, 1923

Oil on canvas, 24 × 20 (61·5 × 51)

Signed and dated 'John 1923' top right corner

The Fitzwilliam Museum, Cambridge

The Hardy portrait is a notable expression of John's new-found respectability in the 1920s. In 1921 he had been elected A.R.A. and in the following year five pictures of his had been hung, including the most generally admired painting of G.B.S., already presented to the Fitzwilliam Museum. Hardy's likeness would soon follow Shaw's to that august collection. John met Hardy at Kingston Maurward on 21st September 1923, and, after several visits to Max Gate, completed the portrait by the middle of the following month. 'An atmosphere of great sympathy and almost complete understanding at once established itself between us,' John records in *Horizon* (December 1942). '. . . I wonder which of the two of us was the more naïve.' When he saw the finished portrait, Hardy remarked: 'I don't know whether that is how I look or not, but that is how I *feel*.' According to Florence Hardy, he also said he would rather have had this portrait bought for the Fitzwilliam 'than receive the Nobel Prize – and he meant it'.

An amusing footnote to the serious occasion was John's reappearance, partly as Meredith, in a mysterious dream where Hardy found himself carrying a heavy child up a ladder to safety, while the Meredith–John chimera looked on unconcernedly. If any meaning can be read into this, it may be that Hardy had always wanted (and been denied) children, while John's prowess in this sphere had rendered him an object of unconscious envy to his sitter. It is hard to see how the author of *Modern Love* fits into the dream-analyst's scheme of things (*The Times Literary Supplement*, 16th June 1972).

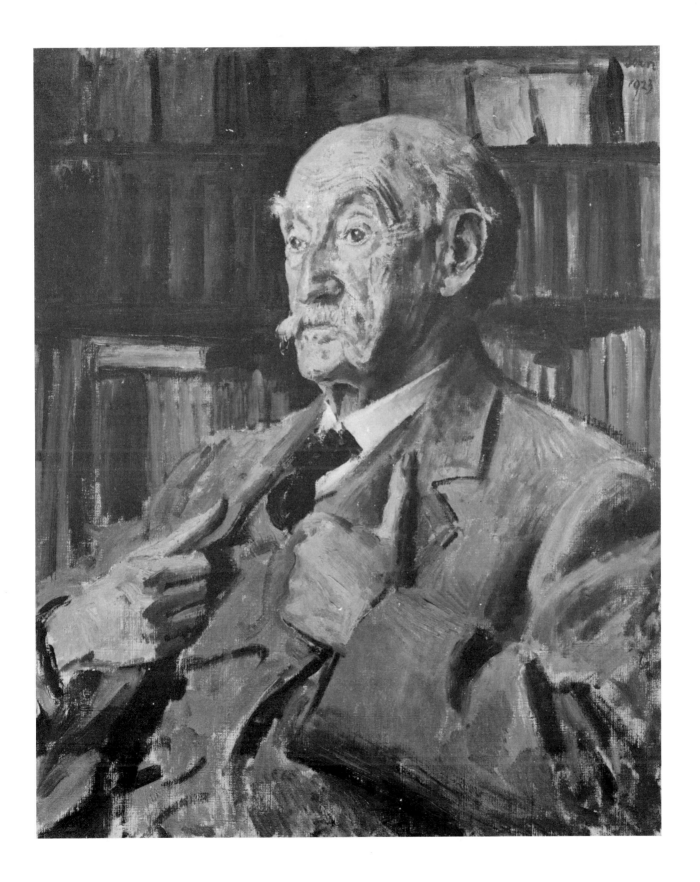

67a VISCOUNT D'ABERNON, 1927–31

Oil on canvas, $90\frac{3}{4} \times 60\frac{1}{2}$ (230·5 × 156)

Signed 'John 1932' bottom right corner

Exhibited R.A., summer 1931 (No. 318); Pittsburgh, 1933
(No. 143); Temple Newsam, 1946 (No. 54)

Collection: Lord D'Abernon; Helen Lady D'Abernon
The Tate Gallery

John paid a visit to Berlin during March and April 1925, one result of
which was his portrait of Gustav Stresemann, who was to share the Nobel
Peace Prize with Briand in the following year, another this full-length
picture of the British Ambassador, Lord D'Abernon. John moved, in fact,
in 'diplomatic circles', and had his own key to a side entrance of our
Embassy. Rare privileges, however, interspersed with rare adventures,
failed to inspire the artist. The Stresemann portrait (now in Buffalo) just
passes, but that of Lord D'Abernon comes as a severe shock to the
admirer of John's best work. In a fever of mingled *Angst* and impatience, it
might seem, he had risked a hit or the wildest miss. In fact, no actual
painting was done in Berlin, where he merely met D'Abernon. Work did
not begin till two years later. And then it proved unremitting, uninspired
labour all the way. In 1933 Homer Saint-Gaudens, of the Carnegie
Institute, Pittsburgh (somewhat overwhelmed, it is true, to be in
correspondence with so noble a sitter), referred to the canvas as the *height
of John's effort,* 'and there is no man on either side of the Atlantic who is
regarded in such high esteem as the painter'. But by then both John and
D'Abernon himself knew that the formal character demanded of such a
picture had never really been in the artist's line. In December 1927,
thanking D'Abernon for a sweetener of £500, John admitted that much
had still to be done. He would have to wait for the dark days to pass,
however: there had been the harrowing experience of trying to complete
Governor Fuller's portrait by artificial light. 'I feel your portrait,' he told
Lord D'Abernon, 'is too fine a scheme to take any such risks with and I
shall return to it later with the greatest enthusiasm.' Such words must have
sounded ominous in the sitter's ear, for an integral part of the agony of
being painted by John was the struggle to make off with one's rightful
property before the disastrous process known as 'improving' began. But a
more cheerful note was sounded in 1929, when Lady D'Abernon learned
from her husband that John had made the face 'less bibulous'. Seen from
five yards off it had become a 'fine costume picture'. As late as July 1931,
John proposed or accepted fresh revisions. But now a second
(prospective) buyer seemed to materialise in the shape of Lord Duveen,
and the Academy's Secretary was putting out feelers about a Chantrey
purchase. That Lord D'Abernon already toyed with the idea of selling his
scarcely-acquired likeness suggests dissatisfaction. But for reasons which
don't concern us, no sale took place, and John received his full £2,000 from
the Ambassador. The work was finally presented to the Tate by Helen
Lady D'Abernon in 1950.

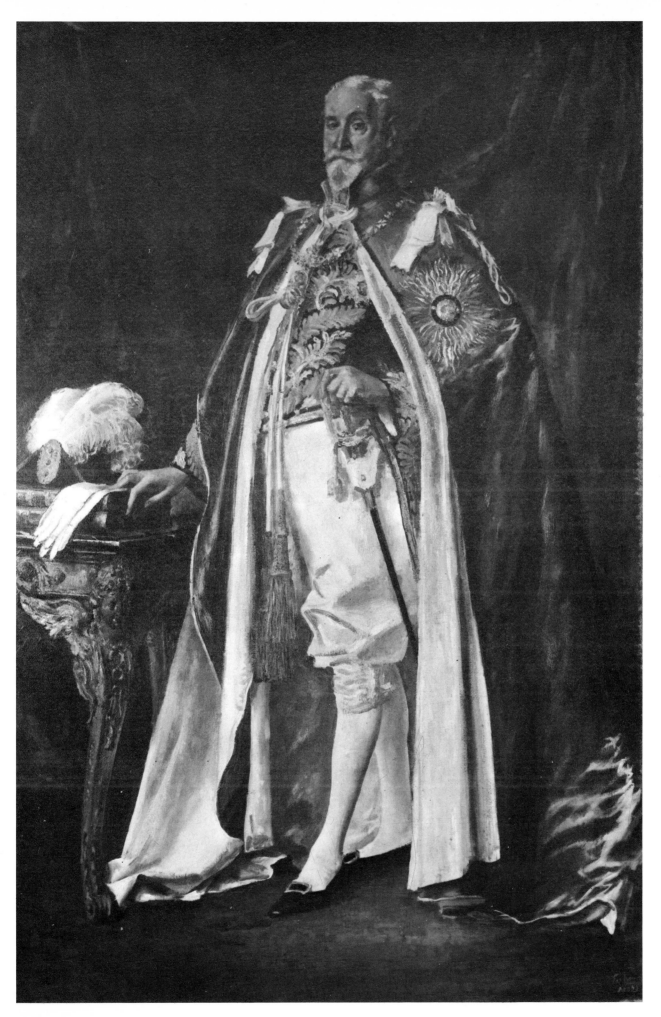

67b VISCOUNT D'ABERNON

Photograph of the subject of the previous painting in his Garter robes

The John Estate

This is a somewhat disquieting photograph, though its practical purpose
was the innocent one of fixing in the artist's mind the correct disposition of
the robes. Not only is there a discrepancy in the likeness: this
discrepancy (the result of many weary alterations) over-advantages the
portly little man who posed. John commonly elongated the sitter's head,
but the amount of painter's surgery that has gone on here seems for once
unacceptable. Lord D'Abernon has also gained twelve inches in height.
The splendid double-flexed curve of the pictured figure has been
conjured out of thin air or from the guardsman who stood for the costume.
No wonder Helen D'Abernon wrote on the back of a print of this
photograph: 'It shows how unlike [my husband] the "parade" portrait
was and is.'

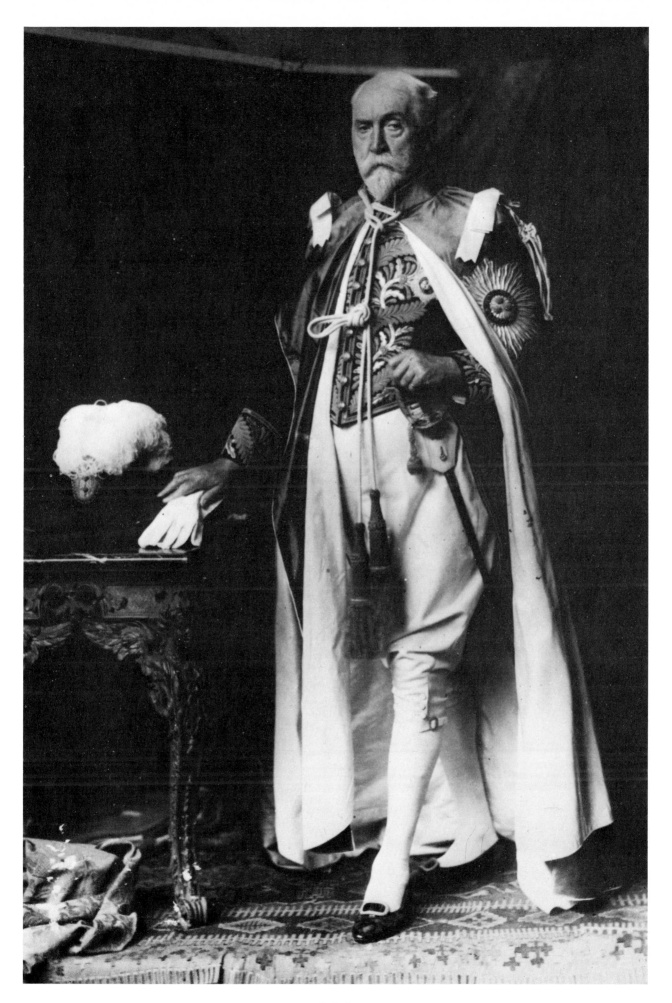

68 THE ARTIST'S DAUGHTER, POPPET, *c.* 1927–8

Oil on canvas, 25 × 18 (63·5 × 45·5)

Signed 'John' bottom left

The National Gallery of Victoria, Melbourne

Since far fewer examples are known, it would be easy to assume that Poppet (born 1912) and Vivien (born 1915) served a less gruelling apprenticeship as models than the boys. Poppet (Mme Pol) can refute this; and Vivien (Mrs White), who has made her own mark as an artist, recalls very clearly the almost continuous sittings she put in right up to the time of her marriage. In the main, she believes, the resulting portraits were unsuccessful; and, indeed, John left no record of the girls to compare with the wonderful anthology of drawings and paintings devoted to his sons. It is the more gratifying, therefore, to discover here and there this generalization contradicted: the charming oil sketch of Vivien as a two-year-old, and this Melbourne 'Poppet' where their father has succeeded in catching all the nuances of high-spirited girlhood. The elder daughter, who inherits Dorelia's exquisite bone-structure, received her name, Romilly John tells us, when Caspar, one of her half-brothers, gazing at the newly-arrived baby, exclaimed: 'What a little poppet!' The approximate date is arrived at from information given in 1932 by Dudley Tooth, who pointed out that negotiations to purchase the portrait for the Chantrey Bequest broke down because the picture had been painted partly in France. Mme Pol confirms this, telling us that sittings took place at the Villa Ste Anne, and so cannot have been later than 1928.

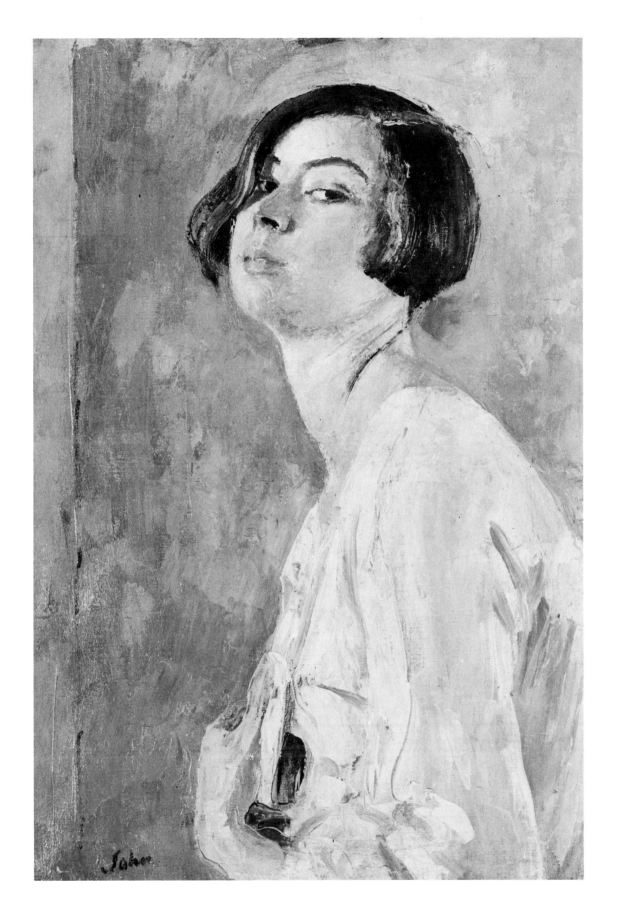

69 THE LITTLE RAILWAY, MARTIGUES, 1928

Oil on canvas, $18\frac{1}{2} \times 21\frac{1}{2}$ ($47 \times 54 \cdot 5$)

Signed 'John' bottom left

Exhibited Temple Newsam, 1946 (No. 48)

The Tate Gallery

John's connection with Martigues, which he had discovered with so much
excitement in 1910, came to an end in 1928 when the Villa Ste Anne was
sold. The 'little railway' in question was that on which one embarked at
Pas des Lanciers, a station on the line from Marseille. Over the years, in
John's estimation, Martigues had changed for the worse. It was no longer
the simple fisherfolk's community, visited by an occasional artist or such
old friends as Roy Campbell, T. W. Earp and Horace de Vere Cole, but,
largely because of the new causeway running along the north shore of the
Etang de Berre, had become part of the ugly modern world.

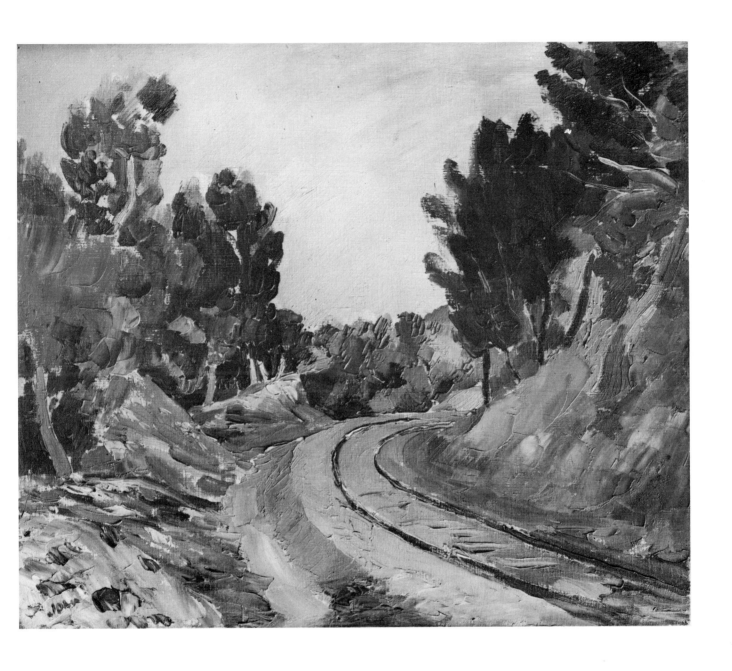

70 JAMES JOYCE, 1930

Chalk on paper

Inscribed, signed and dated 'James Joyce Augustus John Paris 1930' lower right

Present owner untraced

John visited the writer in November 1930. A photograph published in *Chiaroscuro* shows them arm-in-arm, John himself appearing the more anxious of the two to take part in this display of solidarity. Indeed, he complains of the special efforts he had to make to jerk Joyce out of his bourgeois reserve. A number of drawings were made, in which the sitter took a great interest. 'He explained,' says John, 'that the poverty of his beard was due to an early accident to his chin, but I did not feel empowered to restore the missing growth.' In the drawing shown here, however, he has been a hair or two more generous than the camera. The plan was for this drawing to serve as frontispiece to *The Joyce Book*, a volume of Joyce's poems with musical settings by different composers, edited by Herbert Hughes (Sylvan Press and O.U.P., 1933). On 30th October 1930, Joyce wrote to Mrs Herbert Gorman: 'A.J. started my portrait a few days ago with that highly treasonable Stuart royal tie.' But afterwards Joyce was dissatisfied with John's drawings, claiming that they failed to represent accurately the lower part of his face.

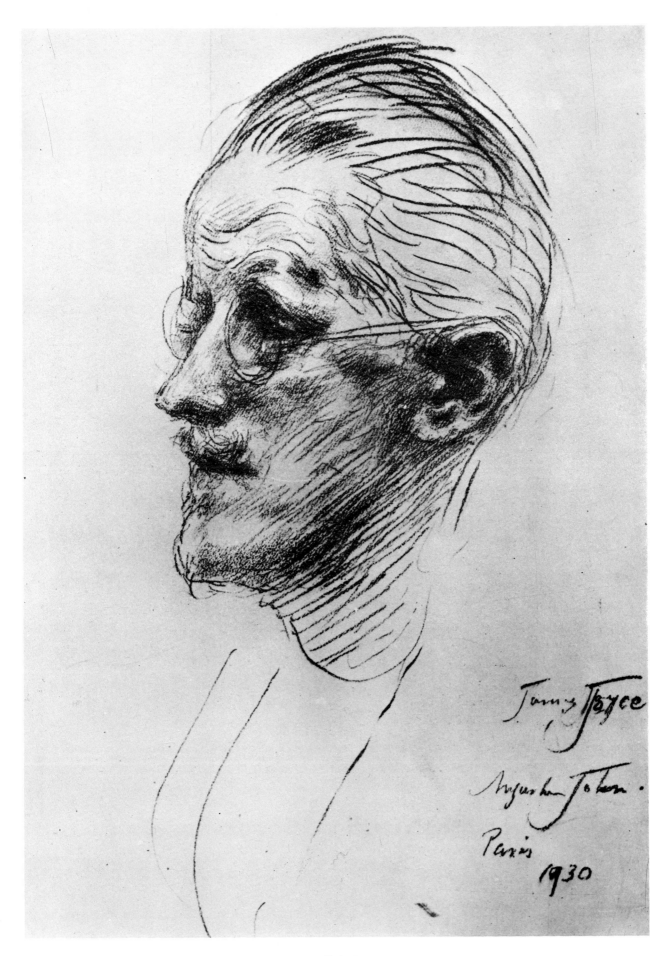

James Joyce

Augustus John.

Paris
1930

71   JAMES JOYCE, 1930

Pencil on paper, 16½ × 12 (42 × 30·5)

Signed 'John' lower right

Exhibited N.G., 1940 (No. 68); Temple Newsam, 1946 (No. 123);
Vassar College, Poughkeepsie, New York, and Wildenstein
Galleries, New York, 1961 (No. 117); Portraits Inc., New York,
1966 (No. 70)

Collections: Lieut-Col. A. J. L. McDonnell; Mr and Mrs
Benjamin Sonnenberg
Mr Cass Canfield

There is no reason to suppose that, because he was domiciled in the world's
art centre, Joyce would have reacted favourably to a drawing so spare that
we might apply to it the label 'School of Paris'. On the contrary, there is
John's evidence that the Joyces existed in an enclave of blissful Irish
philistinism with all the visual equivalents of stewed tea and yesterday's
mutton.

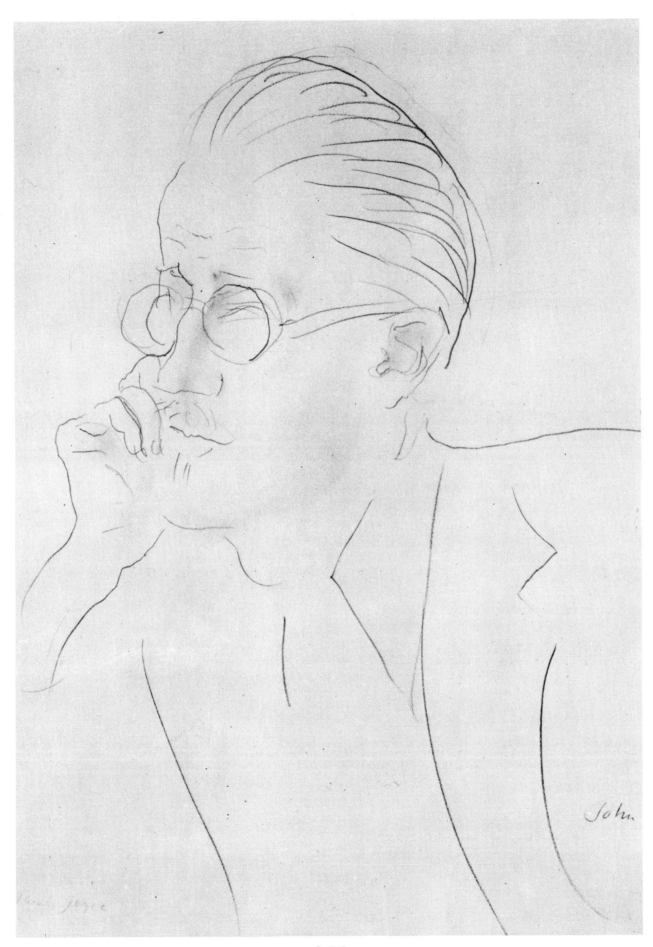

72 JOSEPH HONE, 1932

Oil on canvas, $20 \times 15\frac{3}{4}$ (51×40)

Signed 'John' bottom left

Exhibited 'Contemporary Welsh Art', National Museum of Wales, 1935 (No. 34); Arts Council, 1945–6 (No. 90)

Collections: J. E. Fattorini, Flight-Lieutenant Adams
The Tate Gallery

In April 1957, Joseph Hone (1882–1959), best known for his biography of Yeats, wrote to the Tate Gallery, of this portrait: 'I stayed at Fryern [Court] in the earlier part of the summer of 1932, and it was there that John painted the Tate portrait of me. I have found a letter of his dated August 1932 in which he says, "I would like to do another drawing or two when you return in October, as there is an aspect of you I didn't hit off." I wasn't able to return in October; perhaps it was as well as far as the portrait is concerned – I remember Mrs John [Dorelia] had with difficulty persuaded him not to work on it further.' R. S. Thomas, distinguished poet and Vicar of Eglwysfach, has published some verses in *The Stones of the Field* (1946) which convey the powerful, if unexpected, impression made upon him by this portrait.

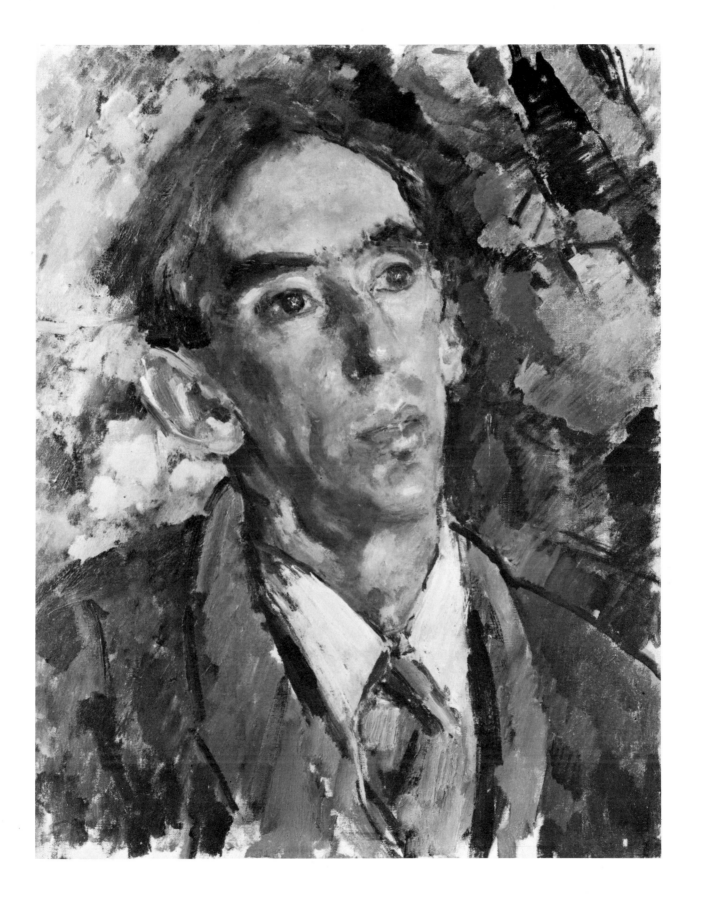

73   DYLAN THOMAS, *c.* 1936

Oil on canvas, 16 × 13½ (40·5 × 34·5)

Exhibited Temple Newsam, 1946 (No. 64); R.A., 1954 (No. 410)

The National Museum of Wales

Dylan Marlais Thomas (1914–1953) had been recognised as an important new poet with the publication of *18 Poems*, a year or two before this likeness was produced. His marriage to Caitlin Macnamara established him in the John household, Francis Macnamara being one of the artist's oldest friends. If John was proud of the connection with a youth of such promise, he did his best to conceal it. The references to Dylan in *Finishing Touches* are heavily sarcastic. Their introduction fittingly took place at the behest of Nina Hamnett in the Fitzroy Tavern, and the acquaintance was improved during many subsequent evenings *chez* Kleinfeld or in the nearby Marquis of Granby. After their marriage, the Thomases frequently came to stay at Caitlin's home, not far from Fryern Court. The likeness has been criticized by Edith Sitwell and by Constantine FitzGibbon, who took exception to the romanticized nose (though nevertheless using the portrait on the dust-jacket of his biography and *Selected Letters* of Dylan). One of the present collaborators, who remembers Thomas very clearly, regards the portrait as an admirable likeness. It was bought from the artist in 1941 by Mrs Thelma Cazalet-Keir for the Contemporary Art Society, on condition of its presentation to the National Museum of Wales.

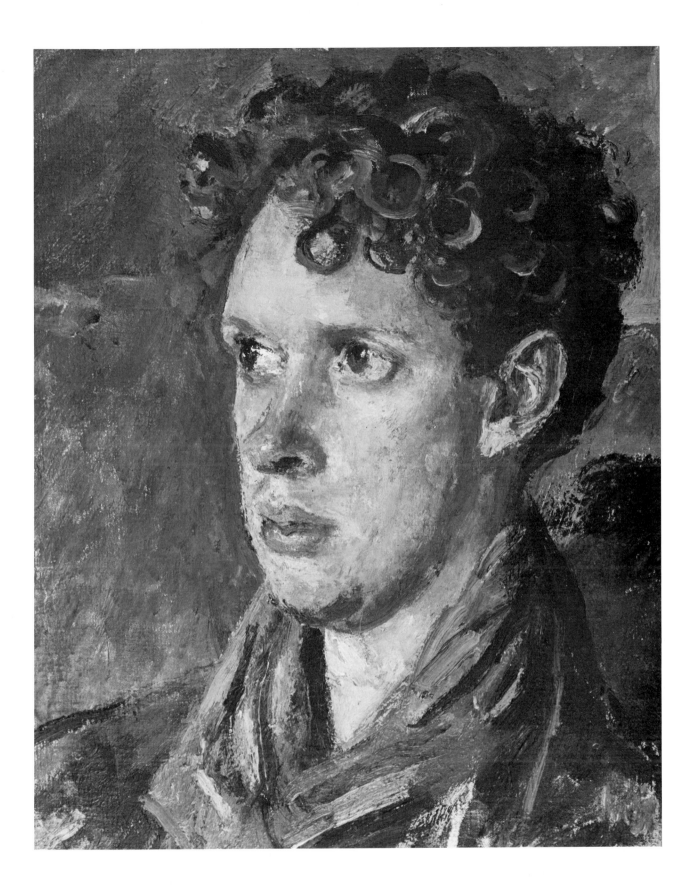

74 TWO JAMAICAN GIRLS, 1937

Oil on canvas, 30 × 25 (76 × 63·5)

Signed 'John' top right corner

Exhibited N.G., 1945 (No. 108); Temple Newsam, 1946 (No. 60);
R.A., 1954 (No. 444)

Collection: with Messrs Tooth
The Walker Art Gallery, Liverpool

The visit to Jamaica took place between March and May 1937. John's extensive use of the amateur models there available resulted in what was to be for him, at very nearly sixty years of age, the St Martin's summer of his creative genius. While in the artist's search for the feminine exotic among the Gypsies and Gitanas these West Indian girls seem to follow naturally enough, they are quite different from their predecessors. John's hand may shake, but there is plenty of power behind it. The earths and umbers which match the Jamaican chambermaids' dusky skins are squeezed from the tube a good deal more generously than would have happened a couple of decades earlier – and slapped into position with the springy blade of a palette-knife. This richness of pigment and broad, plasterer's approach offer an adequate, if not an equal, substitute for the old thin-skinned panels with their ghostly pencil outlines and additions. The sitters (like all John's Jamaican models) were disappointed with their portraits: they had expected to be given white skins!

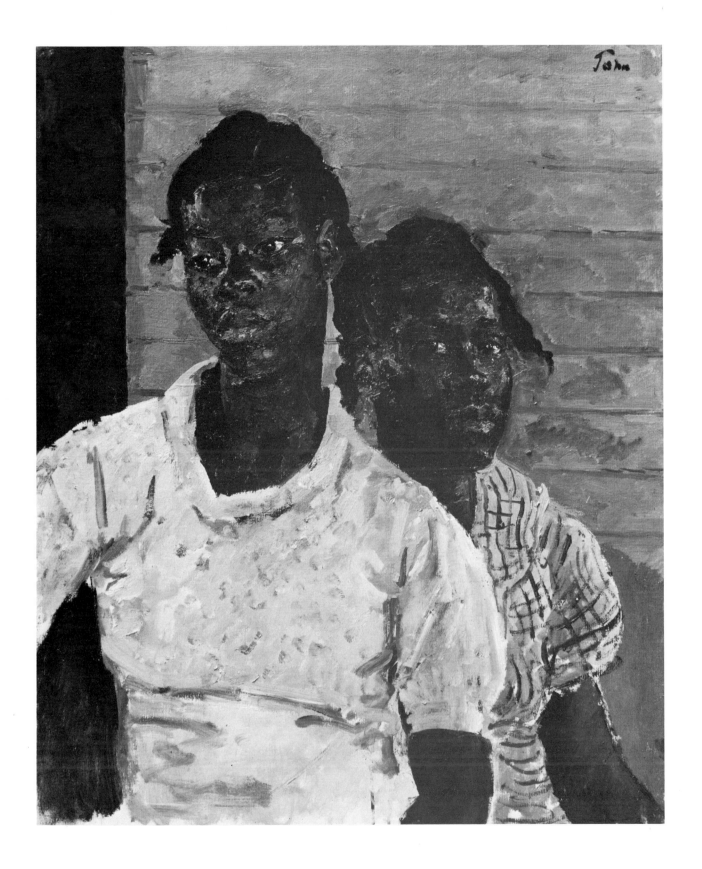

75   ROCKY LANDSCAPE, ST-REMY, *c.* 1938

Oil on canvas, 17 × 21 (43 × 53)

Collection: Hugo Pitman; Mrs Reine Pitman
Mrs R. M. Hughes

The Mas – small farmhouse – de Galeron, St-Rémy-de-Provence, was first
rented by John in 1937, and in the September of the moving-in he paid a
visit to Matthew Smith in nearby Aix. The area seemed propitious:
St-Rémy, with Arles, follows the curve of the Golfe de Lion almost midway
between Montpellier and Marseille. In fact, the landscapes which result
are generally disappointing. John never quite returned to the high promise
of those expeditions before the first war to Wales, to Lord Howard de
Walden's estate at Chirk and to Port-de-Bouc. The Johns had to leave
St-Rémy in a hurry in 1939, but were back again in 1946. The house was
finally relinquished in 1950.

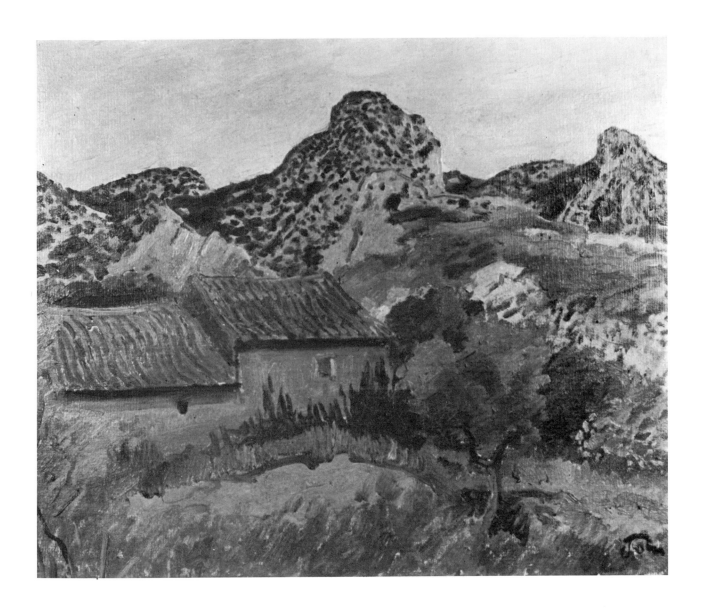

76 BRINSLEY FORD, 1941

Chalk on paper, $17 \times 12\frac{1}{4}$ (43×31)

Signed and dated 'John 1941' lower right

Exhibited Exeter, 1946 (No. 153)

Mr Brinsley Ford

In 1941, John made several drawings of this sitter, who chose for himself the example reproduced. Though John's powers were greatly diminished in the era of the Second World War, a new subtlety can often distinguish his portraits. Here, with the lightest of touches, not only the sitter's outward appearance, but his character as a man, clearly emerges: in this instance, the sympathetic one of distinguished connoisseur and collector. Mr Ford helpfully recalls the sequence of the group of portrait-drawings produced by John from 1941 onwards. It began with a drawing of Thomas Lowinsky, on the strength of which Mr Ford commissioned one of Mrs Ford. This in turn inspired the Sacheverell Sitwells to commission drawings of themselves and their son Reresby. Mr Ford's portrait followed that of his wife, and this led Mr Villiers David to commission portrait-drawings of himself, his friends and his staff. John's charge for such a drawing was £100. Sittings lasted about $2\frac{1}{2}$ hours, though they could be shorter, and it was John's custom to make two or three versions, of which the sitter took his pick.

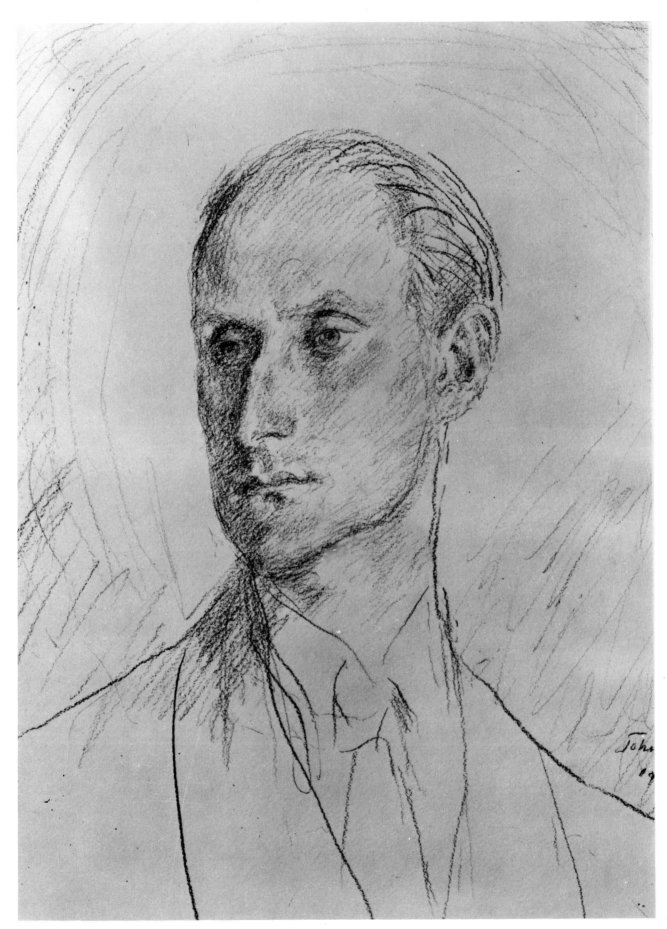

77 SIR MATTHEW SMITH, 1944

Oil on canvas, 24 × 20 (61 × 50·5)

Signed 'John' top right corner

Exhibited Temple Newsam, 1946 (No. 66); Arts Council, 1946 (No. 32); R.A., summer 1950 (No. 3)

The Tate Gallery

Though almost exact contemporaries, Augustus John and Matthew Smith (1879–1959) appear at first sight to have had nothing in common but their education at the Slade. Even there, it is impossible to conceive of a contrast greater than that between Smith's unsuccess and John's triumph. But the time came, just after, if not before, the Second World War, when the critics, deserting John, heaped their praise upon Smith, and the roles were dramatically reversed. John, with his new addiction to prettiness, was slipping out of fashion; Smith was definitely in. But Smith did not disdain to sit for John, and by general consent this is one of the finest of the artist's late portraits and a great deal better, paradoxically, than anything in the same *genre* currently attempted by the sitter. Smith was staying at Fryern with John for part of 1944. One of Smith's portraits of his host is in the Municipal Gallery, Toronto; another is in Miss Pitman's collection.

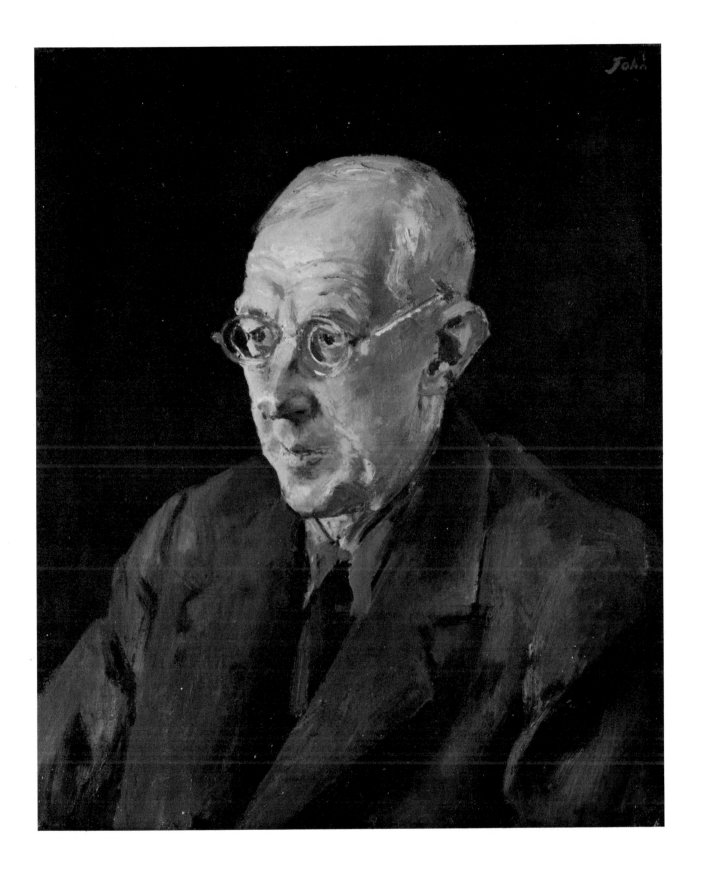

78 CYRIL CONNOLLY, 1945

Red and black chalk on buff paper, 14 × 21 (35·5 × 53·3), *S*

Signed and dated 'John 1945' above centre right

Private Collection

It was Cyril Connolly, founder and editor of *Horizon*, who, by arrangement with Jonathan Cape, published in his magazine the first 'Fragments of Autobiography', later to be filled out under the title of *Chiaroscuro*. (None of the *Horizon* pieces appeared in John's second and posthumous book of reminiscences, *Finishing Touches*: the shreds and patches there having first seen the light in *The London Magazine*, *The Sunday Times* and *The Burlington Magazine*.) Mr Connolly himself informs us that John produced three drawings in one afternoon. The drawing we reproduce was used as the frontispiece to the British and American editions of the sitter's book of essays, *The Condemned Playground*, published in 1945 and 1946, respectively. Indeed, it seems likely to have been designed for the purpose; though John had been gathering new drawings together for an exhibition. By employing black and red chalk in the same drawing, as he did very frequently from the 1940s onwards, John was returning to one of his earliest practices (we have even seen a black and red *ink* drawing of Ida). While very properly dispensing with what Sir Anthony Blunt has referred to as the 'industrious observation' which characterized those very youthful productions, the artist, in his old man's way, has captured a likeness as acutely and delicately as ever.

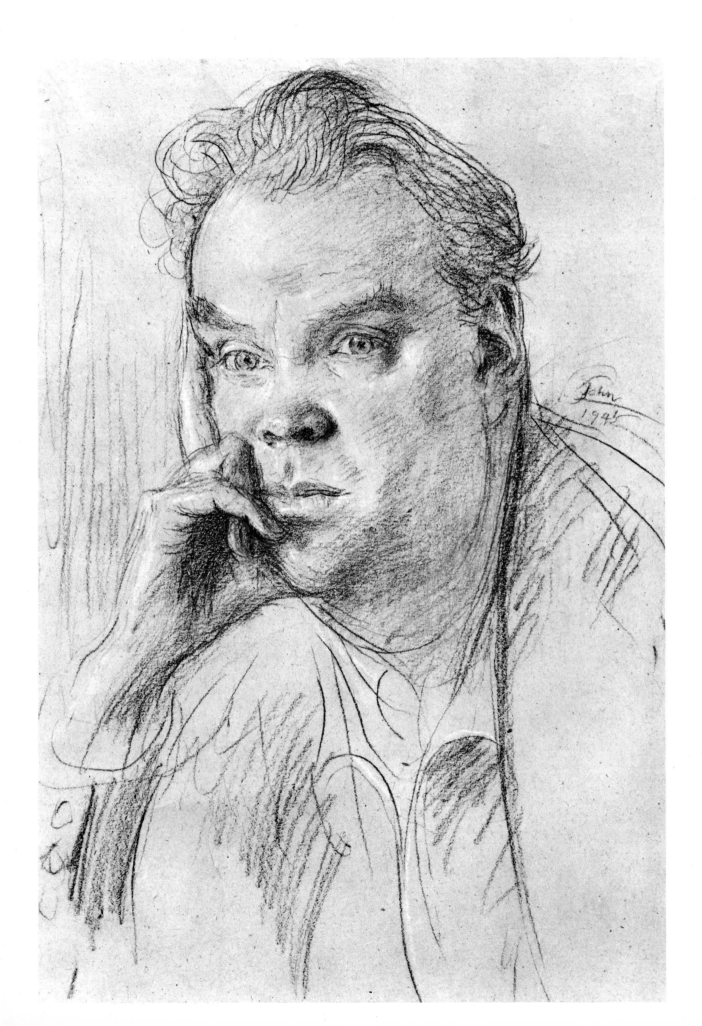

79 SELF-PORTRAIT, *c.* 1950

Oil on canvas, 18 × 15 (45·5 × 38)

Mr William A. Coolidge

Miss Amaryllis Fleming recalls John's habit of painting with his mouth
open: especially when warming up to his task, at which time he would also
be seen to stamp his foot. Increasingly deaf from an early age, the artist
gazed upon people and things with (to the former) a frightening
concentration, revealed physically by the sclerotal white continuously
visible round the pupil. On the colour of these eyes every account differs.
For some biographers they were grey, for others green, for still others
brown. When, however (supported, it seemed, by the pigment on the
canvas), we ourselves opted for brown, a member of the family had to
insist that they were unmistakably blue. It could have been Rembrandt's
example that led John to concentrate more than most artists upon the
self-portrait. This is certainly suggested by the ?1901 picture
(Rothenstein, Pl. 1) as well as by the series of etchings which record his
own features. The finest painting is perhaps the small panel of about 1930
belonging to Mr Charles Bravington, and there are splendid self-portraits
in the collections of Mrs Cazalet-Keir and Mr Edward Cazalet. We have
chosen the present example because it is much less well known and so
forcefully illustrates the points made at the beginning of this note.

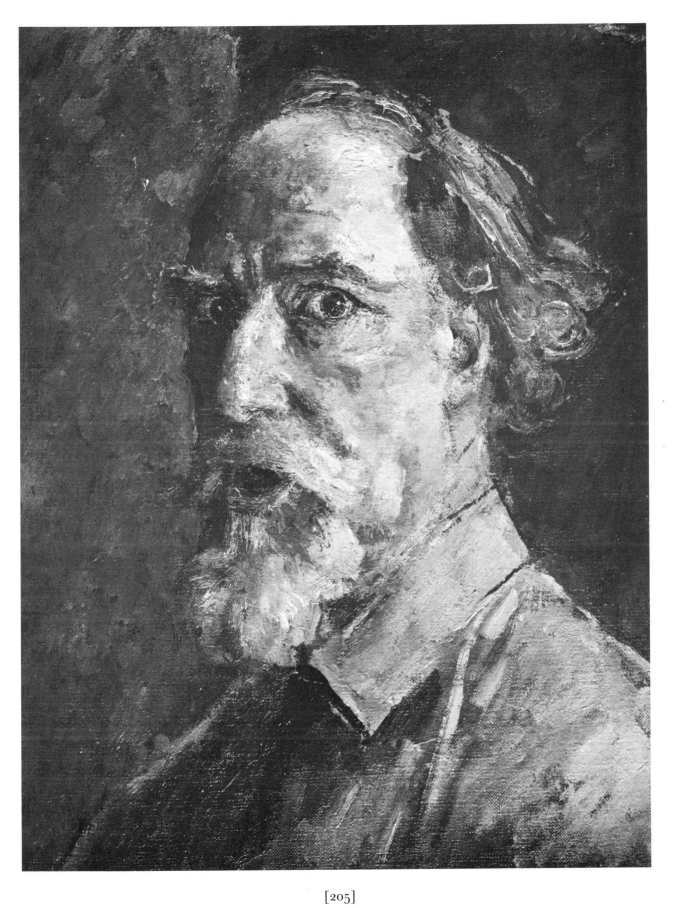

80 JOHN COWPER POWYS, 1955

Chalk on paper

Present owner untraced

His daughter Vivien persuaded a very old and tired Augustus to make the journey to the Powyses' new home at Blaenau Ffestiniog and draw John Cowper's portrait. The latter, six years older than the artist, took to him at once. 'Augustus John simply thrilled me,' Powys wrote to Louis Wilkinson on 8th December 1955, 'because he looked so exactly like a statue of Zeus! When he rose to depart I leapt at him exactly as a devoted Dog of considerable size leaps up at a person he likes, and kissed his Jovian forehead which is certainly the most noble forehead I have ever seen. I kissed it again and again as if it had been marble, holding the godlike old gent so violently in my arms that he couldn't move till the monumental and marmoreal granite of that forehead cooled my feverish devotion. His final drawing [the one reproduced here] was simply of my very soul – I can only say it just *awed* me.' And nearly a year later, Powys added: 'I feel that this amazing old man had the power of seeing clean through me.' In fact, though almost nothing of the essential John, as draughtsman, remains in such trembling comments as this and the slightly later portrait of Gilbert Murray, a certain insight has been revealed and communicates itself to the spectator.

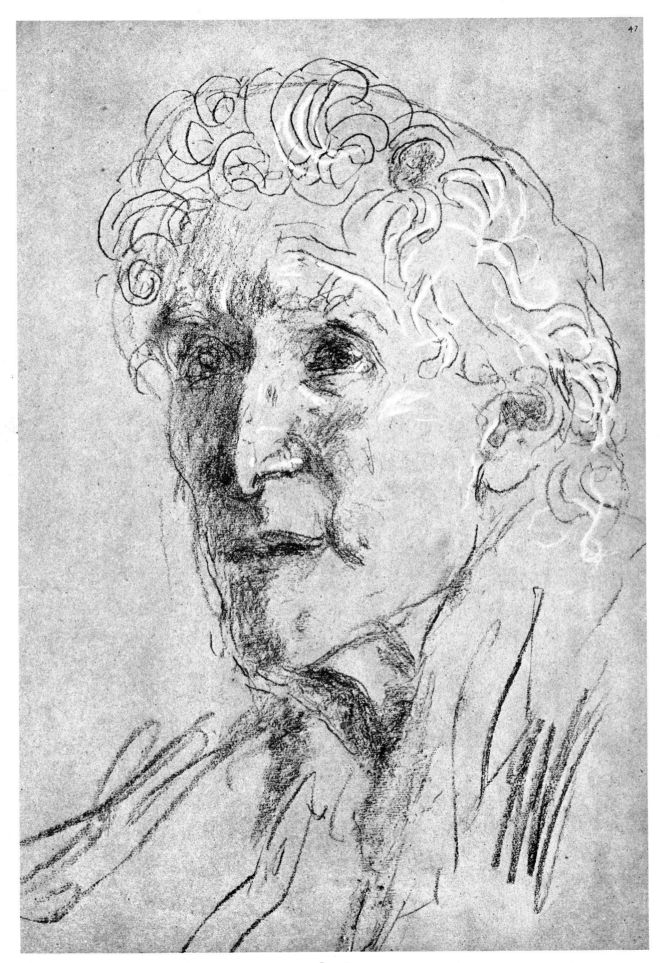

81 DORELIA, before 1959

Oil on canvas, 21 × 17 (53·5 × 43)

Signed and dated (wrongly) 'John 1959' top right

Miss Amaryllis Fleming

This is not the last portrait of Dorelia. Indeed, there are other later
pictures in which the sitter is handled a good deal less gently and is
obviously older. It may be compared with the very interesting late
photograph (with Augustus) taken by Mr Edward Heath and reproduced
in Mrs Thelma Cazalet-Keir's *From the Wings*. For over thirty years
Dorelia did her best to guard Augustus against distractions from his work.
Some intruders were met with silent generosity, in a manner sympathetic
but firm; to others she was coldly polite; to others again invisible. At all
times she carried her secrets well. Her presence, one of generally
cheerful detachment, was always felt – a mixture of formidable common
sense and absolute vagueness on the many matters that did not concern
her. Almost invariably she seemed aloof, but then something trivial would
startle her into laughter – the incompetent way someone cut a slice of
bread – and she would put up her hands to her face and *hoot* with
amusement. Dorelia outlived Augustus by almost nine years. On the
evening of 23rd July 1970, her son Romilly found her lying on the
dining-room floor. She died peacefully in her sleep soon afterwards. The
head is very subtle and beautiful but, as not infrequently occurs in a John
portrait, it makes a rather awkward junction with the shoulders.

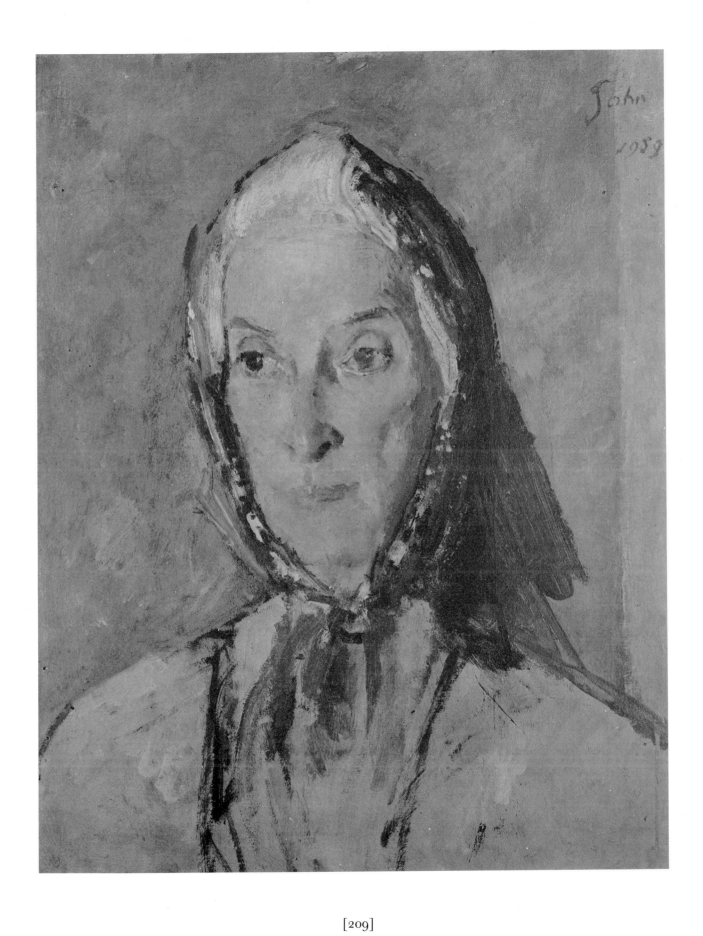

82 STUDY FOR THE CENTRAL PANEL OF A TRIPTYCH, 'LES SAINTES-MARIES', 1960

Pen, ink and wash on patched white paper, $10\frac{5}{8} \times 8\frac{1}{4}$ (27×21)

Signed, dated and inscribed 'John 1960 to Charles Wheeler' bottom right

Sir Charles Wheeler

John visited Saintes-Maries in 1910, and had long been interested in Sara, the Gypsies' saint. The vast triptych he planned dominated the last years of his life when, for the most part, he at last turned his back on commissioned faces and tried to return to his dream world. On 7th March 1949 he writes to Wyndham Lewis of being 'engaged on a long and vast composition'. The sad story of this can be found poignantly told in Sir Charles Wheeler's *High Relief* (1968). John continued work on the picture up to about three weeks before his death. During his last illness he rambled on about a drawing of an ideal town which he said he had finished but which, in fact, did not exist. After his death, vandals broke into his studio and covered the uncompleted work with graffiti and explosions of paint. That was the end.

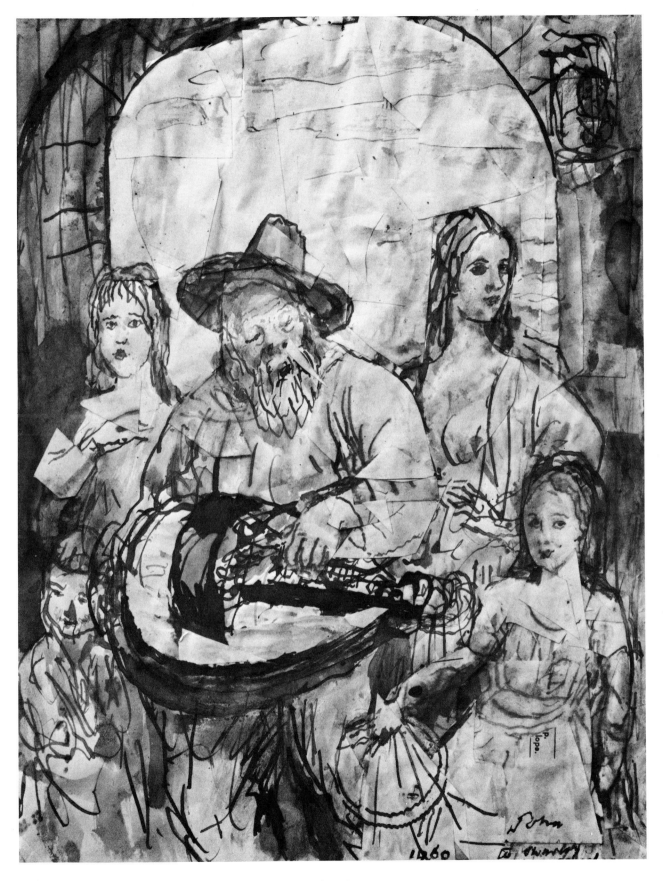

APPENDIX 1

The New English Art Club

As a non-member, John exhibited the following pictures at the N.E.A.C.:

Summer 1899 Miss Spencer Edwards (drawing)
Study (drawing)

Winter 1899 Study in Pen and Wash
Study of a Lady seated (drawing)

Summer 1900 Portrait of William Morgan
Head of an Oriental

Winter 1900 Little Miss Pank

Winter 1902 The Signorina Estelle Dolores
Cerutti
Merikli

After his election to membership, he exhibited:

Summer 1903 A Girl's Head
Haute-Loire
Hark, the Lark
The Wood Folk
A Wild Girl
Study of a Young Girl (drawing)

Winter 1903 Professor John MacDonald
Mackay
Portrait of a Man
Head of John Sampson, Esq
(drawing)
Study of a Girl's Head (drawing)
Head of William Rothenstein, Esq
(drawing)
Study of a Girl (drawing)

Summer 1904 The daughter of Ypocras
Dawn
Joconda
Girl's Head (drawing)
Head of William Orpen
(drawing)
Head of Girl (drawing)

Winter 1904 Ardor
Carlotta
Dorelia
A Portrait of an Old Man
Study of a Girl (drawing)
Goton (drawing)

Summer 1905 Professor J. M. Mackay
Carlotta
The White Feather
Fantasie
Study of a Girl's Head (drawing)
John Sampson, Esq, Head
(drawing)
Head of Girl, Sanguine (drawing)

Winter 1905 Mother and Child
Flora
Bohemians
Study (drawing)
Cupid and Nymphs (drawing)

Summer 1906 A Man's Head (drawing)
A Girl's Head (drawing)
Sir John Brunner
E. K. Muspratt Esq,
Vice-President of the University
of Liverpool

The Meeting in the Lane
Van dwellers

Winter 1906   The Sea-Shore (drawing)
Study for a Portrait (drawing)
The Crab (drawing)
A Girl on the Moor
The Camp
In the Tent

Summer 1907 Study of a Girl (drawing)
Study of a Girl (drawing)
Portrait (drawing)
Study for a Portrait (drawing)
Study of a Head (drawing)
Study of a Head (drawing)

Winter 1907   The River-Side (drawing)
Mother and Child (drawing)
Charles McEvoy (drawing)
Nymph (drawing)
The Nixie (drawing)
The Old Girls of Kinbara

Summer 1908 Three Little Things (drawings)
Study (drawing)
Study (drawing)
A Portrait (drawing)
The Infant Pyramus
Olilai

Summer 1909 The Way Down to the Sea
Portrait of William Nicholson
8 Drawings (4 studies in colour;
2 pencil studies; 1 nude study)

Winter 1909   The Girl on the Cliff
The Man from New York
(John Quinn)
The Camp (drawing)
Head of a Girl (drawing)
Wandering Sinnte (drawing)

Winter 1911   Dr Kuno Meyer
The Rt Hon Harold Chaloner
Dowdall, Lord Mayor of
Liverpool 1909
Forza e Amore

Winter 1912   Calderari: Gypsies of the
Caucasus
The Mumpers

Summer 1913 The World

Winter 1913   Cartoon: the Flute of Pan
Robin
6 Drawings (3 nude studies;
Study for a Portrait; A Girl's
Head; Head of an Architect)

Summer 1915 George Bernard Shaw, Esq
Galway Group
Provençal Composition (drawing)
Galway Shawls (drawing)
Nude Sketch (drawing)
Group of Women (drawing)
Family Group (drawing)
Fisher Folk (drawing)
Nude (drawing)
Portrait (drawing)

Summer 1916 The Laughing Artilleryman
Fresh Herrings
Mr H. A. Barker, 'The
Bone-setter'
The Girl by the Lake
G.B.S.
5 Drawings (3 studies for a panel;
2 studies for a bronze)

Winter 1916   Admiral Lord Fisher of
Kilverston

Summer 1918 A Dancer

Winter 1920   Iris Tree
Portrait of Marquise Salamanca
A Girl's Head (drawing)
L'Argentina

Summer 1920 Sketch for a Picture (drawing)
Nude (drawing)
Composition (drawing)
Nude Study (drawing)

Winter 1921   The Galway Women